C000242889

ARCHITECTURE DEPENDS

ARCHITECTURE DEPENDS

Jeremy Till

The MIT Press
Cambridge, Massachusetts
London, England

MIT Press books may be purchased at special quantity discounts for business or sales promotional use. For information, please email special_sales@mitpress .mit.edu or write to Special Sales Department, The MIT Press, 55 Hayward Street, Cambridge, MA 02142.

This book was set in Scala and Scala Sans by Graphic Composition, Inc. Printed and bound in the United States of America.

Library of Congress Cataloging-in-Publication Data

Till, Jeremy.
Architecture depends / Jeremy Till.
    p. cm.
Includes bibliographical references.
ISBN 978-0-262-01253-9 (hardcover : alk. paper)
    1. Architecture—Philosophy. 2. Architectural practice. I. Title.
NA2540.T55   2009
720.1—dc22
                          2008029578

10 9 8 7 6 5 4 3 2 1

For Sarah
Who was always with me when I wrote this book

Contents

Preface : Mess Is the Law   xi

Introduction : The Elevator Pitch   1

I   **CONTINGENCY   3**

1   **Deluded Detachment   7**
        The Paternoster   7
        Beaux-Arts Mao   11
        2B or Not 2B?   17
        Purity Is a Myth   18

2   **A Semblance of Order   27**
        New Labour Vitruvius   27
        Rogue Objects   29
        Bauman's Order   31
        The Ridding of Contingency   35
        Counting Sheep   41

3   **Coping with Contingency   45**
        A Balance of Colossal Forces   45
        The Juggernaut   48
        Rorty's Retreat   51
        Walking the Girder   54
        Situated Knowledge   55

II   TIME, SPACE, AND LO-FI ARCHITECTURE   63

4   **Time of Waste   67**
    Waste in Transit   67
    Rubbish Theory   70
    Time and Waste   73

5   **Out of Time   77**
    The Terror of Time   77
    From Eternity to Here   80
    Here and Now   84
    Tampering with Time   89

6   **In Time   93**
    Le Temps   93
    Thick Time   95
    Dirty Old Time   100
    The Unfinished   104
    Drawing Time   109
    From Noun to Verb   116

7   **Slack Space   117**
    Making Space   117
    Hard Space   119
    Social Space   125
    Inauthentic Space   127
    Slack Space   133

8   **Lo-Fi Architecture   135**
    Elvis Lives   135
    Exploding into Reality   137
    Monstrous Hybrids   143
    How They'll Tell if Your Building Is Gay   146

III   ARCHITECTURE : A DEPENDENT PROFESSION   149

9   **Architectural Agency   153**
    Lost in Action   153
    Self-Control   156

Contents

Left Brain, Right Brain   159
Remember I'm the Bloody Architect   161
The Crucible   163
The Problem of the Problem   166
Letting Go   169

10   **Imperfect Ethics   171**
Bad Ethics   171
Phony Ethics   174
Social Scales   178
Codes of Misconduct   179
The Ethics of Responsibility   184

11   **Hope against Hope   189**
Gymnasts in the Prison Yard   189
The Flight to Utopia   190
Formative Contexts   191
Angels with Dirty Faces   194

Acknowledgments   197
Notes   201
Bibliography   239
Figure Credits   247
Index   249

Preface : Mess Is the Law

It started to go wrong quite early.

The graffiti went up in the toilet of my School of Architecture sometime in my first year.

Less is more: Mies
Less is a bore: Venturi
Mess is the law: Till

Maybe I should have been flattered to be placed within such a distinguished genealogy of architectural greats, but actually I was hurt. Some wag was acting the schoolroom bully. The wag did not have a prescient sense of my later obsession with the everyday in all its glorious mess; he was mocking my complete inability to master the use of ink pens.

It started to go wrong quite early, my relationship with Architecture.

We had been issued a shopping list in our first week and this included 0.25mm and 0.35mm Rapidograph pens. These were soon put into use in a precedent study exercise, in which each of us had to trace a complete set of drawings of some piece of iconic architecture. This was boot camp pedagogy; by slavishly copying the masters the hope must have been that some of their aura would be transferred to us innocents. Others in my year quickly graduated downward to 0.18mm pens, even to the holy grail of 0.13mm, because these narrower instruments were neater, more professional, and more expert. Somehow these putative Architects managed to keep these needle-thin nibs running smoothly over the tracing paper. For whatever reason (I now put it down to weird bodily electromagnetic forces), my pens clogged up and trailed blobs of ink across the paper. I soon gave up on the 0.25mm and tried to do the whole exercise in 0.35mm. Try tracing the precise minimal lines of Mies van de Rohe's Farnsworth house with a stuttering fat line of ink blots and you will know the meaning of architectural humiliation. In a strange way I have never forgiven Mies. That is why I put him on the front cover with Mark Wallinger gently roughing him up by walking round the precious spaces of Mies's Berlin National Gallery in a bear suit.

My drawings were, indeed, a mess. In terms of my student career this was a disaster. There was an almost precise correlation between the ability to master a 0.13mm Rapidograph and the gaining of good grades. I left the School of Architecture with my tail between my legs.

It has taken me this long to work out that maybe architecture is a mess; not an aesthetic mess but a much more complex social and institutional mess. It has taken me this long to have the confidence to shout back to the wag: "Yes, Mess Is the Law," and be proud of it. It has taken me this long to get to a point of discovering that this mess is not a threat, but an opportunity. This book sets out the case.

ARCHITECTURE DEPENDS

Introduction : The Elevator Pitch

The essential argument of this book is straightforward. During the course of its writing, people have often asked, "What is it about, Jeremy?"

"Short or long?" I ask.

"The elevator pitch, between floors."

So, getting in on the ground floor, I say: "It is based on two premises. First, architecture is a dependent discipline. Second, architecture, as profession and practice, does everything to resist that very dependency. The book explores that resistance."

By this stage we are at the first floor.

"So, what do you mean by dependency?"

"I mean," looking at the indicator clicking from 1 to 2, "that architecture at every stage of its existence—from design through construction to occupation—is buffeted by external forces. Other people, circumstances, and events intervene to upset the architect's best-laid plans. These forces are, to a greater or lesser extent, beyond the direct control of the architect. Architecture is thus shaped more by external conditions than by the internal processes of the architect. Architecture is defined by its very contingency, by its very uncertainty in the face of these outside forces."

"But that is kind of obvious," my elevator companion says, "so what is the big idea?"

"No big idea, but maybe a big problem, namely architects tend to deny this dependency. They feel more comfortable in a world of certain predictions, in linear method, in the pursuit of perfection."

"But that's kind of obvious too. Doesn't sound like much of a book if it just states two truisms."

He has hit a nerve here. I have wondered for years why others never mention an argument that I think is obvious. Is it because it is *so* obvious that it is not said for fear of being seen as simple? Or is it because it is too uncomfortable to say, a kind of taboo that we all know to be the case but fear acknowledging? I am hoping that the latter is right and say as much: "Right, but what if that book is about the clash of those two truisms and the gap that opens up between them? The gap between what architecture—as practice, profession, and object—actually is (in all its dependency and contingency) and what architects want it to be (in all its false perfection). What then?"

He does not answer, but makes a face somewhere between a smile and a grimace (he's an architect, you see), maybe acknowledging his own frailty while at the same time wanting to shrug it off. A both/and face that is appropriate for an argument that, as we shall see, resolves itself in a both/and solution.

"And what if," I continue, pressing home my advantage, "the book argues that we must bridge that gap by opening up to dependency not as a threat but an opportunity? That the inescapable reality of the world must be engaged with and not retreated from. And that in that engagement there is the potential for a reformulation of architectural practice that would resist its present marginalization and find new hope. What then?"

"Then I might buy the book."

We get out together at the fourteenth floor.

I   CONTINGENCY

Part I traces architecture's relationship with contingency. Chapter 1 looks at the way that architecture has avoided engagement with the uncertainties of the world through a retreat into an autonomous realm. It argues that this retreat is deluded. Chapter 2 examines how architects have attempted to maintain a defense system against the overwhelming forces of modernity through maintaining barriers behind which an ordered world can be erected. It argues that this defense is impossible and that only a semblance of order is created. Chapter 3 specifically addresses issues of contingency, working through philosophical and sociological constructions of the term in order to arrive at a point at which contingency is seen as an opportunity for the intentional reformulation of a given context.

1   Deluded Detachment

The Paternoster

We get out at the fourteenth floor; this floor is really there. It is in Sheffield, the entry to another School of Architecture. This school occupies the top six floors of the highest tower block in the city. At the time of its completion in 1966 the tower was the tallest academic building in Europe, its nineteen-story height determined not by the architects (who had initially designed only thirteen stories) but by the University clients in their desire to create a significant landmark. That's architecture's dependency for you.[1]

The building is known as the Arts Tower because the rest of it is occupied by bits of the Faculty of Arts. There is a nice conceit here: architecture crowning the building, literally and symbolically; signaling itself as Mother of the Arts. But there is a problem here as well, because that ascendancy also signals literal and symbolic detachment. We look down at the city below and, at this distance, command it as an abstraction. The voices of people are lost; we just observe their functions. Buildings are reduced to form, roads to flows of traffic. Noises are measured, not listened to. Shapes are classified by type, not sensuously enjoyed. "One's body is no longer clasped by the streets," as Michel de Certeau says, standing prophetically on top of the New York World Trade Center, "nor is it possessed by the rumble of so many differences."[2]

And from below, the city looks back and sees us as remote figures of authority.

The tower thus signifies a removal that allows specific rituals and values to be established at the earliest stages of the nascent architect's education. The architectural critic Reyner Banham identified this symptom in the last article that he wrote before he died. In "A Black Box: The Secret Profession of Architecture" he berates the profession for its retreat into a rarefied and self-referential world. No longer seen as the mother of the arts, or the dominant mode of rational design, architecture, Banham argues, "appears as the exercise of an arcane and privileged aesthetic code."[3] His argument is with architects, not with architecture; he despairs of the former while yearning for the promise of the latter. He identifies the processes of education to be at the heart of the malaise. "Anthropologists," he muses, "have been known to compare the teaching studio to a tribal longhouse; the place and the rituals pursued there are almost unique in the annals of western education. One of the things that sustains this uniqueness is the frequency with which students are discouraged from pursuing modes of design that come from outside the studio."[4] What Banham identifies so clearly is the way that the studio as setting establishes attitudes and values that are then played out in the black box of the profession. Intrusions from outside are restricted in order to allow the internal processes to develop on their own terms.

Notorious among the rituals is the design jury (crit), a strange act of tribal initiation that is played out in schools around the world. Within weeks of arriving in architecture school, students are asked to pin up an initial, and usually clumsy, attempt at architecture on a wall, stand in front of it and talk about it, with tutors then taking the floor to criticize it. The word alone, *crit*, is a stab of negativity. The crit places into a pressure cooker a combination of potentially explosive ingredients: students catatonic with tiredness and fear, tutors (mainly male) charged on power and adrenaline, and an adversarial arena in which actions are as much about showing off as they are about education.[5] Some students survive this; some are deeply scarred by the experience. One of the mistaken arguments for the retention of the crit is that it prepares for the real world—but at what cost? Answer: the development of alien vocabularies (spoken and drawn) understood only by architects, arrogance (attack being seen as the best form of defense in a crit), and a complete inability to listen on the part of both tutor and student. Such are the common traits, among others, which are established in schools of architecture and which then contribute to the formation of the character of the architect. Banham's use of the anthropologist to measure the character of architects is telling. Anthropologists traditionally study societies on the margin and groups under threat of extinction. Banham is thus slyly hinting that these strange characteristics and rituals of the architect may lead to the marginalization and potential extinction of architecture as discipline.

Despite our best efforts at Sheffield to assimilate our students into normal society—to get them literally and figuratively down the tower and out into the streets—I am annually amazed as an amateur anthropologist at how quickly they assume the architectural mantle. Three weeks into their course, at the end of their first project, you see them gathered at the foot of the building, eyes smudged with tiredness, bad hair, three-day-worn clothes. But far from being ashamed of these afflictions, they wear them as badges of honor. It is what sets them apart, signaling their difference from the other students. Garry Stevens identifies this separation very well in his study of the social mores of architecture, describing the studio as a place of "internment [that] produces a socially and mentally homogeneous set of individuals."[6]

A few years ago, an email circulated architecture schools that brilliantly captured the madness of long nights, estrangement, and social dysfunction that result from this detachment. The subject box read: YOU KNOW YOU ARE AN ARCHITECTURE STUDENT WHEN . . .

. . . the alarm clock tells you when to go to sleep
. . . you're not ashamed of drooling in class anymore, especially in the Structures lecture.
. . . you know what UHU tastes like.
. . . you CELEBRATE space and OBSERVE your birthday.
. . . coffee and cokes are tools, not treats.
. . . you think it's possible to CREATE space.
. . . you've fallen asleep in the washroom.
. . . your brother or sister thinks he or she is an only child.
. . . you've listened to all your CDs in less than 48 hours.
. . . you're not seen in public.
. . . you lose your house keys for a week and you don't even notice.
. . . you've brushed your teeth and washed your hair in the school's washroom.
. . . you've discovered the benefits of having none or very short hair.
. . . you've used an entire roll of film to photograph the sidewalk.
. . . you know the exact time the vending machines are refilled.
. . . you always carry your deodorant.
. . . you've danced YMCA with excellent choreography at 3 am and without a single drop of alcohol in your body.
. . . you take notes and messages with a rapidograph and colour markers.
. . . you combine breakfast, lunch and dinner into one single meal.
. . . you see holidays only as extra sleeping time.
. . . you've got more photographs of buildings than of actual people.
. . . you've taken your girlfriend (boyfriend) on a date to a construction site.

. . . you can live without human contact, food or daylight, but if you can't print, it's chaos.
. . . you can use Photoshop, Illustrator and make a web page, but you don't know how to use Excel.
. . . you refer to great architects (dead or alive) by their familiar name as if you knew them. (Frank, Corb, Mies, Rem, Norman . . .)
. . . when someone offers you a Bic pen, you feel offended.

Toward the end of the academic year I forwarded this to all my students, with the message: "This was sent to me and I did not know whether to laugh or cry. Just thought I should send it to you all to let you know you are not alone at this time of year . . ." I was bombarded with return emails, split between those who were laughing and those who were crying. I was less worried about the latter group who, while recognizing their condition, were also distressed by it. The laughers, on the other hand, were hysterically accepting—maybe even enjoying—their strange lot in life.

But at least there was humor. I can find no laughs in the description of another architectural tribe, Miroslav Šik's 1990s atelier at the School of Architecture in Zurich, whose "black uniforms and deliberate isolation bore overtones of a clan; in addition, their interest in discredited architecture, such as that of the Fascist era, was disturbing."[7] Disturbing? I should say so. Not content with detaching themselves from the outside world, this tribe saw fit to remove themselves from their fellow students as well. The attachment to pernicious ideologies arises directly out of their enforced isolation from the real world. It comes as no surprise, therefore, to learn that Šik's pedagogical program was entitled "Analogous Architecture," a set of highly prescriptive exercises in which everything from the program to the style of drawing was imposed by the tutor. While Blackshirts in the studio may be an extreme symbol of the autonomy of architectural education, the symptoms are there throughout the world.

The sense of detachment in the Sheffield tower is accentuated by the provision of a paternoster lift, an endlessly cycling chain of small open boxes rising and falling through the building. The paternoster allows us to move between the six floors of the school of architecture without ever having to encounter people from outside. No sharing of lifts with others; the paternoster allows the school to be a world unto itself. At the top and bottom, the boxes of the paternoster lift disappear into blackness. It looks scary; one imagines that they might flip over as they go over the wheel at the top, but

of course a ratchet track keeps them in the same orientation. However, older students play on the fears of the new students by doing handstands as they pass over the top, and so coming back down upside down to the shrieks of the freshers. The paternoster is horribly like architectural education: a relentlessly circling set of boxes of stuff (ideas, knowledge, skills, techniques) moving through its own world. The movement makes it feel fresh, but in fact the boxes go nowhere very far. And when it all feels a bit dull, a few handstands and other displays of formal gymnastics are thrown in to denote progress. As Le Corbusier says, architects live in the extraordinary world of the acrobat.[8]

Beaux-Arts Mao

The establishment of this autonomous realm in architectural education can be traced back to the French royal architecture academy (Académie Royale d'Architecture) founded in 1671 under Louis XIV, which later gave rise to the École des Beaux-Arts, started in Paris in 1819. The royal academies set the tone: internalized, exclusive, and cutthroat in their competitiveness. In his evidence as to why the academies should be abolished, the painter Jacques-Louis David argued that they were the "last shelters of all the aristocracies . . . they employ cruel means to smother budding talents and take monastic revenge against any young man whose natural gifts put him beyond their tyranny."[9] While the academies were subsequently abolished in 1793, within a week a new School of Architecture was rising from the ashes, with the same professors and administrators, and seemingly the same values. It was this School (run out of the home of the former Academician Julien-David Le Roy) that effectively morphed into the École des Beaux-Arts. Entry to the École was not direct to the school as institution, but to an atelier run by a *patron*. This involved an initiation ceremony "which might consist merely of dodging wet sponges and singing the 'Boulanger March' standing upon a drawing board. More often the initiation was a duel in which the contestants, naked, were each armed with a bucket of paint and a long brush. Afterwards the newest members would swear to observe the atelier rules and would buy food and drink for the group."[10] Clearly such homoerotic play could take place only in an all-male environment, an apartheid that persisted until very recently, as the leading New Urbanist Andrés Duany recounts in his experience of a Beaux-Arts atelier in 1971. He describes cleaning up the sewage sludge deposited into his atelier by rival students as "the kind of thing that would encourage strong bonding among males."[11] Once in, a world unto itself opened up, with the older students teaching the younger ones about "cheese and wine and the flamboyance of dress and manner required of an Ancien Élève of the most influential and finest school of architecture the world has ever seen . . . socialisation was not just a transmittal of architectural culture (and of the sexual lore which is inevitable in male company), but also of manners, mannerisms, and taste."[12]

Plus ça change, plus c'est la même chose. The constitution and aesthetics of the manners, mannerisms, and taste may have changed over the ages, but they still define a particular set of internalized customs in the architecture studio. Garry Stevens describes this process in terms of students identifying with the cultural capital of architecture: "By displaying in all the slight ways of manner, dress and taste that one is becoming what one wishes to be, students absorb cultural capital in the only possible way, by presenting to the studio-master's gaze their whole social being."[13]

Duany is unapologetic in his affirmation of the continuing relevance of the Beaux-Arts model. In his hankering for a return to traditional values, his target is the "tyranny" of schools of architecture run along modernist lines. But his barbs are misplaced, because in fact schools—whether "classical," "modern," or "postmodern"—generally maintain the essentials of the Beaux-Arts ethos. The cult of genius, the unquestioned authority of the *patron,* the emphasis on form, the prescriptive pedagogy, the absurd rituals, the particular socialization, and the internal mores are all alive and kicking in architecture schools. Architectural education still clings to the fundamental pedagogical tenets of the Beaux-Arts, but is distracted from realizing this by the difference of the formal product that emerges at the end. The assumption is that since the outcomes *look* radically different, the processes that lead to those outcomes must also be different; new shapes are conflated with new thoughts. But in fact nothing could be further from the truth. While the product might have moved from classical plans to algorithmic-driven blobs, the underlying principles remain unscathed, most of all the overriding autonomy of the process.

Strangely, Corb (as I now feel bidden to familiarly call him) shares my antipathy to the Beaux-Arts. I say strangely because, as will become apparent, Corb is not a natural ally for my overall argument, but sometimes the sheer energy of his polemic means that one suspends disbelief. One example is *When the Cathedrals Were White,* an account of his trip to the United States in 1935. It is a book that shows him at his best and worst: it is vain beyond belief, politically incorrect, bombastic—and often very observant. In it he tells the story of meeting a Professor of Architecture at the School of Architecture at New York University, an institution that was then run according to strict Beaux-Arts principles. In what Le Corbusier calls a "deeply malignant statement," the professor proudly announces: "*I am no longer a practicing architect,* but I instruct my students in good taste and beauty."[14] Corb pours bile on what this character and his colleagues represent: "they are against life; they represent memory, security, lethargy. In particular they have killed architecture by operating in a vacuum . . . architecture has evaded life in place of being an expression of it."[15] The feeling that not much has changed between David's attack on the eighteenth-century academy, 1935, and now (as represented by that painful email) is reinforced when he notes that the diploma awarded at the end of the Beaux-Arts course "closes everything like a cork. . . . It says: 'It is finished, you have stopped suffering and learning. Henceforth you are free!' The idea of learning has become synonymous with *suffering.*"[16] Le Corbusier is most observant when he identifies what is played out in this vacuum: the acceptance of "forms, methods, concepts, because they exist, without asking why,"[17] delivered "under the ferule of extremely conservative methods."[18] The most explicit manifestation of this conservatism is in the power structures established between students on the one hand, masters on the other. It is, of course, a one-sided relationship: "the masters occupy the throne which they imagine they raised up; from their heads nothing would come except inviolate truths."[19]

This power structure, and association with notions of "truth" and "rightness," remains today. While the École des Beaux-Arts promoted a single version of truth under the rule of Enlightenment reason, today's ateliers are more plural but nonetheless retain the principle that the tutor in some way holds the keys to success, and in order to obtain them the student must follow the rules. In this architectural education fits all too well the patterns and restrictions of conventional education that are so brilliantly exposed by Paolo Freire in his classic work *The Pedagogy of the Oppressed,* a book that almost single-handedly invented the critical pedagogy movement. Freire memorably likens traditional education to a system of banking in which the student is seen as a passive receptacle, there to be filled by the teacher: "The more completely she fills the receptacles, the better teacher she is. The more meekly the receptacles permit themselves to be filled, the better students they are. Education thus becomes an act of depositing, in which the students are the depositories and the teacher is the depositor."[20] Freire's critique of this system centers not only on the basic unacceptability of the resulting power relationship, but also on the way that this relationship can thrive only in a static and closed world. "The teacher talks about reality as if it were motionless, static, compartmentalised and predictable. His task is to fill the students with the contents of his narration—contents which are detached from reality, disconnected from the totality that engendered them and could give them significance."[21] If, he argues, students are presented with an artificial fixity, then it will be impossible for them later to engage with the world in any transformative capacity. The status quo thus remains untouched, just as Le Corbusier noted was the case at the Beaux-Arts. In architecture this disconnected stasis has peculiarly negative effects. The world is seen not as a dynamic social system there to be engaged with, open for transformation, but as a static abstraction, there only to receive mute form.

Architectural education does everything it can to disguise its autonomy and resultant stasis. Briefs for buildings are set in the "real" world on "real" sites, empirical data are collected, engineers are sometimes spoken to, and famous architects are brought in to review the work. But these activities really do nothing to disturb the artificiality of the whole process. A linear route from problem to solution is instigated, unaffected by external forces. Particular events (the crit/jury, the charette,[22] the interim exercise) are introduced to the process in order to create a semblance of disturbance and unpredictability, but these are in fact always determined and overseen by the authority of the tutor. The banking model of education remains more or less untouched by these false contingencies.

However, the main way that architectural education avoids staring the stasis of its own processes in the eye is by confusing radical making with radical thinking. Because things *look* different, from school to school, and from year to year, the assumption is made that the formative educational processes are equally different and equally evolving. The situation is exacerbated in the early twenty-first century by the extraordinary power made available by the computer. Technical determinism enters an unholy alliance with formal determinism, submenus of software programs producing ever more different shapes. In the really "radical" schools conventional software is ditched as rather old-fashioned and replaced with algorithms of the designer's own making; the resultant forms mutate on a yearly basis like an uncontrollable virus. The end-of-year exhibitions are often dazzling, quite literally; such is the shininess and freshness of the surface that one is seduced into believing that something genuinely new is happening. But scratch beneath the veneer and one finds a void, a political and ethical void in which the underlying processes and their social detachment are left unexamined. It is symptomatic of what the Dutch critic Roemer van Toorn calls "Fresh Conservatism," a trend that "presents the normally discreet character of conservatism in a spectacularly fresh manner, as a work of art."[23] It is also symptomatic of the classic mistake of the avant-garde to assume that their avant-garde forms represent avant-garde thinking. In fact the so-called radical gestures of the avant-garde often exist in the most conservative regimes,[24] an argument that can be transferred all too easily to contemporary architectural education. The so-called radicals exist because of, not in spite of, the conservatism that they would presume to challenge. Nowhere is this clearer than in the contemporary fashion in architecture schools for branding your program with a ©, a ™, or a ®, the heady scent of avant-garde irony barely disguising the underlying stench of neoliberalism.[25] The avant-garde will never escape the conservative systems that they attempt to criticize, because in the end both are framed by the same value system, namely that of the production of form and taste.[26]

It is 2003. We are in China. At the time the average Chinese architect was responsible for "designing" 50,000 square meters of floorspace a year, against approximately 1,000 square meters for the average European architect. This differential was reflected in two polls: one in China rated architecture as the third most desirable profession behind IT consultants and business consultants, while in the UK architects were at the bottom of a poll of job satisfaction (the real kick in the teeth being that hairdressers came top).

We are visiting a leading Chinese architecture school, hoping to see how they are adapting to this explosion. The school's history is formative. In the 1930s, some staff were sent to the University of Pennsylvania, which at the time was running along strictly Beaux-Arts lines. On their return, the Chinese professors installed the Beaux-Arts system; it ran through to the 1960s, at which time architecture (as a decadent bourgeois activity) was banished from the academy under the dictates of the Cultural Revolution. Professors and lecturers were sent out to the fields to work, and on their return in the 1970s, postmodernism was overturning the Western architectural world. As the Dean of the Faculty wryly tells us, his school jumped from

the nineteenth century to the twenty-first, missing out modernism on the way. The Beaux-Arts legacy is most apparent in the drawing studio, with its plaster casts of classical torsos, Doric capitals, and Greek gods. It is only two busts of revolutionary workers with their Mao caps that jolt one from Paris to China, and with this jolt comes the recognition of the impotence of these 150-year-old educational techniques in the face of the juggernaut of forces evolving outside.

Just down the corridor from the Beaux-Arts drawing studio is the first-year studio, where we are shown the models from a recent project. The brief was typical of a first-year project anywhere in the world: design a house in the style of a famous architect. There among the various modernist and post-modernist exercises, all done rather better than anywhere else in the world, was a house conspicuously in the style of LAB Architects' Federation Square in Melbourne. This is September 2003. Federation Square was less than a year old. Now that is what I call fresh: the ransacking of images, probably off the net, for instant gratification. Beaux-Arts tradition meets radical form. Two sides of the same coin, that of fresh conservatism.

2B or Not 2B?

I started with education because that is where so many of the values that define the profession are first established. The relationship between the profession and education is complex. It is not completely causal—the actions of the academy do not directly influence the profession and the profession does not directly control education. It is messier than this, like the clumsy embrace of two octopuses. The academy at the same time shapes, and is shaped by, the profession and vice versa. Thus while we might not find the autonomy apparent in education played out directly in the profession and practice, we would expect to find it somewhere in the mix. Architects are no different from any other profession in exerting their independence as a means of defining their territory, their area of control, apart from others. "Autonomy is justified," argues Magali Sarfatti Larson, "by the professional's claim of possessing a special and superior knowledge, which should therefore be free of lay evaluation and protected from inexpert interference."[27]

The autonomy that starts as a professional necessity has social implications. Like any tribe, architects assume particular rituals and certain codes, both visual and linguistic. They often dress according to type and use a specific language. As we have seen, the undertaking of socialization into the tribe starts in the school studio. Our tribe has been studied not just by anthropologists but, rather more worryingly, by psychologists as well; their research shows that by the end of the course, the students are fully assimilated into the social mores of the architectural world.[28] Students enter as normal, situated, humans and come out as rather abnormal, detached, members of the tribe. It is in the nature of such assimilation that one is not fully conscious that it is going on and not fully aware of the consequences when it is over. It is easy to laugh at the traits of others, less easy to identify those of oneself. This is nicely shown in an anecdote told by Reyner Banham. An architect comes across an accident. A man is lying in the street, bleeding profusely. A woman is leaning over him, desperately trying to fashion a tourniquet from her scarf. She calls up to the architect:

"Have you got a pencil to tighten this tourniquet?"

"Will a 2B do?" the architect asks, worriedly.

This kind of social autonomy, for all its gaucheness and moments of absurdity, is maybe understandable. Tribes stick together. What is less comprehensible, and defensible, is when the social autonomy of the profession slips over boundaries and manifests itself as the autonomy of practice or, stranger still, the autonomy of practice's products, namely buildings. How could practice, with all its engagements with others, ever be considered as an independent activity? How could buildings, with all their occupation by others, ever be torn from their social context? The profession and practice are different but often treated as if they are the same. The profession of architecture is a social construct, largely self-defined and self-perpetuating, which is required in order to give architects status and the concomitant power. The practice of architecture is a more nebulous affair. Looking from the outside it is almost laughable to think that architecture, as practice and product, could be seen as autonomous. And yet, from within the black box of the profession of architecture, it somehow seems a sensible move to keep the practice and products inside the walls, there to treat them as autonomous processes and objects. That way you can control them better.

Q: How many architects does it take to change a light bulb?

A: Flos or Arteluce?

Purity Is a Myth

The autonomy of architecture (as practice and product) is a continuing theme of this book. The walls of the black box protect architects from the contingencies of the world beyond, allowing them to develop theories and practices unfettered by others. Georges Bataille gets it dead right in one of the very short pieces he devotes to architecture: "Great monuments," he writes, "are erected like dykes opposing the logic and majesty of authority against all disturbing elements."[29] The metaphor of the dyke is apt. It gives a sense of security but is ultimately fragile in the face of the rising tides of forces beyond; levees will be breached, flooding the impossible purity of the land within with all the toxicity and uncertainty that has so futilely been kept at bay. What happens within the dykes may be called Architecture because the theorists and practitioners so insistently tell us it is, but it is in fact not architecture at all—if, that is, we attach to architecture with a small *a* the physical, environmental, social, political, and economic conditions that inevitably impinge on buildings and their makers. A gap opens up between the architecture as described in the official histories, and the architecture whose story is so rarely told. We need more people who dare to eschew the greats and the specials, and look to the everyday, the social, and the economic as forces that shape architecture.[30]

Seemingly protected by the dyke, Architects live in a state of delusion, worshiping false idols, tempted by a "deferred nirvana."[31] It is hardly surprising, therefore, that the products emerging from behind the walls should get so scarred when they are confronted with the world as it is. How could anything conceived in a vacuum cope with the conditions it has denied were there? "Truth found inside a tightly sealed room," as Lev Shevtsov notes, "is hardly of any use outside; judgements made inside a room which, for fear of draught is never aired, are blown away with the first gust of wind."[32] But this fragility is too much to face. Better then to build the walls still higher, to consolidate the autonomy.

The theoretical justification for the autonomy of architecture reached its peak in the 1970s. By then the failure of the modern movement to deliver on its promises of social redemption was obvious. Architects were under fire from all sides. Jane Jacobs's famous assault on modernist delusions in *The Death and Life of Great American Cities* had been transformed into the populist association of architects with tower blocks (with all their aesthetic and social disgrace), an association that all too conveniently overlooked the fact that tower blocks, at least in the United Kingdom, were not the demented vision of architects with penis complexes but the direct result of the economics of the social housing market in the 1950s and 1960s.[33] In general the reaction of the architectural establishment to these attacks was one of retreat—exceptions being isolated camps in France following the 1968 "revolution" and the community architecture movement of the 1970s.

In the theoretical establishment the prevailing tendency in the 1970s was an obsession with the formal and linguistic aspects of architecture, with intellectual credence being granted by the tenets of structuralism. In their search for the underlying structures of architectural language, theorists in both Europe and America increasingly saw architecture as an abstracted and then autonomous discipline. "Autonomy once more," the Spanish architect and critic Ignasi de Solà-Morales writes of the so-called New York Five, a group of US architects in the 1970s, "an interior game [within which] architecture was a universe sufficient unto itself, nourished on its own history and emerging from the interior of its own rules and protocols."[34] Indeed, for the apologists/promoters/critics (the terms blur in the narcissism of the whole exercise) of the New York Five, their very autonomy was also their very strength. As Arthur Drexler mystifyingly notes in his introduction to a book on the New York Five: "it is *only* architecture, not the salvation of man and the redemption of the earth. For those who like architecture that is no mean feat."[35] Of course Drexler is setting up a false dichotomy—the projects of salvation and redemption, theological overtones and all, were never architecture's duty—but the hyperbole is enough to persuade architects that retreat to their own turf is preferable, even sanctionable, in the face of such impossible tasks. It is enough, it appears, to conduct architecture on its own terms. Indeed, all too often so-called "great" Architecture is defined through its very autonomy, in its very ability to stand over and above the degrading forces of the everyday world.

Probably the most insistent carrier of the message of autonomy was the influential journal *Oppositions,* published in New York in the 1970s. As K. Michael Hays cogently articulates in his introduction to a collection of essays from *Oppositions,* autonomy is the dominant theme that runs though the journal. As he notes, this sets up a tension between architecture as a "closed system" (in the words of Diana Agrest, one of the contributors) and "its contingency on, even determination by, historical forces beyond its control."[36] Hays's argument is that architects and critics set up a defense mechanism against these contingencies and do so by attempting "to recode, to reterritorialize, to reinvent the boundaries and specificities that delimit the discipline."[37] The reaction to any historical crisis or changed social circumstance is not an engagement with the forces that have created that crisis or circumstance, but an internalized redefinition of architecture in the face of them. As a result we see not "architecture's success, but its coming to grief against a historical moment, one that shuts down certain social functions that architecture had previously performed."[38] Of course this reinvention gives the impression that progress is being made in the light of external forces, but in fact each so-called change just entrenches architecture's autonomy still further. Thus when structuralism was superseded by poststructuralism (as external discourse), the internal mechanisms of architecture did not seize on the intellectual possibilities of poststructuralism to reconsider the established social priorities or hierarchies of practice. Vague associations are made between deconstruction as a philosophical concern and deconstructivist architecture, but in the end the thrust of the latter movement is one of formal opportunism. "Form has become contaminated," writes Mark Wigley in his introduction to the exhibition that launched deconstructivist architecture, "deconstruction gains all its force by challenging the very values of harmony, unity, stability and proposing instead a different view of structure."[39] Wigley associates the purity of form with architecture's conservative tendencies, and marks the challenge to that purity as a radical moment—but in fact the new formal complexities are just as conservative as the stabilities they would try to overturn insofar as they consolidate the autonomy of architecture in terms of its formalist preoccupations. The real giveaway is when Wigley explains: "moreover, forms are disturbed and only then given a functional program. Instead of form following function, function follows deformation."[40] Thus even the modernist's nod to the use of the building, albeit severely framed by the rigors of functionalism, is discarded in an exercise that elevates the manipulation of form as the essential activity of architecture.

The most notorious example of this autonomy is the work of one of the New York Five, Peter Eisenman's House VI. At the time, Eisenman was immersed in structuralist readings of architecture, attempting to find the internal rules and ordering principles of modernism.[41] However, he made the classic mistake of confusing a method of analysis with a means of production, and crossed over from being reader to author with barely a thought for the essential differences between these two conditions. Structuralism may indeed be a powerful, if self-absorbed, mode of formal analysis but this does not mean that the rules established through analysis can or should be simply reversed to become systems of production in the hope that the reader/user of the work so produced will inevitably be able to comprehend the underlying systems. Even if the reader/user is aware of something going on, then it is only of an internalized formal discourse; they are effectively sucked into the redundant space of architecture's autonomy. Thus when Eisenman states: "it may be a fundamental act in the making of architecture to take certain regularities which exist in a deep structure and present them systematically so that the user is aware of them,"[42] the obvious retort is "So what?"

But such flippancy flounders in the face of the self-importance of the critic-maker. In a dogmatic assertion of structuralist principles, Eisenman designed a series of houses in the 1970s. Some were built, some remained on paper. All had equal status, and herein lay the rub. Drawing, Building, Text, all elide in the notion of an "architectural project,"[43] in which built and unbuilt assume the same standing. However, the delusion that a drawing is equivalent to building can be sustained only under the rule of autonomy. A text is not a building is not a drawing.[44] Each has its own conditions of production and reception, and any attempt to merge them is doomed to failure, as is demonstrated by the infamous bed in Eisenman's House VI. This is a building predicated on the formal language of architecture and the way that it might be subverted. In his description of the building Eisenman repeatedly uses the word *inversion,* as if this formal attribute alone signifies a radical gesture. The will to "represent a change" is paramount, and if this means functional inconvenience, then so be it. What is primary is "the need to complete a sequence A-B, or to read symmetries in a straight line about a fulcrum or a diagonal line in relation to a datum."[45] Unfortunately, this need—and surely only an architect deep down the abyss of autonomy could identify "the completion of a sequence" as an overriding need—meant that when it came to the bedroom a slot was required, through the floor, up the wall, straight through the bedspace. As the client Suzanne Frank notes with remarkable equanimity: "this inconvenient element . . . forced us to sleep in separate beds which was not our custom."[46] While the bed slot is the best known of the inconveniences inflicted on the Franks (though it should be noted that they entered into the project with eyes fairly wide open), just as telling is Eisenman calling them before the visit of Philip Johnson, the puppet master of American architecture at the time, and entreating Suzanne to remove their daughter's crib from the house. Eisenman's nervousness is almost touching; less so is his assumption that Johnson's architectural sensibility might be so offended by the invasion of everyday life into the perfected autonomy of the House (of Architecture).

It may be easy to dismiss this as just another example of extreme architectural decadence. But this would be to underestimate the hold that theorists such as Eisenman have on the architectural world, in particular in education, and also to overlook the way that initially marginal positions can develop into mainstream orthodoxy. An example of the latter is the Italian architect Aldo Rossi, whose writing was championed by Eisenman through the pages of *Oppositions*. Rossi's *Architecture and the City* became the seminal text in defining an approach to architecture that identified buildings as autonomous types, lifted from history and presented as an "analytical and experimental structure."[47] His writings were supported by a sequence of beautifully drawn projects that, far from Eisenman's alienating abstraction, seduced one into believing in their potential resonances. These drawings were famous throughout the architectural world.

And then they were built.

Like many architects and students, we traveled to Italy to see the cemetery at Modena and the housing at Gallaratese. We tried to find the building that we had seen in the drawings, waiting for people to go, for the sun to set low in order to catch those shadows in the empty arcades. And the more we waited, the more hopeless the task became. The drawing as autonomous object was not there, architecture was. So when some years later I read Solà-Morales, I felt consoled that we were not alone in our failed quest. "The sense of disillusion experienced by many upon seeing a Rossi building," he writes, "derives from the fact that the building asks to be considered objectively or functionally, while its author tries to call attention instead to the process revealed in his drawings, so that the construction of the building is an episode in an architectonic discourse understood as autonomous and thus indifferent to construction or use."[48] Rossi himself acknowledges the gap in his much gentler later book *A Scientific Autobiography*. "What surprises me most in architecture," he writes with seeming—but surely disingenuous—bemusement, "is that a project has one life in its built state but another in its written or drawn state."[49] But far from attempting to make sense of these differences, he continues with his typological experiments.

It was at Rossi's Civic Center in Perugia that I realized that experiment is an unfortunate word to use in architecture. In the center was an empty square, a place signifying public realm but without the public to make it public. Around the edges were arcades, torn from their urban context; no idle chatter, no cafés, just a redundant scenography.[50] Rossi's work, built and drawn, is often compared to that of de Chirico, and standing as an isolated pair with our shadows cast across the piazza, we did indeed feel like figures out of one of those paintings. Melancholy. But it was the strange monument in the middle of the piazza that jolted most. Intended as a pure form to be chiseled by the sun into shadows, the monument was now covered in neo-fascist graffiti. But maybe this is not incidental. As Vincent Scully writes, "fascism haunts the colonnade of the Gallaratese project." We are not in the direct territory of Swiss Blackshirts here, but in a strange

Contingency

world where Scully can immediately follow up with "but it [fascism] is only one of the ghosts. Every classical architect from Le Corbusier to Ledoux and Ictinus is lurking behind the piers."[51] So that's OK then, Scully appears to be saying, as if the presence of fascism is acceptable, even overridden, by placing Rossi in a lineage of great architects, as if in that autonomous genealogy we can overlook the intolerable.

And with that the notion of the autonomy of architecture should come to a juddering halt. It allows architects to detach themselves as humans (social, political, and ethical beings) and then look through the wrong end of the telescope, and so to see the world as an abstraction. One might think that an abstracted world can be ordered, beautified, and perfected, but in the end the real will come to back to bite you. What becomes quickly apparent is that any permanent detachment is deluded. Purity, as the great Brazilian artist Hélio Oiticica says, is a myth.

2 A Semblance of Order

New Labour Vitruvius

I have always had a problem with Vitruvius, the Roman author of the first treatise on architecture. Just because he was first does not necessarily make him right, but his shadow over architecture remains long. "It is not too much to say," writes Arata Isozaki, "that [until the late eighteenth century] the work of the architect was meant to fill in the margins of Vitruvian writing."[1] In many ways the Vitruvian legacy has lasted beyond the late eighteenth century. His triad of commodity, firmness, and delight remains on the architectural rosary, even if the beads have been updated to reflect contemporary concerns with use/function, technology/tectonics, and aesthetics/beauty. There is an unthinking acceptance of a baton being passed from century to century, a "solace in the prescription."[2] This is not to say that buildings should not be usable, stand up, and generally be "delightful" rather than miserable, but these qualities are so self-evident that they should be background beginnings rather than the foreground ends that the Vitruvian dogma suggests.

But my problem is not just with the blandness of the triad; it is more to do with the wider remit of the *Ten Books*. "I decided," Vitruvius writes with a certain immodesty, "that it would be a worthy and most useful thing to bring the whole body of this great discipline to complete order." The ambitious task of calling the discipline to complete order applies not just to the body of professionals—Vitruvius gives precise instructions as to what should be included in an architect's education—but extends to the products of that discipline. "Architecture," he writes, "depends on *ordinatio*, the proper relation of parts of a work taken separately and the provision of proportions for overall symmetry."[3] Here we have the first conflation of the values of profession, practice, and product that is to be repeated throughout architectural history: a prescription of order that applies equally to the knowledge of the profession, the structure of practice, and the appearance of buildings.

As Indra McEwen convincingly shows, the dominating metaphor in the *Ten Books* is that of the body ("the whole body of this great discipline") and the defining feature of the body is its coherence and unity. "Bodies were wholes," she notes, "whose wholeness was, above all, a question of coherence. The agent of coherence—in the body of the world and in all the bodies in it—was *ratio*."[4] Right from the beginning, then, we get the identification of architecture as an act of imposing order, of taking the unruly and making it coherent. However, this is not an aesthetic act alone in terms of *ratio* and symmetry. Vitruvius had greater ambitions than simply defining taste. "I realized," he writes in the preface directed to the emperor Augustus, "that you had care not only for the common life of all men and the regulation of the commonwealth, but also for the fitness of public buildings—that even as, through you, the city was increased with provinces, so public buildings were to provide eminent guarantees for the majesty of empire." McEwen brilliantly shows how this passage, and others supporting it, indicate the wider pretensions of Vitruvius to tie his architectural approach into the imperial program of expansion and authority: "it was not architecture as such that initially attached Vitruvius to Julius Caesar's might. It was, rather, the connection of architecture to *imperium*."[5]

What is happening here is that under the more-or-less benign cloak of aesthetic codes, Vitruvius is slipping in a distinctly nonbenign association with social reform and imperial power. The term *ordering* all too easily conflates the visual with the political. As I have said, just because he was first does not necessarily make him right but it certainly makes Vitruvius influential, because the mistaken (and dangerous) conflation of visual order with social order continues to this day. As we shall see later, this has profound ethical consequences.[6]

My second-year lecture series is called Architecture and Ideas. The first lecture starts with a quote from a critic writing about the house that Sarah and I designed and live in. The critic writes: "It has too many ideas." This is not a compliment. In architecture, having too many ideas is a sign of confusion, whereas one idea rigorously carried through is a mark of order and control.[7] Where in other disciplines having ideas is the lifeblood, in architecture they are edited. To illustrate this intellectual conundrum, I put up a slide with

new blahblah
our aim is true

commodity

firmness

delight

Vitruvius' mantra on it. COMMODITY: FIRMNESS: DELIGHT. "How dumb is that?" I ask. "How empty of ideas is that? Look, if you are a philosopher you at least have Socrates to track back to. If a poet, Sappho. If a playwright, Euripides. If a theater theorist, Aristotle. If a mathematician, Thales and Pythagoras. Those lot are kind of bright. But as architects, whom do we have? A second-rate Roman author, who flattered to deceive, as the fount of our knowledge."[8] Then, because the lecture is at the same time as the UK party political conferences, I add: "It is so bland, so commonsensical, that it could be the Tory conference mission statement," remembering when the Conservative Party election manifesto was called "Time for Common Sense." I got a complaint for that—something to do with political bias—so the next year I changed it to the Labour conference mission statement just to see what would happen, and made an appropriately corporate slide to go with it. No complaints this time, suggesting that the Vitruvian triad is closer to the emollient spin of New Labour's ordering center.

Rogue Objects

In *Civilization and Its Discontents,* Sigmund Freud famously identifies beauty, cleanliness, and order as occupying "a special position among the requirements of civilization."[9] We have just identified the combination of beauty and order in the Vitruvian legacy. Cleanliness adds another dimension: it denotes purity, the removal of waste, whiteness. It is not for nothing, therefore, that modernist architectural beauty is so often associated with pure forms, elimination of decoration, and white walls.[10] And it is not for nothing that this cleanliness is so often associated with some kind of moral order made possible by the actions of the architect/artist. This is a theme that runs from Plato—"The first thing that our artists must do . . . is to wipe the slate of human society and human habits clean . . . after that the first step will be to sketch in the outline of the social system"[11]—to Le Corbusier: "A COAT OF WHITEWASH. We would perform a moral act: *to love purity!* . . . whitewash is extremely moral."[12] In the rush of words, we overlook the offensiveness of the association of visual purity with social morality.

The three terms beauty, cleanliness, and order form a triangle; in fact a Bermuda triangle that eliminates anything that might threaten its formal (and social) perfection. Thus alien objects, dirt, the low, the supposed immoral, are cast aside in the pursuit of purity. If we return to the Vitruvian metaphor of the body, then it is clear that the triangle will tolerate only the classical body. Stallybrass and White identify the classical body as the abiding symbol of high order: "the classical body was far more than an aesthetic standard or model. It structured . . . the characteristically 'high' discourses of philosophy, statecraft, theology and law."[13] The classical body signifies an ordered body of knowledge as well as an ordered system of form. The Vitruvian body on which so much architecture still leans for support is thus much more than a nice metaphor of coherence; it designates a "closed, homogeneous, monumental, centred and symmetrical system."[14]

If the classical body (of architecture, of knowledge) is to be ordered, then it must also in metaphorical terms be healthy. "Order is the oldest concern of political philosophy," Susan Sontag writes in *Illness as Metaphor,* "and if it is plausible to compare the polis to an organism, then it is plausible to compare civil disorder with an illness."[15] Any sign of illness is a threat to order and, as Sontag makes all too clear, the "worst" illness of all is cancer. She shows how illness, and in particular cancer, is often used as a metaphor to describe the malaise of society. "No specific political view seems to have a monopoly of this metaphor. Trotsky called Stalinism the cancer of Marxism," the Gang of Four were called "the cancer of China," and the "standard metaphor of Arab polemics . . . is that Israel is 'a cancer in the heart of the Arab world.'"[16] For the person with cancer, this metaphor has the effect of casting them out as untouchable; cancer is seen as a kind of punishment. For society, the cancerous metaphor demands aggressive treatment in order for a cure to be effected. Cancer must be eliminated if the healthy body is to be reestablished, so for order to be reconstructed.

And so when Le Corbusier declares, in *Precisions*, that "to create architecture is to put into order,"[17] it is no surprise to find that, at the same time, he likens the city (as the thing to be ordered) to a sick organism. Nor is it any surprise to note that the illness that Le Corbusier constantly evokes as metaphor for the sickness of the city, architecture, and the academy is cancer.[18] If the "city has a biological life"[19] which has been infected by illness, then order can be effected only through radical surgery; the primary care of medicine will not suffice: *in city planning 'medical' solutions are a delusion; they resolve nothing, they are very expensive. Surgical solutions resolve.*"[20] Corbusier's metaphor is telling. The stigma of sickness must be eradicated and cancerous elements cut out if a fresh start is to be made. Only then can the quest for ordered perfection be initiated. The Bermuda triangle again: purity, cleanliness, and order eliminating and excluding the rogue objects. "Orderly space is rule-governed space," Zygmunt Bauman writes, and "the rule is a rule in as far as it forbids and excludes."[21]

Some time ago there was a wonderful television series called "Sign of the Times." In it the photographer Martin Parr and social commentator Nicholas Barker quietly observed the British in their homes. As the occupants talked about their design tastes, the camera froze on a single poignant feature, maybe a neo-rococo fireplace with gas flames ("I think we are looking for a look that is established, warm, comfortable, traditional"), maybe a faux antique candelabra ("I'm put off real antiques because to me they look old and sort of spooky"). Generally the effect was too gentle to be mocking, but at times the scene slipped into pathos. One such moment is set in a sparse modernist interior. A woman, voice choked with emotion, is lamenting that her husband will not allow her to have "normal" things such as curtains: the camera dwells on expanses of glazing. When her husband Henry appears, he despairs of the "rogue objects" disturbing his ordered interior. "To come home in the evening," he says, "and to find the kids have carried out their own form of anarchy is just about the last thing I can face."[22]

The rogue objects are his children's toys.

Henry is an architect.

Bauman's Order

Now is a good time to introduce Zygmunt Bauman. He will be with you through the reading of this book, just as he has been with me through the writing of it. I came across Bauman in one of those moments of scavenging among footnotes, a happy accident of reading that brings what has been at the periphery of one's vision right to the center. Of course, he should probably have been central all along: "One of the world's leading social theorists," reads the blurb on the book, and everyone that I now mention him to returns a pitying look as if to question my academic credentials. Everyone, that is, except architects and architectural theorists.[23] This group tend to bypass the foothills of skirmishes with reality and move toward the higher ground of battles with ideals (or their deconstruction), ignoring on the way Dewey's warning that the "construction of ideals in general and their sentimental glorification is easy; the responsibilities of studious thought and action are shirked."[24] There is an intellectual elitism at work here, with the supposedly superior status of philosophical thought being used to prop up the fragile constructions of architectural idea(l)s. Contemporary architectural theory is thus littered with references to philosophical texts with hardly a nod to current social theory. I suspect that architectural theorists have largely ignored Bauman's territory because it is too damn real. It reminds us too constantly of our own fragility, our bodies, our politics. It reminds us, crucially, of others and our responsibilities to them. In the realm of this sociology there is no room for autonomy; indeed, the whole idea of architecture as an autonomous discipline would be treated with the disdain it deserves.

Bauman is too prolific a thinker and writer to summarize here. He has produced almost a book a year for the past fifteen years, and I came to each new one with a mixture of dread and anticipation. Dread that my schedule was going to be knocked still further as I would have to take on board yet more ideas; anticipation that those ideas would, as they so often did, locate my small architectural world into a much wider social and political setting. Bauman gave me confidence and for this I became an unabashed fan; maybe not the best way to write a book (academics are meant to assume an air of detachment), but at least you now know. Time and time again I would find Bauman articulating ideas that appeared to me to have parallels to, and implications for, architectural production.[25] It is not just that he directly addresses issues of dependency and contingency, but that he sees contingency as part of a wider condition of modernity, and so the argument that I was beginning to develop suddenly made sense in terms of its broader social and intellectual context.

Thus when Bauman refers to the "surgical stance which throughout the modern age characterised the attitudes and policies of institutionalised powers,"[26] we can begin to understand that Le Corbusier's excising proclamations are not just the rantings of a self-promoting polemicist but part of a more general attitude. Le Corbusier is seen in the wider picture not as the inventor of modernism (as architectural style and movement), but as an inevitable consequence of modernity (as a condition of society).[27] He is a symptom, not a cause. This simple truth comes as something of a shock to the inhabitants of the black box of architecture, brought up as they are on a determinist diet of cause and effect, in which architectural progress is announced in relation to previous architectural moments. Take, for example, the presumed baton-passing of William Morris to Voysey to Van de Velde to Mackintosh to Wright to Loos to Behrens to Gropius: these are Pevsner's Pioneers of the Modern Movement, a sequence of falling dominos that creates the effect of a completely self-contained world.[28] When Marx says that "men make history but not in circumstances of their own choosing," I am sure that he did not mean to exclude architects, and yet so many of the standard texts of architectural history remain within the tramlines of a self-referential architectural world, ignoring the other circumstances that frame architectural production. Bauman and other social theorists allow us to see that what we may have assumed as an architectural necessity is in fact dependent on a much more powerful pattern of circumstances; they lever us into an acknowledgment of the contingency of architecture. And so to repeat, just to shake the inhabitants from their reverie: Le Corbusier and the others are not a cause of modernism; they are symptoms of modernity.

In this light, what is striking is the way that the principles of architectural modernism fit the more general pattern of the will to order that Bauman identifies as a central feature of modernity. Of all the "impossible tasks that modernity set itself . . . the task of order (more precisely and most importantly, of order as task) stands out."[29] Thus Bauman's argument that "the typically modern practice . . . is the effort to exterminate ambivalence"[30] puts into context Le Corbusier's Law of Ripolin, with its "elimination of the equivocal."[31] It is not just Le Corbusier who fits this pattern, though he is used by Bauman to illustrate certain tendencies in modernism as an expression of the condition of modernity.[32] Bauman describes the modern age as one that has a "vision of an orderly universe . . . the vision was of a hierarchical harmony reflected, as in a mirror, in the uncontested and incontestable pronouncements of reason."[33] In a striking metaphor, Bauman describes the modern state as a gardening state,[34] bringing the unruly, the chaotic, and the fearful (as represented by nature) under the rule of order, regularity, and control (as represented by the garden). It is a metaphor that chimes with Zola's caustic dismissal of a new public square in Paris: "It looks like a bit of nature did something wrong and was put into prison."[35] The ordering of space can thus be seen as part of a much wider ordering of society. Depending on whose argument you follow, architects are mere pawns in an overwhelming regime of power and control, or else architects are active agents in the execution of this power and control.[36] Either way, they are firmly situated in the real conditions that modernity throws up, and not to be seen in some idealized set-apart space.

There are two key, and interrelated, aspects of Bauman's analysis of modernity and its ordering tendencies. On the one hand he argues that the will to order arose out of a fear of disorder. "The kind of society that, retrospectively, came to be called modern," he writes, "emerged out of the discovery that human order is vulnerable, contingent and devoid of reliable foundations. That discovery was shocking. The response to the shock was a dream and an effort to make order solid, obligatory and reliably founded."[37] The important word here is *dream*. The possibility of establishing order over and above the flux of modernity is an illusion. It is an illusion because of the second aspect of his argument, namely that to achieve order one has to eliminate the other of order, but the other of order can never be fully erased. "The struggle for order is not a fight of one definition against another, of one way of articulating reality against a competitive proposal. It is a fight of determination against ambiguity, of semantic precision against ambivalence, of transparency against obscurity, clarity against fuzziness. The other of order is not another order: chaos is its only alternative. The other of order is the miasma of the indeterminate and unpredictable. The other is the uncertainty, that source and archetype of all fear."[38] The gardener gets rid of weeds as part of the controlling of nature. As we shall see with architecture, as with any project of the modern age, the more one attempts to eliminate the other of order, the more it comes back to haunt one. Weeds always come back. The whiter the wall, the quicker it succumbs to dirt. In their pursuit of an idea (and an ideal) of order, architects have to operate in a state of permanent denial of the residual power of the other of order.

Order can thus only really exist as a form of knowledge from which will issue a series of abstracted procedures such as design, manipulation, management, and engineering—these being core activities of the modern age for Bauman.[39] As a form of knowledge, order is subjected to the modern tests of truth and reason and, in a self-legitimating manner, passes them with flying colors. Order is seen as rational and logical because it has been created out of the rules of reason and logic. Nietzsche is very clear about the limits of this closed circuit: "if somebody hides a thing behind a bush, seeks it out and finds it in the selfsame place, then there is not much to boast of respecting this seeking and finding; thus, however, matters stand with the pursuit of seeking and finding 'truth' within the realm of reason."[40] The tests of truth and reason are carried out in a sterile laboratory, doors sealed against the contaminations that the world would inflict. Herein lies the problem that we have already associated with the autonomy of architecture (remember Shevtsov saying: "truth found inside a tightly sealed room is hardly of any use outside"). Ideas developed away from the world may achieve a semblance of purity—of truth and reason—but this purity will always be tormented by the fact that the knowledge has arisen from within the world and eventually will have to return to the world. Agnes Heller summarizes the paradox: "One is confronted with the task of obtaining *true knowledge* about a *world,* whilst being aware that this knowledge is situated in that world."[41] Her solution gives no solace: "in order to overcome this paradox an *Archimedean point outside contemporaneity* must be found. However, this is exactly what cannot be done: the prisonhouse of the present day only allows for illusory escape."[42] We are left with the illusion of order, but closer inspection reveals that the underlying reality is rapidly unraveling that semblance.

Our architect Henry, the one who saw toys as rogue objects, clearly found architecture too unorderly and too unorderable, and so he stopped practicing. Instead he set up a company that manufactures fireplaces, the Platonic Fireplace Company. He finds peace in the controllable gas flame playing over little stone cubes, spheres, and pyramids in a semblance of order.

The Ridding of Contingency

In Edmund Bacon's classic work on town planning, *The Design of Cities,* the titles of the sections are explicit in summarizing the ordering thrust of the argument. Passing through chapters entitled "Impositions of Order," "Development of Order," and "Stirrings of a New Order," one arrives at a page that clearly presents the issues at stake.[43] On it there are two illustrations of Rome. At the top is one of Piranesi's *Vedute di Roma* etchings. The detail of drawing almost overwhelms one in its inclusion of low life, weather, fragments, mess, lovers kissing, broken roads, and vegetating cornices. Each time one looks at it one finds something new. Below is Bacon's interpretation of the same site. A few sparse color-coded lines connecting up isolated monuments; all is understandable in a glance. One can almost

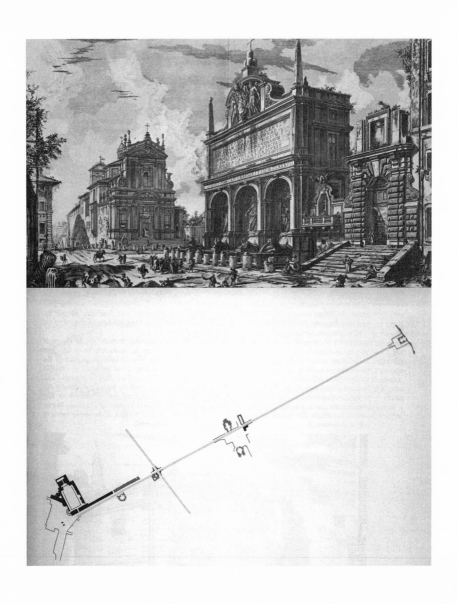

Contingency

sense Bacon's relief in making the drawing, in his ruthless editing of the contingent. Out of sight, out of mind. The world, emptied of uncertainty, is now controlled and controllable. Order all round. Bacon's juxtaposition of the two drawings makes explicit a general architectural tendency, that of ridding the world of contingency the better to manipulate that world into (a semblance of) order.

In a telling passage in *When the Cathedrals Were White,* Le Corbusier is waiting at Bordeaux railway station and notes down what he sees:

The station is disgusting. Not an employee on the crowded platform. An official with a gilded insignia does not know when the Paris train will arrive. At the office of the stationmaster they are evasive, no one knows exactly. General uproar, offensive filthiness, the floor is black, broken up, the immense windows are black. At 9.00pm the express stops at platform no 4 completely cluttered with boxes of vegetables, fish, fruit, hats, returned empty bags.[44]

This short description tells us all we need to know of Le Corbusier's fears, of his "other." Dirt, unruly crowds, broken time, inexact responses, damaged construction, the lack of white, and the contamination of categories (food with clothing). Chaos and transgression all around. But what is really revealing is that Le Corbusier then slyly hints as to why he is in Bordeaux station. He is on his way to Pessac, the new modern quarter that he has designed for Henry Frugès in the suburbs of Bordeaux. It is as if, on his journey from the station to the suburb, Le Corbusier casts off the contingent presences and so arrives at Pessac cleansed. The buildings there are pure, ordered, clean, progressive—everything that Bordeaux station is not. He has accomplished "the miracle of inexpressible space . . . a boundless depth opens up . . . contingent presences are put to flight."[45] Well, he has accomplished this in his head. Once he turns his back, as we shall see, things begin to unravel.

It is important, however, not to see Bacon and Le Corbusier as fringe figures waging lonely wars against disorder. They are part of a much broader trend. If the will to order is an identifying feature of the modern project, then the means to that end lies in the elimination of the other of order; it lies in the ridding of contingency. For Bauman, contingency is the twin of order: "Awareness of the world's contingency and the idea of order as the goal and the outcome of the practice of ordering were born together, as twins; perhaps even Siamese twins." The reason is simple: one does not have the need for order unless one has experienced disorder: "one does not conceive of regularity unless one is buffeted by the unexpected. . . . Contingency was discovered together with the realization that if one wants things and events to be regular, repeatable and predictable, one needs to do something about it; they won't be such on their own."[46] And what one does is to act as the surgeon, separating the Siamese twins, knowing that one will probably be sacrificed so that the privileged one, the one with the better structure, can survive. Contingency cannot be tolerated in the modern project, be it architectural, political, social, or philosophical.

Philosophically, contingency has been demeaned ever since the initial pairing by Aristotle of contingency with necessity.[47] As one of his modal categories, contingency becomes the "not necessary," and in the history of ideas subsequently becomes associated with, at best, the "limitation of reason"[48] or, at worst, with the other of reason, irrationality. If a contingent event is "an element of reality impervious to full rationalization,"[49] then it is not surprising that in the realm of reason which typifies the modern project, the contingent event is dismissed as beneath the dignity of explanation. It is consistent therefore for a philosopher of reason such as Jürgen Habermas to talk of "paralyzing experiences with contingency."[50]

Contingency must be suppressed as a philosophical category if it is not to undermine the authority of reason. Probably the most subtle working of this argument is in Hegel. In order to achieve "the essential task" of his *Science of Logic,* which is "to *overcome* the contingency,"[51] Hegel first introduces the need for contingency, which he beautifully describes as the "unity of actuality and possibility."[52] Contingency adds to reality a certain concreteness which avoids the pitfalls of abstracted thinking.[53] "For Hegel reality would not be self-sufficient if it did not contain its own irrationality."[54] He therefore allows contingency to come to the surface the better to push it down in the establishment of the rule of logic.

I introduce this philosophical interlude of the ridding of contingency not to show off, but as the polished intellectual tip of a much bigger iceberg. For Bauman, modern times are "an era of bitter and relentless war against ambivalence."[55] His most intense example of the war on ambivalence is the Holocaust.[56] This genocide was the elimination of the other, but this terrible act was made possible in the first instance by a dehumanizing of the world brought about by, among other factors, the suppression of ambivalence and contingency in the pursuit of a more ordered and "progressive" society. Bauman's argument is that we should resist the temptation to identify the Holocaust as a one-off event circumscribed by its very "Germanness" and the so-called Jewish problem. Nor should we believe that progressive and supposedly liberalizing tendencies will banish the possibility of such genocide ever happening again. Instead we should see the Holocaust as a consequence of the patterns and processes of modernity, in particular the way that the modern world distances us from taking moral responsibility for our actions.

To go to the furthest shores of humanity (but shores that Bauman argues are maybe not that far from normal life after all) is to begin to understand that the war on ambivalence and the ridding of contingency are not benign processes. It might appear that the normalizing pursuit of order and certainty is self-evidently sensible. Surely the abolishment of uncertainty must mean that our lives are more certain? Surely the collective and measured agreement of morals is better than the subjective response of impulsive individuals? Surely it is better to share common goals than to promote fracturing contradictions? But in fact the normalizing disguises a stealthy process of the marginalization of difference, as William Connolly so convincingly argues in his *Politics and Ambiguity*. "The irony of a normalizing democracy," he writes, "is that it . . . tends to be accompanied by the marginalization of new sectors of the population or newly defined sectors of the self . . . and the suppression of this ambiguity tends to license the insidious extension of normalization into new corners of life."[57] What is normal to one group may be abnormal to another. The problem is that the definitions of the normal are controlled by the powerful and, as generations of feminists have reminded us, this leads to the suppression of various sectors of society. The ridding of contingency, in whatever field, thus inevitably brings political consequences with it, insofar as it is predicated on the establishment of a certain set of values that smother the clamor of different voices beneath. Le Corbusier's abhorrence of the "general uproar" is the other side of his will to impose his value system. All, however, is not lost, because the driving out of contingent presences is not the once-and-for-all act that Le Corbusier and many others would have us believe.

I am on a visit to the McLaren headquarters designed by Norman Foster to house the production facilities, offices, and associated spin-off companies of the Formula One racing group. Many people are saying that this is Foster's ideal project. A heady mix of technology transfer, undisclosed (i.e. huge) budget, speed, minimal tolerances, *Vorsprung durch Technik,* male hormones, and a client (Ron Dennis) who is famously perfectionist and famously demanding. There was a danger that he and Norman (who is thought to share these qualities) might clash, but they are now firm friends (the building

is a success). The two even share the same birthday. How spooky is that? They make cars here, but do not think grease monkeys and porn calendars. Think white gloves and sterile laboratories with sealed doors. I joke that the specification for the cleaning contract must be longer than that for the building contract, but am met with stony faces. Neither do I get many laughs when a group of muscled men in tight black uniforms approach us and I ask if they have come off the production line as well.

I am beginning to lose patience, a decline hastened by a remote-control soap dispenser that has gone berserk and sprayed liquid soap over my expensive new shirt. *Rückschlag durch Technik.* Backlash through technology.[58] It is not just my suppressed anger at the senseless waste of the whole operation, boys with toys in a sport that effectively sanctions global warming. It is not just that the cars on exhibition have a better view than the workers. It is more that there is something deeply disturbing about the silence, the absolute control, and the regime of power that the architecture asserts. "Don't the engineers mind being seen and watched?" I ask, pointing at the huge windows that put the whole process on display. "They get used to it," comes the terse reply that for once eschews the techno-corporate spin used to justify the rest of the building ("Ronspeak," as petrolheads affectionately call it).

Counting Sheep

If Le Corbusier had returned to Pessac in 1964, he would have found a very different vision of modern life to the one he had left for the incoming tenants some thirty-five years before. Open terraces had been filled in. Steel strip windows replaced with divided timber ones complete with vernacular shutters. Pitched roofs added over leaky flat ones. Stick-on bricks, Moorish features, windowsills, and other forms of decoration applied over the original stripped walls. All in all, a straightforward defilement of the master's guiding principles by an ungrateful, even unworthy, public. Or is it?

Philippe Boudon, in his meticulous documentation of the inhabitation of Pessac, argues that the combination of Le Corbusier's initial design and the inhabitants' irrepressible DIY tendencies led to an inevitability that the purity of the original would be overwhelmed by the urges of everyday life. "The fact of the matter," writes Henri Lefebvre, the philosopher of the everyday, in his introduction to Boudon's book, "is that in Pessac Le Corbusier produced a kind of architecture that lent itself to conversion and sculptural ornamentation. . . . And what did the occupants add? Their needs."[59]

Their needs. As simple as that. In fact so simple as to make one wonder why a great philosopher should bother to note it. But it is necessary to state it with full philosophical force in order to acknowledge that architecture can never fully control the actions of users. In Architecture, as it wants to be,

needs are cajoled into functions and thus subjected to normalizing control. Functions (mathematical, scientific, and linear) are, however, very different from needs (full as they are of desires, differences, and demands), and in the end, of course, the needs of the inhabitants at Pessac would well up to claim the architecture. The distance between functions and needs is just one of the many rifts that contribute to the gap between architecture as it wants to be and architecture as it is. I have already fallen foul of this gap in my use of just the architectural "greats" and their writings to introduce my argument. I am effectively setting them up, the better to make them fall into the gap. Clearly not all architects hold to the tenets of these greats, but to a large extent architectural culture has been shaped by them. The architectural scholar Tom Spector has a nice formulation: on the basis of the idea that most Americans consider themselves either rich or pre-rich, he argues that most architects consider themselves either famous or pre-famous. It is thus the values and the currency of the famous that dominate architectural culture: "the masses are encouraged to self-identify with the elites, regardless of whether any realistic possibility of achieving that exalted status exists or not."[60]

While it may be easy to parody the writings of the architectural greats, I do it not out of mere dismissal, but in order to "break up the ordered surfaces" that we might have taken for granted and, in so doing, more positively reconstruct alternatives.[61] The gap between architecture as described in these writings and architecture as it exists in time partially arises out of the crucial mistake of confusing architecture as metaphor with architecture as reality. There is a long tradition of philosophers using the *figure* of the architect to denote rational authority. The *architekton* is used by Aristotle to illustrate the commanding relationship of theory and practice.[62] In the architect, Plato "discovered a figure that under the aegis of 'making' is able to withstand 'becoming.'"[63] And, most forcefully, there is Descartes, who argues that "buildings undertaken and completed by a single architect are usually more attractive and better planned than those which several have tried to patch up by adapting old walls built for different purposes . . . the latter of which . . . you would say is chance rather than the will of man using reason."[64] The banishment of chance, the authority of the individual, the triumph of the rational, the building of the new on cleared ground—these are identified by Descartes as the defining attributes of the architect, and so by analogy are then assumed as the attributes of the philosopher as rational subject. It is an alliance of mutual convenience. For the philosopher there is a necessity to reflect the metaphysical in the physical, because without the material world as grounding the immaterial remains just that—immaterial. So the analogous actions of the architect (as originator of stable constructions) serve as a useful source of legitimation for philosophical discourse. For the architect the reflection of the philosopher (and in particular the Cartesian philosopher of the rational) is a means of establishing authority through establishing a supposedly detached, objective knowledge base. And so the figure of architect/philosopher is created.

In reading Descartes, one might assume that he is referring to the actual actions of the architect, and thus that the figure of the architect/philosopher is based on some kind of worldly reality. It may be necessary for both sides to maintain at least an illusion of this reality—without this illusion the figure loses credence—but it is in fact a conceit. The figure of the architect/philosopher is simply a convenient metaphor. This is revealed most clearly in the relationship being constituted around the common use of language. The terms of architecture are used to underpin the foundations of metaphysics—to structure knowledge. Thus when Descartes speaks in the first paragraph of the *First Meditation* of the necessity *"to start again from the foundations,"*[65] it is made clear that the new philosophy of reason is to be demonstrated in terms of a new construction. Later Heidegger will describe Kant's project in terms of the building trade, with Kant (as architect) laying the foundations from which the construction of metaphysics is projected as a building plan. Kant "draws and sketches" reason's "outline," whose "essential moment" is the "architectonic, the blueprint projected as the essential structure of pure reason."[66]

In these examples, and many others, the language of architecture is being used *metaphorically*. It is the apparent stability and the presumed logic of architecture that appeal to the foundational aspirations of traditional metaphysics, providing a form of legitimation for the construction of a philosophy. The power of this association is such that Heidegger can begin to effect a critique of Western metaphysics through an exposure of the weaknesses of its architectural metaphors. The architectural image of stability disguises an inherent weakness in metaphysics, which in fact is built not on *terra firma* but on an abyss.[67] As Mark Wigley rightly notes, in this context "architecture is a cover and philosophy takes cover in architecture."[68]

This is not to suggest that architects actually read all this difficult stuff and thereby get a deluded sense of their own importance as the mirrors of rational thought. But it is to suggest that the metaphor of architecture as a stable authority is so powerful as to make one believe that this is also the reality of architecture. The danger is not so much when philosophers come to believe in the myths that this metaphor promotes; it is when architects do. The Japanese philosopher Kojin Karatani argues that this has happened: "Platonic architecture is metaphorical. Plato's use of the metaphor of architecture, like that of Descartes, Kant, and Hegel who followed him, should thus be understood as the will to construct an edifice of knowledge on a solid foundation." One result is that "architecture as a metaphor dominated . . . even architecture itself."[69] It is the *metaphorical* will to order, *and no more than that.* We have already seen what happens when one starts to confuse the metaphorical for the real: the deluded belief that architecture can be autonomous; the resulting self-referentiality; the actual will to order; the concomitant suppression of the contingent. To criticize, as I have done, these aspects of architectural culture is to criticize something that is in fact not architecture. It is easy pickings, like kicking a man when he is down, because such architectural culture conceived in all its purity can put up no resistance to the dirty realism of my boot. It is time, therefore, to move to a more grounded description of architecture, away from the dreams and semblances.

In one of his early books, *Della tranquillità dell'animo*, the Renaissance architect and theorist Leon Battista Alberti recommends that to settle oneself in times of stress or anxiety one can find solace in architectural reverie: "and sometimes it has happened that not only have I grown calm in my restlessness of spirit, but I have thought of things most rare and memorable. Sometimes I have designed and built finely proportioned buildings in my mind . . . and I have occupied myself with constructions of this kind until overcome with sleep."[70] Normal people resort to counting sheep to get to sleep. Renaissance architects resort to architectural proportion. Sheep (for urban dwellers) and fine architecture both sit in that twilight zone between day and night, reality and dream—and when one wakes in the morning one is left with no more than a chimeric memory, revealing the perfection of form as a mirage never to be attained.

3   Coping with Contingency

Contingency is, quite simply, the fact that things could be otherwise than they are.
—William Rasch

A Balance of Colossal Forces

Karatani's wake-up call to architects is brutal: "Plato admired the architect as a metaphor but despised the architect as an earthly laborer."[1] This comes as something of a shock. Far from being admitted to the ordered and ordering garden of Plato's Academy, architects are condemned to building the wall around it. The reason for Plato's derision is simple: he despised the architect "because the actual architect, and even architecture itself, are exposed to contingency,"[2] and contingency, as we have seen, does not fit into the ideal scheme of things. The implication is that architecture is not only contingent as a discipline, but irredeemably contingent: no amount of rational will can effect the passage from the reality to the metaphor, from the contingent to the pure. Of course all human actions in any given field are dependent on others to a greater or lesser extent: no one is fully isolated from outside forces. However, architecture is peculiarly exposed to these external dependencies. An accountant, say, may place the fluid finances of a company into the order of a standardized system of measurement. The artist may block the world out during moments of creative conception. The lawyer has recourse to a documented and reasonably stable body of previous case law, even if this is then played out against particular circumstances in the form of "local knowledge."[3] An architect has neither the luxury of solitude, nor the precision of standard methods, nor, as we shall see, the comfort of a stable epistemology. Architecture is dependent on others at every stage of its journey from initial sketch to inhabitation.

One might think that an architectural sketch has a certain innocence, but even these early marks are conditioned by previous experience and present expectations. From then on the whole design process is opened up to the input and control of others—clients, other architects, consultants, potential users, regulators, and so on. While architects may try to calm the resulting flux through the imposition of standard design methodologies, the storm is never abated.[4] Once the design is handed over to the contractor, the building industry inflicts its own set of uncertainties.[5] And when the building is handed over to the client, a whole set of new and still more uncontrollable circumstances move in—the original users, new users, time, historians, new technologies, weather, events, and critics. Architecture is never alone. Daniel Sherer, the translator of the last work of the Italian architectural historian Manfredo Tafuri, makes the point well: "whereas architecture, in searching for definitive solutions to the challenges it confronts, realizes one possibility among many, history places architecture before an open field of possibilities, exposing the most stable plans to unforeseen forces that inevitably disrupt them."[6]

In Karatani's terms, "because architecture is an event, it is always contingent." "Architecture is thus a form of communication conditioned to occur without common rules—it is a communication with the other, who, by definition, does not follow the same set of rules."[7] Again that gap: here between a set of internalized procedures that provide solace to architects, and a seething mass of others who neither understand nor wish to engage with those procedures. Architecture as a discipline is thus far from a linear procedure running along idealized tramlines. It is a balance of colossal forces—the term that Joseph Conrad uses in *Lord Jim* to describe a butterfly; fragile, ephemeral, but astonishingly adapted to its circumstances. It is in a glimpse of the wonder of that balancing act that we might first recognize that contingency is maybe not such a threat to architecture's sanctity after all.

I first came across Kojin Karatani about halfway through writing this book. He was in a reference in David Harvey's *Spaces of Hope*, which in turn was a reference given to me at a seminar I was giving to the Planning Department at Sheffield, which in turn came about following a chance conversation about hope in a lunch queue. Not exactly a direct route to a quote that rattled me badly: "the actual architect, and even architecture itself, are exposed to contingency." Damn, damn, damn, I thought, he has got there before me. The seventy minutes it took for *Architecture as Metaphor* to arrive at Humanities

Reading Room Two in the British Library were very, very, long. When the book came my anxiety was quelled: Karatani redirected but did not overwhelm my argument.

Academics live in fear of being caught out—"But how can you take that seriously, he/she hasn't read XYZ"—and so various risk management strategies are employed. One is to quote absolutely everything; this does not necessarily mean that the writings referred to are even read, let alone critically assessed, but it does cover one's back. The second strategy is to refer only to the great texts, the primary texts, or current leaders in the field. Search for "contingency" in any recent philosophical or cultural studies text, and one is almost always led to Richard Rorty. Any subject is thus framed by the greats, and one can only incrementally shift the arguments around within that frame. The third risk management strategy is to stay firmly within the bounds of one's own discipline. However, all these strategies are bound to fail; there is always another book that one has not read, another idea one has not assimilated. So if research is a combination of diligence (the risk management) and luck, it is acceptable also to welcome the contribution of luck. Finding that reference through chance conversations. Ransacking indexes for compelling conjunctions of terms. Making sense of that snippet of conversation on breakfast radio. Scanning that pile of books on the desk next to you in British Library Humanities Reading Room Two (somehow these are generally more interesting than in Humanities Reading Room One; this a spatial thing: the grounded, darker, denser spaces of Reading Room One seem to attract the serious risk managers, while looser souls gather in the lighter, more open, skyward spaces of Reading Room Two). And so on. Then there are those moments when one reads a book and suddenly has to reconsider the assumptions and ideas that have been developing linearly over the past years. For me Henri Lefebvre's *Production of Space*, Zygmunt Bauman's *Modernity and Ambivalence,* and Bruno Latour's *We Have Never Been Modern* were such books, jolting me sideways into new territories.

My point, to be blunt, is that research is contingent, and none the worse for that if one accepts this contingency as an opportunity for productive synthesis and not as a threat to academic rigor. The contingent researcher purposely crosses over the borderlines of their own discipline, knowing that outsiders so often see the obvious that insiders miss, and knowing that paradigm shifts are frequently initiated from outside and not within a particular field. The contingent researcher welcomes each new book with a sense of curiosity, not with a sense of duty. The contingent researcher enjoys the sideways knocks of new ideas. This is because research is not as linear a procedure as one might believe but is a journey through intellectual rhizomes. (The term is Deleuze and Guattari's; I will be honest here and tell you that I have no more than dipped into the book where they make the argument, *A Thousand Plateaus*. The question is: should I put it in my bibliography as part of my risk management strategy?) However—and this is the vital part of my argument—the contingent researcher is not a relativist. It is not as if any text or idea has equal status or relevance. The journey through the rhizomes is not a random sequence; it has an intended direction—guided by the research question—but the destination is not absolutely fixed. Contingencies that come one's way are thus seen not as competing fragments but as a field of opportunities to be gathered to a greater or lesser extent, and then filtered by the intent of the project. The contingent researcher has to be light enough on his or her feet, and modest enough, to allow that intent to be shaped by other events and ideas, but at the same time purposeful enough not to be overwhelmed by them.

The operation of the contingent researcher, as we shall see, is not that far away from that of the contingent architect.

The Juggernaut

While architecture may be extreme in its contingency, it is not alone in it. The modern world (in all its contingency) has been supremely resistant to accepting the modern project (in all its order). A gap arises between what thinkers would have the world to be and how it really is. We have already encountered this gap separating the ideals and reality of architecture; now we can see that this architectural fissure is part of a much wider epistemological fault line between, on the one hand, the observers of life and, on the other, the believers in reason. While one group (among them Marx, Berman, Bauman) look around them and see that "all that is solid melts into air," another lineage from Descartes through Kant to Habermas will invoke the power of reason to stabilize that flux. This latter intellectual tradition of Enlightenment fundamentalism is still considered to be superior because reason always constructs an intellectual stranglehold over its other. Reason maintains its own terms of reference, and anything beyond these terms (contingency, emotion) is dismissed out of hand as an irrational weakness.[8]

On emerging from Foster's McLaren building, a debate starts. I am left gasping at the vision of a dystopian future of spatial authority through suppression, as they marvel at the transfer of carbon fiber technology from car body to staircase detail. My reaction is visceral, and when I try to explain my views on the building, it comes out as pure emotion. This is a problem. They come back with a reasoned argument as to why the building is a near-perfect marriage of form and technique. They win, as reason always wins over emotion. Stands to reason, dunnit?

It is when the tradition of Enlightenment fundamentalism leaves the sanctuary of philosophical thought and enters the world that the consequences become unpalatable, with unfettered power being imposed under the excuse of better order. To a large extent the insatiable demands of present-day neoliberals are buttressed by this tradition, inasmuch as the free market is justified as the end game of "rational" economics. Thus an apologist for globalization such as Tom Friedman can argue that "the world is flat"—a metaphor he invokes time and time again in his vision of a world in which previous inequalities are supposedly leveled out by a combination of technological advances and corporate capital, a combination driven by the impulse of reason to progress in the name of betterment. "Tom, the playing field is being leveled," he is told by the CEO of one of India's leading high-technology companies, Infosys—completely overlooking the disjunction that his limo has passed rutted roads, rickshaws, beggars, strange smells, in order to reach the Infosys campus. While it is evident that the way is being cleared by technology and Western capital for the emergence of previously latent economies such as India, this does not mean that difference can ever be completely suppressed. The cliché of the McDonaldization of the world hardly disguises the fact that the world is far from flat, that order is far from universal, and that flux is the norm and not the exception to be quelled.[9]

My sympathies lie with those who look first and then think, rather than those who think first and then look for places to impose their thinking. And the world observed is a modern world that resists ordering. There are countless interpretations of modernity, but the most compelling ones come from those who look first and identify the tension between the universalizing drive of the modern project and the uncertainty of the reality. Within this tension there are then different weightings as to whether uncertainty or certainty has the upper hand. Thus on the one hand, the great German social theorist Niklas Luhmann argues that contingency is "modern society's defining feature";[10] on the other, the philosopher Nicholas Smith, for example, considers "human existence to be intelligible only on the assumption of certain limits to contingency."[11] My aim is not to position myself within this spectrum, but to note that its very presence is symptomatic of the turbulence of the modern condition and its interpretations. One of the very best descriptions of the condition of modernity comes from Anthony Giddens, who likens modernity to a juggernaut, "a runaway engine of enormous power which, collectively as human beings, we can drive to some extent but which also threatens to rush out of our control and which could rend itself asunder . . . [we are] caught up in a universe of events we do not fully understand, and which seems in a large part outside of our control."[12] Here architects are no different from the rest of humanity; they are but one of many grappling at the wheel of the juggernaut.

Architects are thus faced with a double bind. Not only is their own discipline intractably contingent, but also the products of that discipline—buildings—are exposed to the contingency of the world. Most other professions or occupations have to deal with one or the other of these conditions, but not both, or else can use the strength of their knowledge base to smother the contingency. In the face of the doubling of contingency, it is not surprising that architects seek succor through deluded attempts in the establishment of certainty and recourse to the Vitruvian triad. To face up to contingency is to stare into the mirror of one's fragility, to see one's shared impotence at the wheel of the juggernaut. Hence the retreat into the illusions of the redemptive potential of the modern project, or else into the decadent diversions of the postmodern project. Architecture was immediately attracted to postmodernity; it offered both a release from the stranglehold of modernism (as an aesthetic) and also a welcome distraction from the failures of the modern project (as social experiment). But the result was ineffectual, mainly because postmodernity was a critique of something that had already disappeared. It stood in opposition to a set of modernist ordering principles that had unraveled in practice, thus only defeating an already vanquished opponent. In this light we can understand the argument that "what Habermas calls the project of modernity is really an escape from it, and what Lyotard calls postmodernity is really the rediscovery of modernity."[13] Habermas, as bearer of the flame of the Enlightenment modern project, describes something that, in denying the contingent reality, is not modernity. Lyotard, while promoting the notion of postmodern rupture and difference, in fact describes the continuing disturbance of modernity. In this light too we can understand that the formal gymnastics of architectural postmodernism (as a style) did little to address the social autonomy of architectural modernism. The visual noise, created in the name of populism and greater meaning, distracted from the fact that PoMo was simply a reworking of a set of internalized codes: the deckchairs may have been arranged into different patterns, but the good ship Architecture plowed on regardless. Although things looked different, the reorganization of the pieces was only formal; the underlying social conditions remained largely ignored.

The versions of modernity that admit to its contingency posit postmodernity not as the irritant of modernity, but as its actuality. Thus Bauman describes postmodernity as modernity without illusions—"modernity reconciled to its own impossibility."[14] The same point is made by Giddens when he opposes the term *postmodernity* with his notion of *radicalized modernity*, replacing the essentially undermining characteristics of the former with the productive potential of the latter.[15] Bauman, Giddens, and others argue that this fitful condition, defined to a greater or lesser extent by contingency, is inescapable and needs to be faced. Postmodernity is not just modernity reconciled to its own impossibility, says Bauman, but also "determined, for better or worse, to live with" that impossibility.[16] If architecture is to face this contingency and live with it, we need to know better what is implied by the term. In what follows I move away from the direct ground of architecture, but the diversion is necessary if we are to come back with a better idea of how to cope with contingency.

Rorty's Retreat

Nearly all the recent interpretations of contingency appear to be magnetically drawn to the version set out by the American philosopher Richard Rorty in *Contingency, Irony, and Solidarity*.[17] This is not to say that all agree with Rorty—in fact his take on contingency is one of the most criticized aspects of his work[18]—but Rorty's stance is often used as a place to start out from. I will do the same, not to tick philosophical boxes but because of the striking way that his version of coping with contingency also describes a tacit architectural behavior. Rorty's starting point is to place contingency in opposition to the foundational claims of traditional metaphysics, and in particular what he terms the "Plato-Kant canon," which has always contrasted contingency with what is universal, necessary, and essential. It is his insistent critique of the truth claims, and what he terms the "final vocabularies," of these foundationalists that shapes Rorty's understanding of contingency. If the truth claims are philosophically dubious,[19] they are also intellectually and socially dangerous because they subsume the freedom of the individual under a set of universal laws. Rorty is convincing in his association of the language of certainty and truth with the articulation of the humiliation of others.[20] Against this domination, Rorty positively champions contingency, releasing it from its previous role as the whipping boy of reason. "Without acknowledging and appropriating contingency," he argues, "we are doomed to spend our conscious lives trying to escape from contingency."[21] This is an argument that might appear to chime with the central thrust of this book, but Rorty's particular appropriation of contingency is fraught with problems.

In order to effect his move to contingency, Rorty proposes that we discard our reliance on the truth-seekers (philosophers, scientists) as potential saviors and instead invest our hopes in what he calls "liberal ironists," a liberal being the type of person who thinks that "cruelty is the worst thing we do," and an ironist being "the sort of person who faces up to the contingency of his or her own most central beliefs and desires."[22] It is with the latter definition that we can begin to identify a central problem with Rorty's take on contingency. If the foundationalists play out their truth game in the public sphere, then the liberal ironists develop their awareness of, and response to, contingency in the privacy of their own belief systems. It is thus consistent that Rorty's heroes are the "strong poets . . . only poets, Nietzsche thought, can grasp contingency."[23] The optimistic ideal of Rorty's society is to let such heroes flourish "in the hope that the poets may eventually make it safe for everybody else."[24] At this moment Rorty's argument slips from a robust critique of foundationalist beliefs into a decadent acceptance of the imaginative impulses of an intellectual elite as potential saviors of society. In Rorty's liberal utopia, these poets are not burdened with the need to act with reformative intent; it is enough for them just to do as they will. "The aim of a just and free society," he argues, "is letting its citizens be as privatistic, 'irrationalist,' and aestheticist as they please so long as they do it in their own time—causing no harm to others and using no resources needed by those less advantaged."[25]

Thus while Rorty makes the important identification of contingency with a certain type of creative freedom, getting us out from under the shackles of doing things in a right or proper way according to the dictates of presumed truth,[26] he then throws away the opportunity of using this creative freedom in a publicly accountable way. Rorty's emphasis is not on the contingent conditions of society but on the contingency of the self which, following Freud, he defines as a "tissue of contingencies." There is thus rigid separation between public and private, with the result that what is achieved in the private world might, but only might, then affect the public realm: "poetic, artistic, philosophical, scientific, or political progress results from the *accidental* coincidence of private obsession with public need."[27] As Richard

Bernstein notes: "it is difficult to understand why anyone who becomes as narcissistic as Rorty advocates would be motivated to assume public responsibilities."[28] The result is an escape into pure solipsism, in which the individual can abrogate any political responsibility. It is exactly the political nonintentionality of Rorty's individualist ironist that allows other powers to develop unhindered so that in the end, as William Connolly observes, Rorty just holds up a tinted mirror to American technocracy.[29]

It appears that Rorty's interpretation of contingency is not only motivated by his stated antipathy to the "final vocabularies" of truth and essence. It is also an escape from dealing with the contingencies of the real world *with intent*—a retreat sanctioned by his reliance on the individual muse. It is here that Rorty's retreat chimes with an architectural belief system. Faced with the intractable contingency of architecture, we have seen how a natural reaction is one of denial and the recourse to impossible ideals. Accompanying this is a belief that salvation may lie in the power of the individual architect to overcome chaos. Thus Walter Gropius, the founder of the Bauhaus, argues in *Apollo in the Democracy* that the problems of society cannot be solved "by intellectual processes or political actions alone." They need a "reawakening in every individual [of] the lost ability to create and understand form."[30] He laments the loss of the poet in our scientific age, and champions the ability of the lone architect to deal with the "spiritual and intellectual confusion" that identifies modern society. Gropius's chosen weapon in the war on chaos is beauty, something that issues from the "inner vision" of the architect. Society, he says, has the duty to nurture this inner vision and also to create the right conditions for the appreciation of the beautiful things arising out of it; without these, *"the desire of the architect to create unity will go on being thwarted."*[31] While Gropius's book is subtitled *The Cultural Obligation of the Architect,* one is left with the overriding impression that what he is proposing is the cultural obligation *to* the architect. "A feeling for beauty and quality," he says, "when it spreads into all levels of society, nourishes the creativeness of the artist and *gives him the needed response.*"[32] There is something of Rorty's narcissism in the idea that it is society's task to provide the right environment to satisfy the aesthetic impulses of the architect-poet. And there is a certain inevitability when the book ends with a homage to four from the pantheon of great architect-poets: Peter Behrens, Frank Lloyd Wright, Ludwig Mies van de Rohe, and Le Corbusier. With both Rorty and Gropius we thus get an internalized method of dealing with the flux of the external world. The ever-present danger of solipsism and potential lack of accountability, let alone lack of political intent, in these private worlds is enough to make us look elsewhere for the means of coping with contingency.

Walking the Girder

In *Die Schwärmer,* Robert Musil describes two types of man: one who is "an able man who needs a solid foundation for himself . . . working on an extended network of girders," the other who is "compelled to look down through the holes in the girders." In his interpretation of this passage, Hilary Putnam identifies the former with a certain brand of optimistic modernism, looking steadfastly ahead and ignoring the inherent dangers, in the construction of a perfected society for New Man. He assigns to the latter the mode of pessimistic modernism, always on the lookout for the pitfalls of modernity, relentlessly deconstructing tradition and so leaving no firm grounds for the establishment of any kind of new redeeming future.[33] However, the latter figure need not be seen as so intrinsically negative. In walking the girder, head up then head down, this figure is aware of both of the possibilities stretching out in front as well as acknowledging the context within which these possibilities are founded. For this figure the girders construct a matrix of certainty and uncertainty, a landscape that must be negotiated. Walking the girder thus faces the contingent reality, but reveals both the dangers and the opportunities within it. As Agnes Heller wisely notes, the contingent person *knows* that she "walks over the abyss, and is therefore in need of a good sense of balance, good reflexes, tremendous luck, and the greatest among them: a network of friends who can hold her hand."[34]

The image of walking the girder introduces the inevitability of coping with contingency in the modern world, but also a certain limit. This is because the image pairs certainty with uncertainty, necessity with contingency, and in this pairing, contingency and uncertainty are never able to throw off the ramifications of their more accepted partners. This pairing is present in the sociologists of contingency such as Bauman and Heller. Bauman documents the inevitability of facing up to contingency better than anyone, but his account remains in the shadow of the other of contingency, order. He urges us to "transfer contingency from the vocabulary of dashed hopes into that of the opportunity, from the language of domination into that of emancipation,"[35] but in that one sentence the pall of domination perhaps still oversees the opportunity's prospects for release. As long as contingency is understood as the castoff of order, it remains in thrall to it. Thus when Bauman says that "postmodernity is the age of contingency *für sich*, of self-conscious contingency,"[36] and elsewhere that "we are *bound* to live with contingency for the foreseeable future," there is a sense of resignation to contingency as one's fate, which may in turn restrict the means of dealing with that fate productively. The same is true of Heller, who finds contingency lurking in the wreckage of certainty. Her individuals are ones who have "transformed his or her contingency into his or her destiny" but, while aware of their own contingency, are "unhappy with this awareness."[37]

Bauman argues that "nerves of steel" should be the "feature that the contingent being . . . needs most," but such a tough attitude is required only if contingency is manifested as the other of order.[38] While contingency throws up uncertainties to deal with, these uncertainties are a threat to overcome with steely resistance only if they appear to be cast out from the realm of certainty. What if instead one follows the line of the Buddhist thinker Sogyal Rinpoche? "The constant uncertainty may make everything seem bleak and almost hopeless," he writes, "but if you look more deeply at it, you will see that its very nature creates gaps, spaces in which profound chance and opportunities for transformation are continuously flowering—if, that is, they can be seen and seized."[39] What Rinpoche beautifully identifies is the *transformative* potential latent in uncertainty and the freedom that comes with it. Where order and certainty close things down into fixed ways of doing things, contingency and uncertainty open up liberating possibilities for action. In this light contingency is more than just fate; it is truly an opportunity.

In order to move toward this more positive character for contingency we need to be rid of its pair—to take contingency on its own terms and not on the terms of a philosophical genealogy of weakness. This means reworking the relationship of contingency and necessity. As Louis Althusser writes: "instead of thinking of contingency as a modality of or an exception to the necessary, one must think of necessity as the becoming-necessary of contingent encounters."[40] To do this we need to escape from the shadow of Enlightenment philosophy and its assertion of the right of reason. We need, in effect, to say that we have never been modern.

Situated Knowledge

You shut down the wireless Internet connection, put on your iPod and nestle down with a Frappuccino®. You pick up a book. *We Have Never Been Modern.*[41]

Stupid title, you think, laughable really.

But four pages in you are hooked. By the end your initial skepticism is overwhelmed. This is not to say that Bruno Latour's astounding book is "right," in fact final correctness is something that he would probably challenge as an idea, but it certainly knocks some major assumptions on the head. The premise is simple—you get what it says on the package—but the implications are complex.

The argument goes something like this. Once there was a time when "social needs and natural reality, meanings and mechanisms, signs and things"[42] were blended together. It was a time when objects, as products of both nature and society, were understood as part of complex networks. Anthropologists could observe this time through tracing those networks, "weaving together the real, the social and the narrated." In this time a building, as one such hybrid object, could be understood as the intersection of a range of forces, from the political to the natural, from the real to the metaphorical. A balance, indeed, of colossal forces.

And then the modern age presumed to intervene. With its ruthless program of purification, the modern project separated out the parts: nature/society, making/thinking, history/story, human/nonhuman. Now the natural sciences, as their own sphere of knowledge, could define what nature was, leaving the philosophers to determine what society might be. But these two spheres must never meet; hybrids must be eliminated and networks broken. "All the subtle pathways leading continuously from circumstances to universals," which Latour identified in the "premodern" age, "have been broken off by the modern epistemologists, and we have found ourselves with pitiful contingencies on one side and necessary Laws on the other—without, of course, being able to conceptualize their relations."[43] In this modern age, architecture is evaluated against strictly "objective" criteria derived from the natural sciences (function, proportion, rationalism, technique) or else against strictly cultural criteria as a pure creation arising *ab initio* (aesthetics, the metaphor of foundations and its deconstructive undermining). Its very contingency is thus suppressed, along with its status as what Latour calls a "quasi-object." These quasi-objects "are in between the two poles [of Nature and Society;] . . . [they] are much more social, much more fabricated, much more collective than the 'hard' parts of nature, but they are in no way the arbitrary receptacles of a fully fledged society."[44] Quasi-objects, with all their hybridity, are part of the networks that the modern project ruled out of court.

Latour's crucial observation, almost so simple that it has been overlooked by others, is that these quasi-objects have never gone away. Far from being eliminated by the modern project, they have proliferated under it.

First there were the skyscrapers of postmodern architecture; then Khomeini's Islamic revolution, which no one managed to peg as revolutionary or reactionary. From then on, the exceptions have popped up without cease. No one knows whether the reintroduction of the bear in the Pyrenees, kolkhozes, aerosols, the Green Revolution, the anti-smallpox vaccine, Star Wars, the Muslim religion, partridge hunting, the French Revolution, service industries, labor unions, cold fusion, Bolshevism, relativity, Slovak nationalism, commercial sailboats, and so on, are outmoded, up to date, futuristic, atemporal, nonexistent, or permanent.[45]

While various strategies were invented to deal with this proliferation,[46] none worked. Thus by the end of the twentieth century, the proliferation had "exploded modern temporality along with its Constitution. The modern's flight into the future ground to a halt . . . with the multiplication of exceptions that nobody could situate in the regular flow of time." So if the modern age has never delivered on its promises, and if the postmodernists have done no more than "disperse the elements that the modernizers grouped together in a well-ordered cluster,"[47] where does this leave us? Not as returning to the "premodern" (because that would assume that the project of modernity had been carried out successfully), but as *non*-modern. "We have never been modern in the sense of the Constitution (of the modern project). No one has ever been modern. Modernity has never begun."[48] Things and life are "modern," but this does not mean that they accord to the sacrament of the modern project. In this light, "modernity is," says Latour, "much more than an illusion and much less than an essence."[49] This is not to say that the present age has not thrown up new forms of technology and living (wireless Internet, iPods, and all). As a historian of science Latour is all too well aware of these modern things, but sees them not as mere products of technological progress, but as part of a much more complex network of social, economic, *and* technological forces. The Frappuccino® is not just a benign form of enjoyment, but tied into issues of globalization, high-street rents, taste, persuasion, and so on.

Latour's formulation is important because it relieves the pressure on the modern project, in particular the pressure of perfection and of keeping things in separate categories. It allows things and processes, including architecture, to be treated as they are: as quasi-objects in their own right rather than as artificially separated and purified constructions of the modern world. Architecture can be placed back at the intersection of the human and the nonhuman, the particular and the general, but not in a manner that recalls some nostalgic state of pre-Faustian virtue (Latour's amodernity is definitively not wistful for a lost past). Networks are reestablished that "allow us to pass with continuity from the local to the global, from the human to the nonhuman," and it is these networks that once again form the basis for the interpretation of the overlapping spheres of science, culture—and architecture.

For the purposes of my argument, the main pressure that Latour relieves is that on contingency. Far from being the "pitiful" partner in the struggle for reason, contingency just is. It is there. "The history of human beings," says Latour, "is going to remain contingent, agitated by sound and fury."[50] It is there to be dealt with on its own terms and not on the terms of others, and in particular not as the despised partner of order. This immediately absolves contingency from the charge of relativism, in which it is argued that because nothing is certain everything must be relative. The charge is made from the camp of objective reason. "If things are not necessary and might turn out in any of a multitude of ways," it goes, "then that means that processes are beyond control and order; every action has equal status or relevance. If there are no absolutes then everything must be relative. All actions and all outcomes are thus equally good or equally bad. Where does this lead us as rational beings?" However, this charge, based as it is on the assumption of an absolute, is framed by that assumption, and thus self-determining. "Unable to accommodate the idea of a world conceived otherwise," argues Barbara Herrnstein Smith, "objectivist thought concludes that, in the absence of its own conceptualizations, there could not be a world or any thought at all."[51] The result is a phony war: the rational modernists dismiss the contingent amodernists out of hand, the amodernists do not accept the modernists' terms; it is a "game of pure non-engagement."[52]

More important is to differentiate the open, and ultimately weak, choices sanctioned by the relativist position from the intentional, and in the long run strong, judgments that are necessary in the contingent world. The relativist position would lead to a weak model of contingency in which one's actions lose any sense of responsibility and in which, say, the architect is permitted to indulge in whatever formal or technical gesture they see fit. Indeed, many have argued that the multiple masks that architectural postmodernism wears are symptomatic of a collapse into a relativist world devoid of social values. Latour, by releasing contingency from the grip of order, allows us to see that the contingent world is not the same as the relativist world, while at the same time permitting the use of language and a set of consequences far richer than the modernists ever sanctioned. He also allows us to avoid the "performative paradox" that the rational modernists so delight in accusing contingency of.[53] "If the modern world is contingent," this charge goes, "and if this description is necessarily part of the modernism that it describes, then the description must also be contingent. It too must be partial, weakened, and limited, and thus not worth taking account of."[54] This charge too, however, is based on the overriding assumption that the world *could* be a certain place, and that any challenge to that certainty is necessarily weak. It dismisses contingency because it does not accord with the rules of modernism. But if those rules are found to be wanting, then contingency is released from their clutches: it is allowed to be an inevitable condition of life that must be dealt with on its own terms.

So what are those terms? Contingency asks of us to make choices. The contingent world is one in which "choice becomes destiny," as the Italian thinker Alberto Melucci writes. "The imperative that immediately arises from uncertainty is therefore the necessity to choose . . . it is impossible not to choose among the options available in any situation."[55] But this does not mean that all these choices are completely open—that "anything goes" as it might under a relativist regime in which "uncertainty is uncertainly dealt with," and in which one might resort to chance as the means of making choice.[56] For two reasons, the making of choice in the contingent world is both far from relativist and far from being absolutely determined. First because we engage with those choices with a degree of intent and vision; there is an end in sight and a hope driving that end. Where in the modern project the end is overseen by values of truth and reason, and thus to a large extent predetermined, in the contingent world the exact end is uncertain and the choices made along the way are exposed to other forces, and in particular the hopes and intents of others. Contingency thus demands that we share our destinies; it does not overpower the intents that people bring to the table, it just shapes them and obliges them to be less dogmatic. Dealing with contingency thus calls for one to have a vision but, at the same time, to be modest and light-footed enough to allow that vision to be adjusted to the circumstances. The second reason that the making of choice is neither relativist nor determinist is because we enter into those choices as sentient, knowing, and situated people, not as innocents abroad in the detached knowledge of others. We bring to those choices a concrete background, which informs—but does not absolutely determine—the way that we deal with them. This is very different from deferring to the jurisdiction of the rationalist project, in which decisions are made according to the higher authority of "objective" reason and truth. The "modern" individual is absolved from taking responsibility for the ultimate effect of these decisions because they are seen as part of a system that transcends the particular. The contingent field, on the other hand, deflates any delusions of knowledge being played out in a detached realm, and brings it firmly down to earth. Because contingent choices are grounded in concrete reality, we are made to be aware of the effect of any decisions we come to, and this means it is impossible to ignore the political and social aspects of future outcomes. We necessarily use our personal experience and the experiences of others to project the possible consequences of our decisions, and in this projection the contingent world relies on situated knowledge.

The term situated knowledge comes from feminist thinking, and in particular Donna Haraway's seminal contribution.[57] Haraway starts by arguing that we should not dismiss out of hand the notion of objectivity. If we do, then we are doomed to the other of objectivity, subjectivity, and in this move condemned to a marginal position. Such is the fate of women under the objectivist regime. Instead she proposes an alternative objectivity, one based on "situated knowledge." From this standpoint, "objectivity turns out to be about particular and specific embodiment, and definitely not about the false vision promising transcendence of all limits and responsibility . . . in this way we might become answerable for what we learn how to see."[58] Haraway's notion of situated knowledge provides firm pointers as to how we might cope with contingency, and how the choices contingency throws up might be dealt with. First, because "we might become answerable," situated knowledge implies that we take responsibility for our "enabling practices," and positions them firmly in the political and ethical arena. Secondly, situated knowledge sees opportunities in the particular and does not look for problems to be solved in the universal scheme of things—just as the landscape architect Lancelot "Capability" Brown, when looking at the untamed estate of a new client, would not ask: "So what's the problem?" but instead would propose: "What are the capabilities of the place?" Situated knowledge works with the particular, but this is seen as a strength, not a weakness: "the only way to find a larger vision is to be somewhere in particular."[59] There is something inherently optimistic in this approach, but this optimism is situated, not idealistic. Thirdly, situated knowledge is partial knowledge (partial in being both not complete and also partisan), but this self-confessed partiality, in all its honesty and modesty, is a bonus, not a deficit. It does not presume to have universal relevance or authority, but this does not mean it is irrelevant. Situated knowledge works more humbly, gathering the past in order to shape better (but not perfect) futures, "from points of view which can never be known in advance, which promise something quite extraordinary, that is, knowledge potent for constructing worlds less organised by axes of domination."[60] Situated knowledge is thus responsible, particular, and partial, and in all these three qualities forms a basis on which to make the choices that the contingent world throws up.

I could go on, attempting to develop a "theory of contingency," but others have done it better before me,[61] and in a way it is wrong to develop a theory for something that resists that enveloping term. There is a concomitant danger that a theory of contingency would universalize a state of flux, allowing nothing firm to be entertained and dissolving all intent. The American philosopher John Dewey provides a good argument as to both the opportunities and the limits of contingency. "Contingency is a necessary, *although not sufficient*, condition of freedom," he wrote in 1929. "In a world which is completely tight and exact in all its constituents, there would be no room for freedom. Contingency, while it gives room for that freedom, does not fill that room."[62] The contingent scene is thus infused by other values. I am therefore not proposing contingency as the one and only condition that shapes contemporary life, and with it architecture. I am only suggesting that contingency is a pivotal feature, and needs to be taken into account rather than avoided as a potential threat. In this contingency situates us in the real world, providing opportunities for transformative change while avoiding the siren calls of ideals.

If a "theory of contingency" is inadvisable, then maybe it is better to develop a praxis of contingency; the rest of the book will be spent doing this through the particular lens of architecture. While the focus is on architecture, this does not mean that the praxis of contingency described is not relevant to other areas. My hunch is that architecture is the contingent discipline par excellence, and if we can deal with rather than deny that contingency, architecture may be seen as an exemplary form of transformative practice and lessons as to how to cope with contingency may be learned from its practice. But architects will deserve this attention only if they give up their delusions of autonomy and engage with others in their messy, complex lives. Then, maybe, mess will be the law.

II TIME, SPACE, AND LO-FI ARCHITECTURE

In 1942, Sigfried Giedion published *Space, Time and Architecture,* a book that subsequently went through five editions and remains in print today. The book propelled twentieth-century architecture; many of Giedion's central themes of aesthetic progress, technical determinism, and architecture as expression of *Zeitgeist* remain with us today, even if the criteria by which those categories are judged have shifted.

Giedion's book, with its celebration of the transitory and fluid moments of modernity, might be read as a manifesto for contingency. However, nothing could be further from the truth. He talks approvingly of Frank Lloyd Wright being impressed by the Japanese house as "a supreme study in elimination—not only of dirt, but the elimination, too, of the *insignificant,*" and then argues that, for the American house, Wright "accomplished just such an elimination, a rejection of the confused and trivial."[1] Dirt, the insignificant, the trivial, and the confused: all these are conditions that must be overcome in Giedion's, modernism's, and modernity's war on contingency. All these, too, are aspects that will come back to the surface in part II.

Giedion's key move is to treat architecture as an "index" of aspects of modernity; he seizes these transitory elements and makes them available for representation in architecture. He thus aestheticizes and technicizes the modern flux, and with this rids it of its contingency. His central concept of space-time, which he relates to contemporary developments in science and art, effectively freezes time and empties space of its social content.

This part of the book consciously inverts and challenges Giedion's polemic. By readmitting the transitory, fluid, and contingent aspects of modernity back into architecture, the fullness of time is released from his frozen vignettes and his empty space is repopulated. Where Giedion started with space (in order to better objectify it), I start with time, because time is the medium that most clearly upsets any notions of static idealized perfection in architecture, so that when I get to "space," it is space that is redolent with social possibilities. And when I get to architecture, it comes out as a lo-fi antidote to the high icons that populate the pages of Giedion's book.

4   Time of Waste

Waste in Transit

It was one of those emails that one dreads. "Please can you do a few words of thanks after the John Carr Memorial Lecture. The lecturer is Peter Guthrie. The subject is Construction Waste." I couldn't say no (it came from on high). This was duty, not pleasure.

The opening statement of the lecture signaled that Professor Guthrie had a somewhat different take on construction waste than I expected. "Sustainable development is a term of political duplicity." My notes, which I still have, bear testament to an expansive story in which skips and landfill become signals of a much wider malaise in modern life:

"approx 50% UK landfill = construction waste = 17.5mill tonnes." (A Mini car is my measure of what a tonne looks like. That is a lot of Minis.)

"Less than 35% construction waste recycled."[1]

"Introduction of landfill tax = more illegal flytipping + hiding toxic waste (more ££ to landfill) under inert waste ⇒ environmental timebomb."

"As resources run out, landfills will become the mines of the future."

In Professor Guthrie's hands, construction waste became a network of social, economic, and environmental issues, building to a vision of a sustainable nightmare. But what really stands out in my notes is a single phrase, in capitals and underlined:

ALL ARCHITECTURE IS BUT WASTE IN TRANSIT!!

This was a precisely targeted barb, going straight to the heart of architectural anxieties. How could architecture be waste, a word whose original meaning in Old and Middle English referred to an environment that was unsuitable to sustain human habitation?[2] If he had said "architecture is waste waiting to happen" (maybe a more accurate description given the landfill figures), at least we architects could have held up the cross of eternity to ward off the devilish moment of collapse into ruins; we could have asserted the metaphor of grounded stability to cover the cracks of reality. But waste *in transit*. What can we do about that? Tidy it up a bit, put it into neater piles (let's call them roofs, walls, floors, windows, and so on), stick them together and sit back to wait for the inevitable to happen as the physical and social glue unravels. Construction, after all, if traced back to its Latin roots, means no more than to pile together (*con:* together; *struere:* to pile); demolition just takes those piles and rearranges them.

Construction and demolition are closer than most architects would dare admit. Cedric Price was aware of this when he joined the Federation of Demolition Contractors as its only architect member. But most architects do not share Cedric's sense of both humor and prescience; for them the distinction of construction over demolition is fundamental. As Robert Smithson so rightly points out, "certain architects hate bulldozers and steam shovels. With such equipment construction takes on the look of destruction ... they seem to turn the terrain into unfinished cities of organized wreckage."[3] In order to maintain dignity it is essential to separate construction from demolition; only this will disassociate the profession from any of the connotations of wreckage. This happens quite literally on site: the demolition contract is often let separately from the main contract, and always to a separate subcontractor. Architects will have no business with demolition contractors; to control them would be to associate with disorder. We like to come to a cleared site, *"to start again from the foundations"* (and so play out the dream of Descartes's architect/philosopher). This way we can exorcize the specter of demolition (previous and potential) that haunts all construction.

A hint that the line between waste and Architecture is not so defined as we may think is given by Le Corbusier in his description of a journey through the mining area of Flanders. He sees something out of the train windows and has a revelation: "What is that, a mirage? Gigantic pyramids rising from the plains are silhouetted against the sky all the way to the horizon. . . . My emotion was intense. These sublime monuments . . . " For a moment he dreams he is outside Cairo among the Pyramids of Giza, only to be rudely awakened: "No, not at all! Those are not masterpieces, they are not works of art. They are simply schist wastes. And at once I measure the abyss which opens up between the aspect of a thing and the quality of the spirit that has brought it into being. . . . Here there is nothing more than an industrial enterprise in which no elevated intention is involved."[4]

What Le Corbusier exposes is that the two states of matter, slagheap and eternal pyramid, are kept apart only by the most fragile of defenses—an appeal to spirit and the notion of intent. The pyramid is not classified as waste because it is the product of intentional human action guided by the mystery of the spirit. Demolition and construction, waste and order, are kept apart through disciplinary policing of the boundary between the two. As Mary Douglas so famously noted, nothing is *intrinsically* dirty, and waste is not an internal quality of an object. Dirt and waste are merely the products of systems of social classification. "Where there is dirt, there is system," she says. In our particular society certain definitions of cleanliness and order are privileged, and these in turn define dirt and waste as their other, the things to be eliminated, "in so far as ordering involves rejecting inappropriate elements."[5] But what Douglas, as an anthropologist, so compellingly reveals is that these systems of classification vary across societies, so what is rejected by one group will be completely acceptable to another. Guthrie's barb is so sharp because it consciously upsets our accepted system of classification. To denote architecture (that presumed sanctuary of order) as waste is to flood the discipline with doubt as to its real status. It is not that architecture actually *is* waste (because nothing is intrinsically waste), but more that we should be aware that buildings can all too easily slip over into a territory where waste and its associations are all too present. "Architecture is but waste in transit" reminds us all too vividly that architecture cannot be definitively seen as the other of waste, namely stable order. Maybe buildings are more like the items that Marian and Nick, characters in Don DeLillo's *Underworld,* observe on supermarket shelves: "Marian and I saw products as garbage even when they sat gleaming on store shelves . . . we didn't say, What kind of casserole will that make? We said, What kind of garbage will that make? How does it measure up as waste, we asked."[6] Maybe, then, we should consider buildings in the same light, as things that one day will be waste, not just to answer the sustainable imperative (can it be reused, can it be disassembled, what can one do to delay the moment of waste, where can that waste go?), but because in the end it is a more honest appraisal of the fate of buildings.

Soon after landfill tax was introduced in the UK, huge mounds of rubble, mainly concrete, began to appear around the fringes of our cities. It was cheaper to pile it up than to dump it, though no one had really worked out a use for this matter out of place. The old had to give way to the new, but there was nowhere for the old to be hidden from sight. The two were in equilibrium:

the more new architecture there was, the higher the mounds of waste grew. The effect was particularly striking on the train journey into Liverpool Street station, where one could see the tower blocks rising out of the City of London across the mounds of rubble that filled the wastelands of Stratford. We saw an opportunity here for the house that we were building: we decided to constrain these piles of waste in wire cages and call them walls, two states of matter divided by little more than naming. The practice, of course, was rather more tricky than the theory. Wire cages have particular sized holes, and concrete crushers have particular sized filters. Unfortunately the two generally don't match, and most crushed concrete would slip through the holes in our chosen wire cages. This meant venturing out into these piles of waste to find a crusher with a larger filter. I cut an incongruous figure circumnavigating London on my bike and entering into these wastelands tape measure in hand. These are territories on the margin (of the economy, of the city, of what is proper) run by people on the margin. At one point I had a gun pulled on me (". . . only joking, mate, just thought you looked a bit of a wanker"), and decided to give up my effete tracking system. I did not belong in this other world with its own set of rules. In the end we found the right stuff with one phone call from our foreman to his brother, who drives one of the trucks moving piles of stuff in various states of cohesion around the country. We paid less per ton for our lumps of discarded concrete than we did to have our own demolition waste taken away. Economically this part of the building is, indeed, rubbish.

Rubbish Theory

The future is but the obsolete in reverse.
—Vladimir Nabokov

In a way, waste is too benign a word. Let's call it rubbish to get the full depth of its associations. "Rubbish is immortal," says the narrator of Ivan Klima's novel *Love and Garbage*, "it pervades the air, swells up in water, dissolves, rots, disintegrates, changes into gas, into smoke, into soot, it travels the world and gradually engulfs it."[7] Rubbish is always with us but at the same time always against us: it upsets our sense of propriety, and therefore we do everything we can to hide it and then be rid of it. So it is a brave person who takes on the task of writing a theory of rubbish, but this is what Michael Thompson did in his book *Rubbish Theory*, a text that twenty-five years after its publication has cult status among those interested in the social construction of matter. Thompson's argument has revealing insights into architecture, which in itself is a social construction of matter. He argues that "in our culture, objects are assigned to one or other of two overt categories, which I label 'transient' and 'durable.' Objects in the transient category decrease in value over time and have finite life-spans. Objects in the durable category increase in value over time and have (ideally) infinite life-spans."[8] He then notes that these two categories are insufficient to describe the actual behavior of objects. What happens when the value of the transient object decreases to the extent that it is worthless? The answer is that it assumes the status of rubbish and, in order to fully understand the social control of value, this third category has to be added to the other two. Thompson's bold claim is that objects can move from the transient to the rubbish category, and from the rubbish to the durable category, but that no other transactions are possible. It is not possible to move from the durable to the rubbish (because durable things are by definition increasing in value) or from the rubbish to the transient (because that would reverse the endemic state of decline of the transient object).[9] As with Mary Douglas, with whom he worked,[10] Thompson is clear that the assignment of objects to the various categories is not down to their inherent physical or aesthetic properties, but due to qualities that they have as a result of "the social process of endowment," a process that is in a state of continual flux. Objects, including buildings, are exposed to "social malleability" in the determination of their value to society, and thus their place within one of the three categories.[11]

In terms of architecture, the analysis is sobering. While architects may dream of their buildings coming into the world as fully fledged durable items with enduring value, the reality is that they *always* enter the social realm as transient objects, subject right from the beginning to decline in value and an inexorable slide to the status of rubbish. Some conditions (maybe buildings in relatively stable cultural circumstances or those designed by famous architects) may delay this progress, but Thompson's argument is that it gets to them all in the end. Only once they have reached the bottom can they in some circumstances be transferred to the status of durable. Thompson's example is the standard Georgian terraced house in the inner London boroughs such as Islington. From a bourgeois beginning these had declined in the twentieth century until by the 1950s they had reached the status of rubbish. Off the radar of estate agents, and the great and good, these rotting terraces were either cleared as slums (moving out the rubbish people who occupied the rubbish buildings) or succumbed to the endless cycles of what Thompson calls the Ron-and-Cliffs, the working classes who "have no access to durability . . . committed to a world in which there is only transience and rubbish. In consequence, Ron-and-Cliff can see no future except demolition."[12] The Ron-and-Cliffs botch houses together only to move out quicker. They are opposite to the "Knockers-through," the middle-class pioneers who saw the opportunity to move these rubbish tips into the durable category. The Knockers-through (so-called because they would knock-through the main rooms to form a kitchen-dining room in the basement and a large living room on the ground floor) used perseverance and critical mass to effect the transfer of their houses to the durable category, a transfer confirmed as permanent by the later imposition of conservation orders and the inexorable logic of the marketplace.

A good illustration of Thompson's theory can be found in the story of Sarah Wigglesworth's parents. They were early pioneers in Islington, buying their large and decayed Georgian house in 1956 for almost nothing (cash), befitting its rubbish status. They immediately knocked-through the ground and basement floors. The house was later listed on the register of historic buildings and the surrounding area designated a conservation area, conferring the mark of durability. When the house was eventually sold in 2004 for a sum of money befitting its durable status (more than cash), the new owners immediately unknocked-it-through, putting back faux versions of the original cornices and restoring the dividing walls. Gordon Wigglesworth's rather masterful modernist interventions and knocking-through were clearly too much a reminder of the house's early rubbish era.

It is possible to query the structure of Thompson's argument, and he does so himself. Does the durable always remain durable? Can it ever return to the state of rubbish? Can anything enter the system as a fully fledged durable object (a question to soothe architects' fears)? What about Parliament Buildings (but tell that to the viewers of Channel 4's *Demolition* program, who consigned the new Scottish Parliament to their rubbish dump by voting it onto the list of buildings they would like to see demolished)? However, the beauty of Thompson's argument is not in its perfection but in its provocation: "the delightful consequence of this hypothesis is that, in order to study the social control of value, we have to study rubbish."[13] Architecture in this light is defined not by its stability but by its potential obsolescence, subject to a process of physical decline and social change. This process of change is not directly related to the physical properties of the architecture, even though these clearly impinge on it. "The 'lastingness' [of a building] is not imposed by the intrinsic physical properties, but by the social system . . . it is not a 'natural process' but tied up with cultural categories."[14] Architects

Time, Space, and Lo-Fi Architecture

have no direct control over this social system; rubbish theory thus exposes architecture to two fears: time and dependency.

Just opposite our house, the local Council have seen to fit to erect a huge rubbish dump. Well, that is what we will call it as long as it smells and casts stigma. Rubbish is indeed dumped there, and then taken away later. The Council are, of course, aware of the stigma of rubbish and therefore officially designate the building a "waste transfer station," as if the word transfer will signify a transient state of waste always on the move, and in this transience make it more acceptable. If you go round to the local agents trying to flog the new apartments up the road from the "station," they have another spin on it. Ask them, pretending to be a prospective purchaser, "What about the rubbish dump?" and they throw their hands up in horror: "No, no, no, it is a recycling facility," as if, just as if, you will be buying into some sustainable lifestyle with associated feelgood factor.

But these agents are not selling the apartments that actually wrap around the station. Initially the developers tried the argument that "the new facilities can take their place in the city in a way which reflects pride in the provision of public services."[15] The subsequent outcry from the local community suggested that the developer's faith in public pride was misplaced when it came to rubbish dumps. So the scheme was redesigned and the dump hidden away behind a wall of housing which wrapped around its sides. The out of sight, out of mind argument appeared to sway the Council, who then gave the go-ahead (over the still vociferous complaints of the locals who knew that out of sight was not out of stigma, let alone out of nostril). This housing is not for sale because it is designated for "keyworkers": nurses, teachers, firemen, and maybe even rubbish collectors. This new underclass will live their lives quite literally with their backs up against a wall of waste. Rubbish tip, rubbish people, all rubbish, always will be. Call it a waste transfer station, call it a recycling facility, but words don't rub out rubbish. Rubbish is immortal.

Time and Waste

In Italo Calvino's city of Leonia the streets are cleaned meticulously every night so that the inhabitants can wake up every morning to a city cleansed and refreshed. But beyond the city boundaries mountains of waste form, which the inhabitants choose to ignore. It is only when Marco Polo comes that he, as an outsider, can point to the perversity of the condition that the Leonians are living in. One can have permanent newness, he notes, but it is an illusion. It comes at a price, and that price is the making permanent of rubbish, a fate worse, perhaps, than the ephemeral charms of progress.

Calvino's point remains relevant. "Where there is design," says Zygmunt Bauman, "there is waste."[16] The production of newness, whether in buildings or other commodities, is always shadowed by waste. The two exist in equilibrium, as Don DeLillo muses. Looking out from Fresh Kills landfill site on Staten Island across to the then standing World Trade Center, one of his characters senses "a poetic balance between that idea [the WTC] and this one [Fresh Kills]." And, just like Le Corbusier, DeLillo's character, looking at the mountain of waste in the landfill, "imagined he was watching the construction of the Great Pyramid at Giza."[17] The subsequent fate of the World Trade Center only heightens the pathos of DeLillo's observations on the equilibrium of construction and destruction.

The designed object, in all its freshness, attempts to freeze time in order to capture a state of perfection; its shadow, waste, commits the unforgivable crime and reminds us of decay, and with this the passage of time. This is why John Scanlan, in his brilliant book *On Garbage,* says that "garbage is also the broken knowledge that lies in the wake of (and in the way of) progress."[18] Waste is the unwelcome handmaiden of progress, its cyclical processes intervening in the instant moments of advancement. Walter Benjamin's Angel of History is blown by a storm that "drives him irresistibly to the future, to which his back is turned, while the pile of debris before him grows to the sky. What we call progress is this storm."[19] The poignancy of Benjamin's image lies in the impotence of the angel to intervene—"the angel would like to stay, awaken the dead and make whole what had been smashed"—and also in the impossibility of escaping from the vision—"his eyes are staring, his mouth open." Waste and progress are intractably joined and, unlike Benjamin's Angel, the commonest reaction is look away from this horror, pretend that the piles of rubbish are not there while celebrating the freshness of the instant.

The artist who most consciously addressed this connection of waste and progress is Robert Smithson. In his Earthworks, machines of construction/destruction (bulldozers/rubble trucks) are sent to create something (art) out of nothing (waste).[20] "One wants to retreat into the cool room of reason," he writes of his most famous work, *Spiral Jetty,* a spiral of rocks emerging from a salt lake in Utah, "but no . . . purity is put in jeopardy. Logical purity suddenly finds itself in a bog." The resulting work is at the same time natural/artificial, of the land/of the water, stable/decaying, emerging from the lake/returning to the lake, and so on. Smithson plays on ambiguities and the way that these upset our tendency to separate things out.

"No sense wondering about classification and categories, there were none."[21] He enjoys the temporality that waste brings with it, and in particular the notion of entropy, that uncertain and uncontrollable aspect of time which disturbs any idea of linear routes to progress.

The point here is not to celebrate waste as an aesthetic in its own right; rather, it is to address two issues. First, the way that waste upsets our systems of classification, and second, that waste introduces time to architecture. Waste brings us face to face with the destructive potential of time and the inevitability of time. The point is best made by Scanlan when he writes that "garbage becomes . . . the evidence of our failure to escape 'natural' time. Deteriorating matter embodies a time that exists beyond our rational time: in this shadow world, time is always running matter down, breaking things into pieces, or removing the sheen of glossy surfaces."[22] Like the Leonians, it is easier to turn away from the shadow and to follow the light of progress, believing it will lead us away from the discomfort of time (and architects, it is clear, are not alone in this turning away). But learning from the fictional Marco Polo, we should know the futility of this denial. I introduce waste to architecture not—I repeat—to assert that architecture equates to waste,[23] but in order to bring time to architecture.

5   Out of Time

The Terror of Time

In one photograph a fish lies on a table in a modernist room. In another picture, the fish has been replaced with a loaf of bread. The photographs have been reproduced time and time again, multiplying the loaves and fishes and embedding them into the creed of architectural modernism. But this is not the only miracle that Le Corbusier achieves in these seminal photographs of the Villas Stein and Savoye. The real triumph of these *tableaux* is to abolish time within architecture. You know the scene isn't real because there is a teapot and jug of milk on the table as well as the fish, and who drinks tea with fish in France? Le Corbusier's photographs are consciously manipulated to banish normal domestic inhabitation;[1] they are indeed "still lives."

The record of modern architecture is captured by such pictures of buildings caught at an idealized moment before time enters to disturb the perfection of the scene. The photograph allows us to forget what has come before (the pain of extended labor to achieve the delivery of the fully formed building) and what is to come after (the affront of time as dirt, users, change, and weather move in). It freezes time or, rather, freezes out time. Architectural photography "lifts the building out of time, out of breath,"[2] and in this provides solace for architects who can dream for a moment that architecture is a stable power existing over and above the tides of time.

As many others have argued, such is the power, or even seduction, of this dream that the architectural photograph becomes not just the site of reproduction of architecture but also the site of production of architecture.[3] It is not so much the overstated urban myth that architects design buildings with a view to specific photographs of them, but more that photography becomes the primary point of reference for architecture. Architects are no

Time, Space, and Lo-Fi Architecture

great semioticians; they do not have the time to deconstruct the meaning of the front cover of *Architectural Review* (a holy grail as a site for architectural (re)production), the image just sits there to be absorbed passively. If the photography presents a certain sense of architecture out of time, and photography is the main means of transmission of architectural culture, then that frozen image is the one that is aspired to.

However, if the absorption of the image is somewhat passive, the construction of it is less so. In freezing time, architects would have it that they can control time. It is a control that attempts to banish those elements of time that present a challenge to the immutable authority of architecture. As the American philosopher Karsten Harries rightly notes, architects live in the "terror of time."[4] Time is therefore engaged with as an enemy of architecture. This is why Aldo Rossi sees architecture as "the confrontation of a precise form with time and the elements, a confrontation which lasted until the form was destroyed in the process of this combat."[5] Although there is a resignation here about the futility of the combat, this does not stop all the attempts of architects to put up a good fight. The battle with time is engaged by removing from it the most dangerous (but also of course most essential) element, that of flux. Conditions of cyclical time (seasons, night, weather) or linear time (programmatic change, dirt, ageing, social drift) are therefore either denied or manipulated to organize Harries's "defence against the terror of time . . . to abolish time within time."[6]

In order to marshal this defense, a number of strategies are used. The first is to deny time is there at all; as Georges Bataille scathingly notes, the presumed essence of architecture is the "canceling of time."[7] The second strategy is to state boldly and loudly that architecture's role is to express the timeless, the eternal. The third is to accept that time passes, but erect physical barriers to halt the flow through recourse to Vitruvian notions of stability and durability. Finally, when the inevitability of time is accepted—because all the first three strategies are doomed to failure—time is admitted to architecture but only on very strict conditions: it is ordered into a linear sequence of frozen instants as a representation of progress that rids time of its uncertainty. It is worth examining each of these strategies in turn—not to mock their hopelessness, but to understand them as symptomatic of architecture's denial of dependency. Time's complexity, manifested most clearly in the tension between the cyclical aspects of life and the linear ones, brings uncertainty to architecture, and it is easier to look away from this than to embrace it. As we shall see, however, this denial is not architecture's alone: time's very multiplicity presents a threat to the ordered and ordering system of modernity as a whole.

It is before the days of mobile phones. Sarah and I are on a brief holiday to recover after delivering the manuscript for *The Everyday and Architecture*. We just need to finalize the front cover, and so I am ringing a picture editor in London from a beach café in Dorset. We have chosen the image that we wanted to use: one of Timothy Hursley's radiant photographs of the Rural Studio. But the picture editor is having nothing of it. "It's the wrong shape." "Then crop it." "It's too busy, we normally do clean." "This is the everyday," I reply. "It just feels wrong," she says. "Why, tell me why?" I insist. "Well, maybe it's because it has got a person in and we have never had one of those on the front cover," she says. "Then it's about time you did. If you don't use it, we'll pull the manuscript." "You can't," she says, "we have a contract." I am beginning to raise my voice, and in losing my temper beginning to lose the argument. I still remember the expressions on the faces of the parents around the polished pine tables full of English cream teas as I explode: "You bastards! It's because it's a black man, isn't it?"—or, rather, I remember their body language as they instinctively move to protect their children from the deranged Londoner swinging round on the end of a telephone cord. "I'm sorry. We can't use that image." (And in that studied politeness the battle is won.) The picture is changed. Still a Hursley, still of the Rural Studio, but with a bike instead of a man. The only tiny victory snatched from the jaws of defeat is that the bike was thrown down in a heap. A bit of mess, as if someone had just exited stage left: a small trace of time across a front cover whose gloss normally shook off such stains.

From Eternity to Here

Walter Gropius, on a trip to Japan, describes a visit to the stone garden of Ryoanji as "one of my really overwhelming experiences . . . the absence of any time-bound, man-made object, or of plants, takes the garden out of the realm of perishable values."[8] Time is banished here (and with it, note, the specter of waste). In order to gain entrance to the garden one used to have the choice of either singing with the monks for half an hour or else taking up a brush and tracing over calligraphics as forms of mental preparation. One effectively has to cast off time in order enter the timeless; the place out of time cannot be adulterated with traces of time that the unprepared person would bring with them.

Time, Space, and Lo-Fi Architecture

The pursuit of this timeless zone was one of the strategies with which the modernists reacted to the new temporality of modernity. The standard version of modernist time, Bruno Latour notwithstanding, is predicated on a rupture from the past. As Michel Serres notes: "the temporal rupture is the equivalent of a dogmatic expulsion,"[9] and brings with it new and uncontrollable forces—the so-called Faustian pact.[10] The time of modernity is therefore typified by qualities that are the antithesis to the weight of tradition—fluidity, speed, and the instant. On the one hand this is seen as something to be celebrated and represented, as capturing the spirit of the age, but on the other hand this temporal flux brings with it uncertainty, disorder, and chaos, all of which are clearly to be avoided. This leads to a division in modernist approaches.[11] First those who celebrate the rupture with the past and develop an aesthetic of the new temporality in terms of speed and movement (crudely put, the futurists) and then those who would escape from the flux and attempt to establish an autonomous field that overrides the presentness of the present (crudely put, the "classical" modernists such as Mies van de Rohe and Louis Kahn). Le Corbusier, as was his expedient wont, played whichever of the two games suited best, or sometimes both at the same time as in the iconic juxtaposition of pictures of motor cars with the Parthenon in *Vers une architecture*.

In fact both these tendencies, while superficially opposite in character, are absolutely similar in their attitude to time, inasmuch as both banish time from their work: one by freezing it into an aesthetic instant, the other by sidestepping it. The most paradoxical figures are the classical modernists. How can they have it both ways? How can they *at the same time* stand outside history in an appeal to the eternal *and* locate themselves precisely in the present in an appeal to the *Zeitgeist*? How can Mies say in the same lecture that architecture must "carry and drive our age" and also be "founded on eternal truths of . . . order, space and proportion,"[12] and keep a straight face? The answers are possible only when time as flux is taken out of the equation, because then the eternal and the present can coalesce and so be made available for representation as pure form. Gropius will thus describe Mies as "relentlessly distilling the permanent from the transitory and fashionable . . . resolutely discarding anything superfluous."[13] The language (relentlessly, ruthlessly) is quite disturbing in its dogma, but one needs this overriding sense of self-belief in order to dismiss time as superfluous so as to achieve the miracle of the "eternal present." Giedion uses this apparently oxymoronic phrase in his books *The Eternal Present*,[14] and so does the philosopher Peter Osborne in *The Politics of Time*. But where Giedion uses it as a term of approbation (with Mies one of the figures on whom he bestows its approval), Osborne points to its impossibility. The "eternal present" rids the past of its "fundamental pastness" and obliterates the "radical futurity of the future."[15] The eternal present thus breaks the present's connections with both past and future, and so abolishes time from the present.[16]

The quest for eternity is thus both intellectually problematic and actually doomed to failure. A slightly less extreme version of the same approach is to assert the supposed stability of architecture in the face of the flux of time. "When we build," writes Ruskin, "let us think that we build forever."[17] The "let us think" is telling here: it does not exude complete confidence but sets an aspiration. At one level it is difficult not to agree with the basic Vitruvian premise of "firmness." However, too often this form of technical stability is conflated with cultural stability in which buildings are seen to stand over the social flux that time brings with it. While it may be true, as Bataille notes, that "society entrusts its desire to endure to architecture,"[18] it is equally true that architects all too willingly accept this mission, ignoring all the evidence that it is a mission impossible. Thus Aldo Rossi can claim that "places are stronger than people, the fixed scene stronger than the transitory succession of events. This is the theoretical basis . . . of architecture itself."[19] This, however, places the "stable" cart of architecture before the bucking horse of the forces of time, when in fact the two must coexist in a state of dynamic tension.

Time, Space, and Lo-Fi Architecture

The appeal to stability, constructional, cultural, and temporal, is another of architecture's defenses against contingency. Steven Groák, in his short classic *The Idea of Building,* is particularly clear in outlining the issues at stake when architecture meets the instabilities of the world. He describes the process of architectural production and occupation as containing "many errors, omissions, smudged definitions, conflicts and fragmentations, discontinuities, failures of building program and failures of building performance, disturbances of the supposed stable pattern." In the face of such disturbances architects erect an "orthodox framework of stability [that] treats such anomalies as problems to be overcome or eliminated."[20] Historically this recourse to stability has been achieved both technically and representationally. For the latter, notions of type (architectural forms that exist through time) and harmony (an aesthetic principle that exists over time—"harmony, like the plan, casts time to the outside")[21] are employed to provide a semblance of permanence. However, this representation of stability by no means equates to the reality of stability; indeed, the distance between representation and reality becomes the fault line through which temporality worms its way into the heart of architecture's fiction of endurance. Eternity and stability are thus terms of denial. The more one tries to escape time, the more it will rush in to fill the voids one has left. "Time is what changes and evolves: eternity remains simple," writes Meister Eckhart.[22] Better then to deal with time in all its complexities; better then to move from the simple eternity to the complex here.

It is the early 1990s, before blobs and bloids had really taken over the architectural gene bank. A resistant line of pure architecture existed in the form of hardline minimalism, holding up the eternal flame to ward off the invasive incomers. Its proponents talked in haikus of timeless values, touching the spirit, and finding the essence. It was around this period that one of these bearers of truth took his students on a study trip. There are not that many of these purist buildings in existence (they take a very rich and a very tolerant client), so the trip is to one of his own buildings. The students are slightly surprised that a whole day has been set aside to see one building, but dutifully turn up on time. They are instructed that they can only be let in two at a time, in silence. Anything more would disturb the inner spirit of the place. So in they go, two by two, into a sanctuary from the fallen world beyond. The others wait outside and (this being a field trip) drink cheap red wine; steadily; in the full sun. Seven hours of this later and the last two are finally let in. The combination of heatstroke and alcohol trounces their ability to pay even the

most basic homage. Indeed, just limited concentration on architectural niceties (those shadow gapsh are peshky little things to focus on) overwhelms
the synapses of one of them. Something gives. He lurches around looking
for the bathroom, all lined in that expensive limestone with little holes and
fossils in it. But in his confused state he cannot find the toilet ("it's that thing
that looks like an altar," they joked afterward). Despite the cleaner's best
efforts (resorting in the end to using a toothbrush in those tiny limestone
crevices) the stain of seven hours of cheap red wine remains. Never did the
eternal feel so corrupted, so brought into the now, but as the other students
say later that night—mercilessly joshing the perpetrator—it was an accident
waiting to happen.

Here and Now

The here is an appealing term for architects because it represents instant
freshness. The argument that modernism could, or rather should, represent the spirit of the new age was made most forcefully by Sigfried Giedion
in *Space, Time and Architecture,* which is for many the canonical theoretical
work of the modernist movement. Giedion's central demand is that modern
architecture has an obligation, often couched in moral terms, to represent
the *Zeitgeist*. This can be achieved both technically (through the use of so-
called progressive technologies) and aesthetically. For the latter, Giedion
proposes that the modern age is characterized by a new conception of
space-time whose first expression is in the synthetic cubism of Picasso and
Braque. He sees it as the task of architecture to represent this space-time
condition in a way that "corrects cubism's aberrations," in that cubism's
"symbols were not rational."[23] This entailed a purist representation of the
movement and interpenetration that characterized the modern space-time
condition. Thus for Giedion the production of modernist architecture is
"based in *representations* of movement and its correlates—interpenetration
and simultaneity," so that Gropius's Werkbund Fabrik staircases "seem like
movement seized and immobilised in space."[24] The key word here is *immo-
bilize*. The aestheticization of the *Zeitgeist* necessarily cancels time out of
it; the problem of immobilized movement, a contradiction in terms if ever
there was one, is forgotten in the seduction of progressive form.

What is clear is that this canceling of time and the amnesia induced by
novel form is not limited to Giedion's particular brand or period of modernism. Modernism as architectural movement and style arises out of the condition of modernity and, as Henri Lefebvre notes, the "manifest expulsion

Time, Space, and Lo-Fi Architecture

of time is arguably one of the hallmarks of modernity."[25] Lefebvre here is not suggesting the complete ridding of time, but the ordering of time so as to eliminate the marks of lived time. This ordering is indicative of a general tendency of nineteenth- and twentieth-century modernity in its ability to see itself in specific relation to other epochs. "Modernity is . . . perhaps more than anything else," argues Bauman, "*the history of time:* modernity is the time when time has a history."[26] Modernity is not merely placed "in a linear sequence of chronological time," but assumes a transcendence over the past and with this "a reorientation towards the future."[27] The temporality of Western modernity is necessarily linear, a succession of instants driven by a relentless forward urge. Progress *must* be announced if one is to avoid being sucked back in to the mire of the past or being tarnished by association with the faded charms of a previous instant.[28] And what better vehicle for announcement than the visible might of architecture? Le Corbusier is very clear about the power of the architectural instant: "it commands our attention, masters our spirits, dominates, imposes, subjugates. Such is the argumentation of architecture."[29] Buildings are thus used as markers for the successive moments of modernity.

Architects are all too happy to comply with this demand because these progressive marks help to establish their identity and with it their place in the marketplace—whether it is the external marketplace of economic capital or the internalized architectural marketplace of symbolic capital.[30] If capital is inherently restless and if that restlessness is expressed through the endless progress of commodities feeding the insatiable desire of the consumer—a desire that capital instigates in order to perpetuate itself[31]— then it is easy to see how architects become tied firmly into the modernist capitalist economy. Their commodity—the design of buildings as objects— has to signal its progressive tendencies so as to survive, and in order to do this turns to technology and aesthetics. Progress is announced through the employment of ever-newer technologies (hence the conspicuous success of the hi-tech movement in the external marketplace) or the display of ever-fresher forms and surfaces (hence the conspicuous success of the "radical" formalists in the internal marketplace). Best of all is if you can combine the two, hence the unstoppable drive of Norman Foster to the top of both economic league tables and architectural league tables as his practice plays both the progressive technical card and the progressive formal card.

What is at stake here is the freezing of time into a set of instant aesthetic moments. We have seen how this was achieved in the early modernist period through confining time within the frame of the photograph. In a way the reliance on the photograph is a confession of the fragility of architecture in the face of time; the shift of attention from the object itself to the representation of the object signals a retreat into a more controllable but less real realm. But as Stewart Brand notes in his crucial book *How Buildings Learn*, the photograph is the second of two instants in time that dominate contemporary architecture. The other is the moment of the client's instruction to go ahead with the project, when "the beguiling qualities of the renderings and model of the building-to-be overwhelm the client's resistance . . . so that shallow guesses are frozen as deep decisions."[32] The canceling of time at this key moment effectively freezes the flux of the design process, removing it from any contingencies, most importantly the input of the client and future users.

Late modernists have a much more powerful tool than the photograph or balsa model to effect this removal. The computer brings the distancing of architecture from the temporality of the world right to the start of the design process. Its immense power tricks its users (the designers) and viewers (potential clients) into believing that what is on the screen is what will be achieved on site, taking all too seriously the claims of WYSIWYG (what you see is what you get). The mirage is further enhanced in the way that the computer, by allowing its objects to move or to be "walked through," apparently allows the release of time, breathing life into the frozen vignettes. But this is no more than an extreme form of temporal coercion. As Solà-Morales notes, the modernist *promenade architecturale* (a defined route through a sequence of architectural experiences) "is not a diversity but an itinerary that admits the possibility of control . . . [it is] time organized from the linear viewpoint."[33] The computer walkthrough takes the *promenade architecturale* and stuffs it into a representational straitjacket, thus establishing the control over time still further.

The final, and most compelling, bonus that the computer gives is that it allows architects to indulge in their quest for fresh form. In a classic display of technical determinism, new shapes are evolved because they *can* be there (at least representationally; the actual technicalities of making these shapes is lagging some way behind and often relies on Victorian levels of craft) and not because they *need* to be there. Best of all, the very latest computer technology in the form of CNC (Computer Numerical Control) machines allows the two-dimensional drawings to become three-dimensional models, reinforcing the semblance of reality while forgetting that they have been conceived out of time. Thus the imperative of progressive display is satisfied at the same time as the illusion of temporal reality is given. In fact

Time, Space, and Lo-Fi Architecture

the virtual reality of the computer is just that, virtual. Laurie Anderson's pithy reminder that she will not believe in virtual reality until they learn how to put in dirt is overlooked in the rush for more "realistic" imagery. Anderson's dirt is not to be taken literally; it is a mark of temporality, and the metaphorical lack of it is a signal of timelessness. So the more "real" the computer-generated image, the more it excludes time by petrifying its flux—passing sun reduced to static reflections, weather to radiant blue skies, people to happy lifestyle images. It takes a brave architect, such as Les K Architectures, to break these rules and allow time to creep into the image while accepting that the two dimensions of the page can never present the fullness of life.

An associated effect of the computer's confusion of representation and reality is that it reinforces architecture's autonomy. In severing time from the architectural scene, while giving the illusion that it is there, architects are provided the luxury of preoccupying themselves with form alone, undisturbed by the social and physical flux of contemporary life. As the American artist Gordon Matta-Clark observes, "when a thing does not have any life at all, it seems to have a lot of manipulation for manipulation's sake." If we remove architecture from time, there is not much left to do apart from play with formal and technical devices. The contemporary obsession with morphologies and formal taxonomies arises because the generative power of the computer has created a vast array of new shapes which apparently need classifying, a tsunami of form that overwhelms any critical faculties. There is so much visual noise in the internal systems of architecture that one cannot hear the external world. "Though the parochialism of these especially recent developments is often obscured by the virtuosity of their results," writes Sanford Kwinter in *Architectures of Time*, "they have never managed to hide their fundamental aimlessness, the inevitable result of cultures whose intellectual activity has become severed from its foundations in social, historical and economic life."[34] Out of time effectively becomes out of this world.

Arguments are made that current notions of complexity (scientific and social) should be reflected in so-called complex form (for which read 1980s linear disjunctions, 1990s folds or bloids, and whatever the current year's algorithm throws up in the 2000s). The wizardry of the surfaces distracts from the breathtaking naivety of these arguments. There is something desperate in the belief that generating formal complexity in the computer is necessarily going to lead to occupational and social complexity in the final building. As Henri Lefebvre continually reminds us, spatial (for which read social) complexity is down to far more than mere formal or physical attributes. Drawing pictures, or even building representations, of something does not equate to equaling it; just as with Giedion, aestheticizing the present condition is to rid it of its defining feature, namely its multiple temporality. But more to the point, why *should* architecture stand for the here and now? Why, in Bob Evans's terms, have we moved from the notion that a building is "an opportunity to improve the human condition," to a time when it is conceived of as "an opportunity to express the human condition"?[35] I suspect the answer is disturbingly simple: *it looks good*. The freezing of time allows the architect to edit the world, appropriating the bits that are full of aesthetic or technical potential and discarding those that are not. The argument appears to be that there's lots of new media and technology out there, so let's represent them. Well, there's also lots of poverty out there, but I don't see much of that informing contemporary architectural discourse. Poverty doesn't look good; media and technology do. The problem is that in the aestheticization of this freshness, the architect uncritically celebrates the conditions associated with the dominance of media and technology; on the one hand the saturation of private lives by corporate capital, on the other issues of the environmental crisis brought on by the decadent exploitation of natural resources through technical means.

It is the new millennium. Blobs are with us but beginning to look tired already. With the year-on-year doubling of computer speed one gets a year-on-year doubling of formal complexity. New morphologies mutate like uncontrollable viruses; future architectural historians will have to know more about the submenus of certain software packages than about stylistic chains of influence. I am in an architecture school, talking to the librarian. She laments that students are no longer reading or that, when they do, they prefer texts on biological evolution to architectural theory. I try to cheer her up by saying that at least her pathetically small budget doesn't need to stretch so far. Later, I am talking to a group of design tutors.

"We have," says one, fixing me in the eye, "we have to get a CNC milling machine." No "it would be nice"; this is a necessity.

"Why?" I ask.

"In order to keep up," another responds.

"And how much is one of these miracles?"

A sum ten times the library budget is mentioned. I blink, and in that blinking reveal that I am not a progressive zealot. Later, in a bar with my guard down, this is confirmed as I ramble: "So that's it. The future of architecture. Illiterate button-punchers." The looks exchanged round the table say more than words ever could. They have sensed a Luddite.

Tampering with Time

"Keep off time, time is untouchable, one must not provoke it! Isn't it enough for you to have space? Space is for human beings, you can swing about in space, turn somersaults, fall down, jump from star to star. But for goodness' sake, don't tamper with time."
—Bruno Schulz: *Sanatorium under the Sign of the Hourglass*[36]

In pursuing this argument against the "progressives," I am treading on dangerous ground. The charge will be laid that if one is not looking forward, then one must be looking back; maybe even that one is complicit with the traditionalists. But in fact progressives and traditionalists share the same attitude to time. The traditionalists' abrupt appropriation of past architectural moments attempts to summon up a previous aesthetic in an instant, and with it the values attached to that aesthetic. Just add people to these perfected images and the hope is that they will assume the virtues of that frozen moment in time. Poundbury, Prince Charles's development in Dorset, is perhaps the most explicit example of an attempt to conjoin moral and aesthetic values in a wistful effort to return to a seventeenth-century town pattern, and with it to restore the supposed social values associated with that pattern. The same is true with probably the most infamous of all

these vignettes of frozen history, Disney's Town of Celebration in Florida. It is all too easy for critics to do a hatchet job on Celebration's conflation of historic styles, corporate capitalism, and social determinism.[37] However, a more subtle and even-handed reading is provided by the cultural historian Andrew Ross, who spent a year living there. What he notes is that the architectural strictures of the New Urbanists (on whose principles Celebration is largely but not wholly based) are simply not enough to ensure the return to the kind of values of community, sociability, and harmony that they yearn for. Apart from the fact that the neotraditionalist buildings at Celebration are incredibly badly built and often do not meet basic functional requirements (thus failing two out of three of the Vitruvian tests), Ross chronicles a much more complex intersection of social and economic forces than architecture alone can address. Failings in school, the demise of the main retail quarter, and problems in the social mix[38] all indicate that catching a moment (or rather, at Celebration, a hodgepodge of different moments) of historical instants is not enough; they will get overwhelmed by the winds of contemporary life.

In all instant mixes the result can never hope to match the complexity of the original. "Just add water"—let's say to instant mashed potato—becomes "just add people"—let's say to instant Tuscany. Both fail miserably. Time, as James Joyce reminds us, is too slippery to re-create from

Time, Space, and Lo-Fi Architecture

nothing. ("Can't bring back time. Like holding water in your hand.") Ross's observation that the social determinist dogma of the New Urbanists is as unvarying as that of the modernists is telling here, as is his chronicle as to how the New Urbanists are no different from modernist architects in their desperation to get their polemic enacted. In both cases the expediency is sometimes breathtaking, whether it is Andrés Duany (the high priest of the New Urbanists) making the case for the tenets of corporate capital as an acceptable basis for running these new communities or the great modernists' association with fascism (Le Corbusier with Vichy France[39] or Mies with the Nazis). By lifting architecture out of time one lifts it out of the world, and this apparently abrogates even the most basic political awareness, let alone responsibility. As Hans Jonas writes: "Platonic eros, directed at eternity, at the non-temporal, is not responsible for its object . . . only for the changeable and the perishable can one be responsible."[40] Jonas argues that the temporal brings with it a moral responsibility. Once the future of an object or person is acknowledged, the ethical consequences of one's actions toward that object or person have to be accounted for. In contrast, "what time cannot effect and to which nothing can happen is an object not of responsibility but of emulation."[41] The atemporal architect in his or her aesthetic emulation, of the past or of a fiction of a future, thus eschews any wider responsibility. The traditionalists and the progressives are therefore but two sides of the same conservative—and amoral—coin; the only real difference between the two camps is that the traditionalists are more honest in admitting to their conservative tendencies.

The traditionalists and the progressives are eventually joined by an attitude toward time in which instant pasts or instant futures are represented in static formalist gestures that necessarily cancel out the very time that they are trying to summon. This is an avowedly modernist approach that effectively, despite Bruno Schulz's warning, tampers with time. Once the modern break from the past has been made, time can be divided into discrete moments each of which becomes available for isolated representation. The moment of a past era or of a soon-to-be future is equivalent inasmuch as each has been artificially torn from a dynamic continuity. This is why Bruno Latour can argue that "the idea of an identical repetition of the past and that of a radical rupture with any past are two symmetrical results of a single conception of time."[42] Latour is also clear as to why these figments of the past should reappear in the supposedly modern era. One might think that the modern era should be represented by pure progress, but as we have seen, it is impossible for modernity to maintain its purity: Latour's quasi-objects (exemplified, remember, by postmodern architecture) return to disturb it. Thus although "the moderns have a peculiar propensity for understanding that time passes as if it were really abolishing the past behind it," in reality "the past remains, therefore, and even returns."[43] The architectural traditionalists' recourse to the past is thus just as much a symptom of modernity as the formal gestures of the futurists, however uncomfortable this identification might be for the New Urbanists with their moralizing antimodernist cant. One cannot abolish time within time, but this is the conceit that modernists (and architectural postmodernists as part of the same game) attempt to pull off. It is a game that reduces architecture to an object for which one can absolve oneself of any real responsibility—an object that, when placed into a wider chain of exchanges, becomes primarily a commodity of capital exchange rather than a crucible of social exchange.

Gropius's identification of the rock garden at Ryoanji as a world set apart is shared by many. The Japanese architect Kenzo Tange writes: "in the stone garden of the Ryoanji, an emotion making us feel that we are shedding our self overcomes us."[44] But Tange also astutely notes the price that comes with this casting off: "Why is it," he asks, "that we experience a strong feeling of resistance nevertheless? Is it not directed against the magic spell which draws us away from reality and makes us lose our own selves?" The canceling of time in Ryoanji is also a canceling of reality. To aspire to eternal values may be an ideal for some, but it is a delusory one because in the end the thing that will most quickly shatter architecture's false mask of autonomy is time. As the argument about waste suggested, architecture *necessarily* has to accommodate temporality; thus to describe something that exists out of time is to describe something that is not architecture. It is therefore necessary to reverse the modernist equation that tampers with time, to move from seeing time as held in architecture to understanding architecture in time.

Time, Space, and Lo-Fi Architecture

6   In Time

Le Temps

Bruno Latour is in conversation with his fellow French intellectual Michel
Serres. Latour is generously playing the innocent to Serres's wise man in
order to draw out what he already knows.

Bruno Latour: It is obvious to us moderns that, as we advance in time,
each successive stage outstrips the preceding one.
Michel Serres: But that's not time.
Bruno Latour: That's what you need to explain to me—why this passage
of time is not time.
Michel Serres: That's not time, only a simple line.[1]

As we have seen, time as a simple line has a certain attraction to architects
and modernists alike. The line places time into an ordered sequence of
instants, a definition that was first proposed by Aristotle and has been persistent ever since. The trouble is that the line coerces time into something
that it is not. "Time is paradoxical," says Serres later in the interview, "it folds
or twists; it is as various as the dance of flames in a brazier, here interrupted,
there vertical, mobile, and unexpected."[2] But then, Serres and Latour have
an advantage. They are French, and so use the same word for time and the
weather: *le temps*. This is not a linguistic accident: "at a profound level they
are the same thing." The weather proceeds in a line of successive seasons,
but this regularity is continually disturbed by short-term uncertainties (. . .
an Indian summer), instant events (. . . that sudden downpour), and long-
term patterns (. . . global warming). In the same way the linearity of time
as described by the calendar (yesterday, today, tomorrow) is overlaid with

cyclical time (day/night, yearly cycles); and as if the resulting flux of the intersection of these external characters of time were not enough, it is further complicated by the introduction of the human dimensions of time, both personal (memories and anticipations) and shared (histories and futures).

The very essence of time is its lack of essence; any version of time is bound to be disarranged by another. "We live all the patterns of time simultaneously," says the Italian sociologist Alberto Melucci, "the recurring circle of memory and project, the linear projection of the arrow as an intention and a goal, the exalted condensation of the point, or the experience of losing ourselves in disconnected fragments. It is often difficult to reconcile these patterns, since each one of them brings us to the borders of the others."[3] The resulting instability is the cause of the architects' terror of time; it presents a force beyond their control, which is why they either remove themselves from it through false notions of eternity or else attempt to arrange it into a line of "nows."

This reaction to the uncertainty of time is by no means unique to architects but is symptomatic of a much wider tradition that asserts the power of the intellect over time. Thus, for instance, in anthropology the dynamics of social interaction through time are typically ordered into neat packages of time called epochs. These are defined through physical time—dates and timescales that document demographic changes in a supposedly neutral manner—and typological time in which time becomes the measure of patterns of social behavior (industrial versus peasant societies, the traditional versus the modern era).[4] But as Johannes Fabian argues in *Time and the Other*, these approaches necessarily abstract time, removing the documenter (the anthropologist) from the scene they are documenting. The scene is thus stripped of its defining features in order to fit into a more universalized notion of time and society, and in particular a notion based on Western values. The contingency of the specifics is overwhelmed by the ordering of the system. Fabian's key notion is that of coevalness—the sharing of time with others and the sharing of the time of the other—and in anthropology's attitude to time he sees the "denial of coevalness."[5] A distance opens up between observer and observed which turns the world into a set of petrified relations, emptied of their social and political content. Fabian talks of the "scandal" of these petrified relations. Exactly the same is true of architects' attitude to time when they attempt to freeze time and take architecture out of time. They become detached from the scene that they are designing, thereby distancing themselves from it as a site of political and social significance. At a temporal distance, the user becomes an abstraction and so available to be subjected to determinist methods of analysis and design

Time, Space, and Lo-Fi Architecture

such as functionalism, just as the distant tribe is corralled into determinist behavior patterns under the rule of structuralist anthropology.[6]

How can these scenes be released from their straitjackets? To quote Marx out of context, "these petrified relations must be forced to dance by singing to them their own melody."[7] It is a temporal melody. Time must be admitted to architecture. Architects must admit to time. They need to get coeval, to share the time of others, and maybe the best way to start is to look out of the window at *le temps*, at the weather as a reminder of the immediacy, multiplicity, interconnectedness, and power of time.

Thick Time

Immediate, multiple, connected, and powerful. These are the conditions of time that architecture needs to face up to. In its *immediacy*, time cannot be escaped. One has to be alert to what Robert Smithson calls the "temporal surfaces," aware of time as experienced rather than of some abstracted and eventually ideological construct of it.[8] In its *multiplicity*, time presents a diversity that architecture has to accept—the linear, the cyclical, the personal, the instant explosion of the event, the *longue durée*—and, in order to do that, has to relinquish its mythology of stability and strength. This is why Ignasi de Solà-Morales identifies his notion of "weak architecture" so strongly with the multiplicity of time: "the diversity of time becomes absolutely central . . . to weak architecture."[9] Architecture is here a framework that can accommodate the multiplicity of time rather than a barrier erected against the tides of time or a reification of a single version of time. Architecture needs to be a setting that allows these diverse temporal conditions to coexist. Not just the event, but the potential for the event being overlaid on a regular ritual. Not just a building that responds to cyclic rhythms (of life, of the seasons, of the world), but one that allows these to unfold against the linear aspects (of decay, of change). In its *connectedness*, time places architecture in a dynamic continuity, aware of the past, projecting to the future. The here-and-now is seen not as an instant to be satisfied but as part of an "expanded present," or of what may be designated "Thick Time." And finally, in its very *powerfulness*, time brings to architecture forces which it cannot resist—weather, dirt, occupation—and therefore must admit to. Maybe it is all too easy to say all this and less easy to enact it, but this paragraph is in a certain way a statement of intent for the book.

My argument here is that time, and not space, should be seen as the primary context in which architecture is conceived. This may at first look like a complete reversal of the normal emphasis on space in architecture. Any notions of time's conquest of space or of space's of time prove to be Pyrrhic victories, because the two cannot be separated, and so the triumph of one over the other is the vanquishing of something stripped of its fullness.[10] So when I suggest time as the primary context for architecture, it is not to reassert the modernist myth of the conquest of space through time, but rather to establish the principle of bringing time to space. Or, to put it another way, to think of temporalized space—space full of time—rather than spatialized time—the latter of which, as we saw with Giedion, inevitably leads in its reification and aestheticization to a completely emasculated version of time. If, as Lefebvre suggests, "with the advent of modernity, time has vanished from social space,"[11] then we need to find ways of reintroducing it. The foregrounding of space tends toward its abstraction; against this, by positing time as the key context for architecture, space becomes active, social, and is released from the hold of static formalism.

"We must acknowledge," writes Steven Groák, "that in reality buildings have to be understood in terms of several different timescales over which they change, in terms of moving images and ideas in flux."[12] And if time is the primary context for architecture, and if the context of time is one of contingency and uncertainty, then it is the first context out of which we can begin to develop notions of how to deal with that contingency: to understand architecture as a contingent discipline, one must grapple with an understanding of time. I use the word *grapple* knowingly; great, great minds have wrestled with the slippery beast of time, so where should we mere mortals start? Aristotle, St. Augustine, Kant, Einstein, Heidegger, Bergson, Whitehead, or Ricoeur? My advice is none of these; they become black holes in which, quite literally, one can lose a lot of time. Start with what you know, what you see, what you experience; start with the everyday; start with Smithson's "temporal surfaces," which are there waiting to be found if one just puts on the time-based spectacles; put aside your clock and look for all those other aspects of time as lived which I have hinted at above: the linear, the cyclical, the instant, the memory, the event, the ritual. Lived time: you will find it in the streets, you will find it in the everyday. You will find the best understanding of lived time in your own, human, experience of it. Most poignantly, you will find it in novels; share your time with their time.[13] Most explicitly, you will find lived time in James Joyce, in *Ulysses*.

It is Joyce more than any philosopher who most acutely describes time as lived, and so indicates the impossibility of placing it into a neat set of categories. In *Ulysses*, he weaves threads of epic time (the time of the Homeric

Time, Space, and Lo-Fi Architecture

gods), natural cyclical time (the rivers, the shifting sands), historical cyclical time (the repetitive sense of Ireland's identity), linear historical time (the particular chronological response to colonization), personal time (Joyce's own life reinscribed in the pages), fuzzy time (memories snatched), focused time (the endless newspapers), their future time, my future time (when will I finish it?) . . . and so on and on. The relationship of these threads is always restless, so that no one temporal modality predominates over the others. In *Ulysses* the present is never seen as held in the thrall of the past, but the two coexist in a continually evolving relationship—a present in which the anticipation of the future is always at hand ("Coming events cast their shadows before them," muses Bloom, the hero of *Ulysses*). Time in *Ulysses* inheres in the commonplace objects and situations of Dublin. Joyce's time, as he follows Bloom, Dedalus, and their friends through the streets of Dublin, is the time of the everyday, but it is by no means ordinary, summoning up as it does the richness of multiple and coincident modes of time. Time is revealed through the literary device of the epiphany, "the moment in which the soul of the commonest object seems to us radiant," in a sudden "revelation of the whatness of the thing."[14] These epiphanies in all their immediate ordinariness, but eventual complexity, give to *Ulysses* a concentration on the everyday as the place of extraordinarily productive potential. Normally everyday time is seen to be subsumed by more ascendant temporal modes. On the one hand the linear time of progress, in its concentration on the iconic and the one-off, has no place for the quotidian; on the other hand cyclical time is generally represented only through the grand narratives of the gods. The architect Adolf Loos's identification of the tomb and the monument as the only true moments of architecture (everything else is mere building) confirms these ascendant modes as paradigms for the architect, because these two types stand outside the time of the everyday. Joyce's triumph is to contextualize multiple modes of time through the everyday. In *Ulysses* other times, ascendant, personal, cyclical, historical, and so on, are seen through, and thereby reformulated by, the time of the everyday. The same is possible with architecture, allowing the time of the everyday, lived time, to dismantle Loos's crude barrier between architecture and building.

Joyce's time of the everyday elides with philosophical readings of everyday time. "The everyday," notes Henri Lefebvre, "is situated at the intersection of two modes of repetition: the cyclical, which dominates in nature, and the linear, which dominates in processes known as 'rational.'"[15] Lefebvre (who, not surprisingly, was a great reader of Joyce)[16] argues that the everyday is subject to constant repetitions and cycles, but is also open to randomness and chance. The everyday is the result of "a myriad repetitive practices,"[17] and thus accumulates traces of the past, but in its very incompleteness is always accessible to reformulation, and thus orientated toward the future. In Lefebvre's memorable phrase, the everyday is thus the place where "the riddle of recurrence intercepts the theory of becoming."[18] Everyday time is thus thick time, a temporal space that critically gathers the past and also projects the future.

As Melucci notes, "fluid and enfolding, the experience of time is characterised by a sense of thickness and a density that our definitions seldom provide."[19] Thick time forces us to relinquish any notion of time, or architecture, as a set of instants. Thick time is time of the extended present that avoids mere repetition of past times or the instant celebration of new futures. Thick time is where the interception of recurrence and becoming provides the space for action, but not in an easy linear manner ("Hold to the now, the here," says Joyce, "through which all future plunges to the past"). In the course of design, thick time catalyzes action through bringing experiences together with hopes. Experience alone is not enough, because that means that one is doomed to endless repetitions of the status quo without any transformative insight. Hope alone is not enough because, as we shall see in part III of this book, that can lead to deluded dreams of perfected worlds created and inhabited from scratch.[20] By infusing the process of design with both experiences and hopes (of architects, of the other designers, of users, of clients) thick time brings architecture to the world as lived. As we have seen, out of time is out of this world. To be in (thick) time, however, is to be in the world, not a world of static objects but a world of social and temporal exchanges, and if these exchanges are reflected upon in the course of design, it is all the more likely that the resultant buildings will be able to accept the multiplicity of time in the future. "We are brewers and exchangers of time,"[21] says Michel Serres, and thus architecture needs to take in these exchanges.

Probably the most sustained investigation of buildings in time is Stewart Brand's book *How Buildings Learn*. The argument of the book is direct: buildings change and grow over time, but designers of buildings do not take these temporal aspects into account. Indeed, not only do they not take them into account, they often deny them altogether. "Architecture, we imagine, is permanent. And so our buildings thwart us. Because they discount time, they misuse time."[22] Brand's book has never found much favor in the architectural community, though it rightly remains popular beyond. Part of the reason may be the way he illustrates his argument through a dialogue between "high architecture," generally cast as the villain of the piece, and vernacular or everyday architecture, generally seen to possess the temporal virtues he is promoting. Architects instinctively bristle at the vernacular; it threatens their very existence since, by definition, it is beyond the complete control of the professional. But the real reason for architects' antipathy to Brand's argument is that he confronts the architect's terror of time head on. He welcomes time into building, and in so doing challenges all those architectural preoccupations with stasis and perfection. Brand insistently criticizes the architectural "greats" for their disavowal of time, repeating the popular tales of leaky roofs, rusting pipes, and awkward inflexibility.

It is not surprising, therefore, that an architectural great, Richard Rogers, should take such umbrage at Brand's observations on his buildings, which were made in the first American edition but excised from subsequent British editions under the threat of legal action from the architect. The differences between the two are less to do with the accuracy of Brand's architectural observations (which are no more harsh than, say, a theater critic might use on a flawed but magnificent play) and more to do with their irreconcilable attitude toward time. The musician, artist, and thinker Brian Eno suggests as much. Eno, a good friend of Brand, was brought in as an intermediary to reach an agreement between Rogers and Brand. As Eno notes, with his characteristic perceptiveness, "there are many futures and only one status quo. This is why conservatives mostly agree and radicals always argue. Richard Rogers and Stewart Brand—two people who are, in some way or the other, trying to make the future, but disagreeing about how it should be done."[23] Brand wants to "embrace and exploit time's depth."[24] Rogers professes to share something of the same attitude: "one of the things which we are searching for is a form of architecture which, unlike classical architecture, is not perfect and finite upon completion . . . we are looking for an architecture rather like some music and poetry which can actually be changed by the users, an architecture of improvisation."[25] However, the evidence would indicate that this improvisation is overseen by the strictures of the architecture. In 1994, when Gae Aulenti moved a set of solid-looking boxes into the Centre Pompidou designed by Rogers and Piano, the original architects were less than pleased: "it is like they are putting a plaster cast on a leg," commented Renzo Piano wryly.[26] This suggests that their building was not quite as flexible as they had led us to believe; it can change, but only on our terms, was the message. More telling were the comments of Dominique Bozo, the director of the Centre Pompidou who commissioned Aulenti to create spaces more sympathetic to the permanent art collection. Piano and Rogers "reduced everything to the ephemeral . . . the Centre's concept aimed at being 'contemporary' . . . they should have been more cautious, have known that the present never lasts." The building, for Bozo, effectively tampered with time, its flexibility being a frozen image located at a particular point in time.

In the end, what Rogers managed to expunge from Brand's book were all the references to the fact that his buildings had suffered the affront of uncontrollable time. In challenging Rogers's control over time, Brand was challenging his very definition as an Architect; hence, maybe, the uncharacteristic reaction on Rogers's part.

It is 1991. Paris. Another field trip. I am outside the Beaubourg, using the slope of the piazza in front of it to lecture to my students. I love the Beaubourg, you have to be a misanthrope not to, but it has been a long day of extolling the greats, and Piano & Rogers are getting a somewhat skeptical overview (little knowing that Piano himself will later mock his masterpiece much better than I ever could as a parody of the technological imagery of our time, thus deflating all those hi-tech pretensions and confusing lots of acolytes into the bargain).[27] Suddenly, stage front, Richard Rogers emerges from the front door, less than fifty meters away. I freeze, terrified he might have heard me. "Go get him," the students shout. He would have come over, I am sure; he is smiling, he is always generous. But I stay rooted; overwhelmed, spooked even, by this coincidence, by the timing of his entry: Rogers truly does control time in his buildings. The evidence is there in the fading light.

Dirty Old Time

James Joyce is spending Christmas 1940, two weeks before he dies, in Switzerland. His hosts are his friends the architectural writer Sigfried Giedion and the art critic Carola Giedion-Welcker. Giedion has just finished *Space, Time and Architecture,* the book that was to do more than any in the freezing of time in architecture. Joyce has reached the end of his exploration of the flux of life. The documenter of paralyzed time sits with the author of unstable time. The former talks of a nearby group of modernist houses that he commissioned some years before, designed by his compatriot Marcel Breuer, all white and neat. But Joyce is "much opposed. 'Look at these fine walls and windows' he says, admiring the wall's thickness and window's smallness: in comparison with this solidity the Breuer houses seem to him sterile and commonplace." Giedion, one guesses, admonishes him for his fixation with tradition, extolling the power of modernism to be rid of time and stains. Joyce, "mocking Swiss cleanliness and order," responds: "You don't know how wonderful dirt is."[28]

In all their simplicity, there is something devastating about these words of Joyce, these words that were among his very last to be recorded. "You don't know how wonderful dirt is." In raising the specter of dirt, he goes straight to the heart of Giedion's (and his associated architects') anxieties about time. The issue is not so much dirt per se, but dirt as the signal of the encroachment of time into the sterile perfection of architecture. Modernism's obsession with cleanliness is well documented. The clearest example is in the title and content of Le Corbusier's book *When the Cathedrals Were White*, a paean of praise for an era of freshness and cleanliness that he thinks he has rediscovered in the United States, but which has been lost in dirty old (and old-fashioned) France.[29] Dirt represents the other that must be overcome. The tarnish of the past was to be eliminated, and this could be effected with quite disarming ease through a coat of white. This is made clear in Corbusier's *Law of Ripolin* (Ripolin being a form of modern whitewash): "there are no more dirty, dark corners . . . . on white walls these accretions of dead things from the past world would be intolerable; they would leave a stain."[30] Memories are selective here. Le Corbusier insists that the Acropolis was "white and dazzling,"[31] because that fitted with his call for newness, when in fact the Parthenon and other buildings were painted and colored. Countless historians have corralled modernism's earliest show homes, the Stuttgart Weissenhofsiedlung, into an image of pure whiteness, when approximately a third of the buildings were highly colored and another third various shades of off-white. Mark Wigley is right to explain this as a "strategic silence" necessary to maintain the myth of modernism as a universal single trajectory, defined in this case by its very whiteness.[32] White represents more, much more, than just a lack of color. In its purity it also signals a moral cleansing, as Le Corbusier makes clear: "A COAT OF WHITEWASH. We would perform a moral act: *to love purity*!"[33] Whitewash cleanses not just the stains of dirt, but also the impure society that has inflicted those stains. It marks a new beginning.

White is, of course, quite hopeless in carrying its burden of representing a new era. It can only represent the instant moment of the fresh beginning; after that it is condemned to grubby failure. The whiter the wall, the more fragile its defense against time. Ask any cleaner. So as whiteness failed (literally and metaphorically), new cleansing weapons were introduced on the side of modernism, as exemplified most clearly in the work of the hi-tech architects who deployed technology in their battle with the pall of time. Ripolin gave way to metals, glasses, and plastics, whiteness to shininess and transparency. If ever there is an example of the way that the hi-tech movement is obsessed more by the image of technology than the reality of it, it is here.[34] In the reduction of hi-tech to an aesthetic, the main emphasis is not so much that the buildings should *actually* deny time, but that they should *look* as if they could. It is clear that these hi-tech boys (for so they are, almost to a man) have never done the housework; any common sense would tell them that the shinier the surface the more apparent the dirt, the tarnish—the temporal changes.

Time, Space, and Lo-Fi Architecture

It was when cleaning cradles hunched over the top of buildings became an aesthetic in their own right that one sensed the whole thing had gone too far. "Come and get us," the cradles appear to shout to Father Time, "throw what you will at us and we will shrug it off." But in fact all the cradles do is to provide the *illusion* of buildings standing over time. Along with the spectacle of trained mountaineers clambering in specially developed suckered boots over I. M. Pei's Louvre Pyramid, polishing cloths in hand, the cradles are signals of desperation. In a classic example of technological determinism, one technology (the cradle, the suckered boots) is employed to solve the problem caused by another technology (the shiny surface), without first questioning the efficacy of technology in the face of time, dirty old time.

Now it is 1998. Paris again. Less than twenty years after it was completed, the Beaubourg is covered in billowing cloth. Signs have been erected by the Ministry of Culture: "Centre Georges Pompidou: Restauration: Façade Ouest." Under its shrouds, like a cathedral, this great building is being accorded the honor of restoration. The cleaners are at work, removing what the bright colors could not shake off. It is suddenly a magnificent old, but soon to be new again, building. It may have failed some of the tests of time (why else would it need restoration quite so quickly?),[35] but it has passed the greatest temporal test of all: it has been designated durable, something above time.

The Unfinished

My reading of Joyce's statement "You don't know how wonderful dirt is" is not a celebration of the aesthetics of dirt. I am not advocating that buildings should be designed avowedly to get dirty. My plea is for an acknowledgment of architecture being situated in and through time. The Italian historian Manfredo Tafuri identifies this temporality operating in the magnificent 1950s work of the Milanese architects BPR, for whom "the many legacies combined in a project gave rise to contaminations, to works that were in some way 'dirty.'"[36]

At the most direct level the acceptance of time in architecture includes the idea that weathering "is a form of completion,"[37] a concept developed by David Leatherbarrow and Mohsen Mostafavi, who see buildings as necessarily incomplete when they are just finished, and that the weather is an agent of positive transformation toward completion. While Leatherbarrow and Mostafavi see this action as indicative of a wider sensibility about architecture and human temporality, it is possible to reduce weathering to another aesthetic device in the architect's toolbox, as exploited brilliantly by Herzog and de Meuron in buildings such as the Studio Rémy Zaugg, with its concrete surfaces gradually returning to a memory of mossy rock faces. Here and elsewhere, dirt is reclassified from being the enemy of architecture to its aesthetic ally, but there is the concomitant danger that this very aestheticism, while "dirty" and temporal, is just as removed from the vicissitudes of the social world as the whiteness that it replaces.

The idea of architecture in time therefore needs to extend further than the exterior surface being completed by weathering. Temporality in architecture begins at the moment of conception in thick time, and it continues through the life of the buildings, bringing with it the forces of entropy, use, and change. Of these three, entropy is potentially the most upsetting to architects. In the modern project of architecture, use (under the guise of function) can purportedly be determined, and change (under the guise of flexibility) can supposedly be limited to areas within the architect's direct control. But entropy is something else. It denotes a condition of ongoing uncertainty and with it the potential decline into disorder, something beyond the jurisdiction of any professional body. One aspect of the modern project, in its quest for purity and unfettered ideals, can be seen as an ongoing battle to halt the processes of entropy. The archprophet of modernity, Buckminster Fuller, took particular exception to entropy, even going so far

as to invent his own term, *synotropy*, to counter what he saw as the negative connotations of entropy.

But what if, instead of attempting to resist the irresistible force of entropy, one "collaborated" with it?[38] The term was used in this sense by Robert Smithson, who set out his stall in direct opposition to the ordering tendency of modernity, with its monuments "built not for the ages but rather against the ages."[39] For Smithson, entropy takes on both a negative and a positive connotation. The negative one follows the Second Law of Thermodynamics: a gradual draining of energy until one reaches a state of inactive equilibrium, a condition of "all-encompassing sameness" that he finds in the "slurbs, urban sprawl, and the infinite number of housing developments of the post-war boom," all of which have contributed to "the architecture of entropy." The resulting banality and emptiness are not what Smithson aspires to in his collaboration with entropy.[40] What he looks for is an engagement with the active aspects of entropy's inevitable disturbance of stability and highly developed structures. This is, for Smithson, a positive reformulation that contributes to the continuous remaking of stuff (his art, architecture) over time.

Perhaps the most poignant trace of this entropic process in Smithson's own work is in the *Spiral Jetty*, that seemingly simple arrangement of brown rocks projecting out into a lonely salt lake in Utah. Smithson died shortly after completing—no, that should be starting—*Spiral Jetty*, and over the succeeding years his work disappeared under the rising water. However, in recent years, as the waters have retreated, the jetty has again been revealed, somehow shrunken and with the sharpness of the rocks softened by luminous white encrustations. It is all too easy, and enjoyable, to be seduced by Smithson's aesthetic here but, as with all great works of art, the lessons are not solely in the object as matter but in the object qua idea. And the burning idea under the searing skies of Utah is that the work is never finished. Smithson, as artist, only starts what entropic time continues. He collaborates with entropy.

To transfer this argument to architecture brings further complexities. Architecture is subjected not only to the elemental forces of time (the weather, physical decay) but also to the social forces of time (users, changing function, economic obsolescence). But this added entropy does not overrule the possibility of collaborating with it. In fact it reinforces it. The architect only starts what time and others continue. Entropic time is seen not as an affront, but as a partner in a process of design that continues long

Time, Space, and Lo-Fi Architecture

after the architect has left the scene. However, to accept this collaboration demands a change in architectural priorities away from architecture as a frozen moment of "completion," and toward an acceptance of what Lars Lerup calls "building the unfinished."[41] This does not necessarily mean literally, physically, unfinished but unfinished in the sense that it allows "for the possibility of appropriation" by its users.[42] "Human action . . . is a complicated matrix with unknown combinations, the result of which is considerable unpredictability, a marvellous unfinishedness and openness. When this fact is brushed aside, ignored or forgotten the importance of architecture becomes simply utilitarian, design becomes dull, repetitive and mechanical," and so, Lerup argues, "the designer must learn how to live comfortably with the imprecisions of our understanding of human behavior."[43] It is clear that Lerup sees this notion of unfinishedness not as a threat to the sanctity of architectural control, but as an opportunity for spatial invention in which the user's voice is heard throughout the architectural process.

There are very few architects who openly subscribe to the notion of the unfinished. Perhaps the best known is Herman Hertzberger, whose principles of spatial appropriation and temporal acceptance chime with many of the arguments in this book.[44] He thus describes his Diagoon Dwellings as "in principle unfinished . . . the actual design should be seen as a provisional framework that must still be filled in."[45] Internal balconies, external terraces, a protected corner outside—all of these and more anticipate being taken over so that the dwelling is completed not by Hertzberger but by the occupants. The flexibility in the Diagoon houses arises from the provision of slack space that can "absorb and accommodate the influences of changing times and situations."[46] It is therefore about the making of space, but also about leaving space for interpretation.

What is clear from Hertzberger and other architects who successfully pursue the notion of the unfinished is that this is far from a laissez-faire approach to architecture in which the architect merely provides a neutral background for the users to operate on. Instead, building the unfinished compels the architect to project multiple actions onto the building. Where the functionalist or behaviorist architect attempts to determine use in a fixed and singular manner, the architect of the unfinished mentally inhabits the spaces of their future building in myriad ways in order to test them for their openness to appropriation, and then makes adjustments when the whole feels too constricted. The important thing is that it is conceptually unfinished in order to allow time to take its inevitable course in a positive manner.

I am on a trip somewhere in Europe, judging buildings for the RIBA Awards. To enter a building for the awards one has to fill out a form, including a box noting the "Date of Completion." Buildings that are more than a year old are somehow perceived by their architects as past their sell-by date, and so in the pursuit of freshness there is a rush to get buildings in just as soon as they are "complete," even if this means pushing the meaning of that term to the limits. As judges we often see buildings whose "date of completion" is suspiciously close to the date of our visit. On this particular trip my patience with this temporal meddling finally snaps as we drive six hours between two buildings, one completely empty, the other with the builders still applying the whitewash. We resolve to do something. "How about two boxes on the form next year?" I propose at the next meeting of the Awards Group, "One for 'Date of Completion,' the other for 'Date of Commencement.'" "Oh, Jeremy, get real," someone sniggers. So we settle on just one box. "Date of Occupation." A small but, in my mind, quite significant step in the annals of temporal architecture.

Drawing Time

In order to allow time into architecture, we need to track back to the start of the architectural process, or at least to where it begins for so many architects, namely the sketch.[47] A recent book collects together a particular genre of architectural sketch, those drawn on dinner napkins to quickly explore an idea. The book, only slightly tongue in cheek, panders to the myth that all great buildings start their life as sketches on napkins in restaurants or (more likely now) on airline dinner trays, the status of the architect being revealed by whether the napkin is first, business, or economy class. One architect, Rem Koolhaas, demanded a tablecloth from the editor. This was seen by one reviewer of the book as a trait of architectural arrogance, but I guess that Koolhaas was gently disparaging the commonly held belief that "it should be possible to sketch the concept of a good building in less than ten seconds"[48] A tablecloth is a more realistic platform for the initiation of the complexities of architecture than a mere napkin.

It is a problem of delusion, and probably of ego, to believe that a sketch can, or indeed should, capture a building's essence. The sketch is deemed to contain traces of both the impulsive marks of the intuitive genius and the considered mark of logical thinking, thus perpetuating the abiding myth that architecture is the meeting of art and science. The use of the sketch was formalized most dramatically in the Beaux-Arts educational exercise of *l'esquisse,* in which students had twelve hours to lay down the essentials of their design, which were then frozen. Over the next three months they worked up these initial gestures, always conscious that they would be failed if the final design varied from the initial sketch. The whole process firmly establishes the belief that the sketch is the manifestation of inner urges and that the better the sketch as anticipation of the final building, the greater the imbuement of those urges with the spirit of genius.

A sketch is necessarily reductive, and one of the inevitable casualties is time. The reliance on the sketch as the initiator of so much architectural production inexorably leads to a fixation on form and type, as manifested in a product, as opposed to a consideration of use and time, as might be developed in a process. The real confusion with the sketch lies in its combined use both as a means of capturing an idea and as the starting point for the production of architecture. From the Renaissance onward, the architectural drawing (including the sketch) has played a twin role, that of representing something out there (an idea, a condition) and that of producing something soon to be out there (an architectural object, a building). The problem is that the two roles of drawing are confused. Typically one might wish to represent an idea out there—let's say that of a classical ideal (in the Renaissance), of order (in modernity), or complexity (in the contemporary era). Ideas are difficult enough to express in words; try pinning them down within the reductive codes of architectural language, and something is bound to give. A severe editing takes place and a yawning gap opens up between the idea/condition and its representation. As Henri Lefebvre notes, architectural knowledge "suffers from the delusion that 'objective' knowledge of 'reality' can be attained by means of graphic representation."[49] The gap is disguised by technique—in the Renaissance through the birth of perspective and systems of proportion, in modernity through the development of abstracted ordering systems such as the grid and its distortions, and in the contemporary era through the tools provided by the computer. In all cases what happens is that the technique of the drawing becomes the ground for working out ideas divorced from their initial (social and temporal) context; technique alone carries all the intellectual and representational burden, eventually becoming an end unto itself, rather than a means to an end. The result is autonomy in the processes of architectural production, driven by an internalized obsession with the various modes and codes of architectural representation.

With this fixation on technique it is all too easy to slip from drawing as a means of representation to drawing as a means of production, bringing exactly the same codes and methods from one activity to another very different one.[50] The argument would appear to be that if architectural drawing can successfully *represent* a set of presumed virtues, then surely that same technique can be used to *deliver* those virtues back to the world. Thus, to give three examples: perspective, first employed as the representation of symbolic form and embodied space in the early Renaissance, soon becomes an instrument of architectural production. It is for this reason that Dalibor Vesely sees perspective as the "first plausible anticipation of modernity," with the instrumental power of perspectival representation overwhelming its role in the communication of phenomenal reality.[51] Second, geometry and ratio, first used to identify and represent proportional systems in the pursuit of an ideal, become prime mechanisms in the composition and production of plans and elevations from Alberti through Palladio to Le Corbusier. Third, the complex geometrical patterns that presume to map contemporary flux are then all too easily employed as templates for "complex" architectural form. In all cases, the result is that "the formal representation of reality" is no longer distinguished from "the mathematical representation of technical knowledge."[52] The means of communicative representation thus flips over to become precisely the means of production, hoping that in this shift the drawing will remain as a perfect mirror, allowing the seamless translation from idea to architectural object. The employment of the same techniques through all stages of representation gives the semblance that ideas and interpretations of reality are being carried intact from one end of the process to the other.

But this hope falls on two swords. First, as we have seen, the drawing, in its editing and abstraction, fails to represent the fullness of the conditions it is addressing, but this failure is disguised, particularly in the contemporary era, by the virtuosity of the technique. Secondly, as Bob Evans notes wryly, "what comes out is not always the same as what goes in";[53] what goes into the drawing, in terms of ideas and techniques to represent those ideas, is different from what emerges as the matter of the architectural object. "There is," Evans continues, "a blind spot between the drawing and its object, because we can never be quite certain, before the event, how things will travel and what will happen to them on the way."[54] The whole journey from idea to drawing to building is one of uncertainty, and yet, as Evans argues, "architecture has been thought of as an attempt at maximum preservation in which both meaning and likeness are transported from idea through drawing to building with minimum loss."[55] The vehicle for this journey is the drawing, and such is the faith in its power to translate that one ends up with the conviction that the drawing is equivalent to the architectural object that it produces, and in turn the conviction that the mute architectural object is equivalent to the temporal building that emerges from the process. What is clear is that the drawing, in all its rigid two-dimensionality, cannot be the same as the architectural object in all its three-dimensionality and spatiality, and even more that the architectural object, as a collection of static forms, cannot begin to presume to be the same as the building in all its sociality and temporality. However, architects rely on the "reassurance of sufficient affinity between paper and wall,"[56] to such an extent that it blocks out the lumps and differences in the translation from drawing to architectural object to building. The drawing becomes the center of their attention—a security blanket that, in smothering (they wish, they hope) external contingencies, asserts their control over architectural production.

The focus on the drawing is inculcated in architectural education. This may be inevitable: with so much dependent on the visual evidence of the individual portfolio, the drawing is privileged as the means of communication and the basis for assessment, and so virtuosity is rewarded over other aspects of production. It is in architecture school that the internalized codes of architectural representation are first learned and then taken for granted. The assumption is that these codes are transparent, whereas all the evidence points to fundamental misunderstandings by nonarchitects of even "simple" drawing codes such as floor plans. It is in the schools also that the idea of equivalence between drawing–architectural object–building is first established. "You are not drawing buildings," I say endlessly to my students, "you are drawing ideas." But it takes a brave soul to listen to me in the face of validating bodies which demand pictures of "buildings" in order to satisfy the criteria. The closest that students may get is images of architectural objects: plans, sections, and elevations of things that resemble the bare bones of potential architecture, but never approach the temporality, or corporality, of the flesh of buildings.

My argument is not with the virtuosity of the drawing or with the sketch per se, but with the notion that these internalized codes can represent the fullness of architecture at the expense of other means of spatial communication. It is the apparent ease with which the standard modes of representation suppress the contingency of architecture that is both their strength and their weakness. The strength lies in the restraint that the drawing and model apply to the external flux within which architecture is ultimately situated. They are a means of control, and the architect is the agent of control in a display of professional authority. As Henri Lefebvre points out, while drawing in codes may appear a benign activity, it is in fact the nexus for the production of a certain type of "abstract" space. "The tendency to make reductions of this kind," he argues, referring to architectural representations, "is a tendency that degrades space."[57] Here he points to the ultimate weakness of architectural representation: in editing the world, and then transferring this emasculation through into the production of buildings, architecture is eventually powerless in the face of forces that, while purportedly and all too conveniently canceled, will come back to haunt it. Of all these forces it is time that hovers most threateningly over the deathless body of architecture; something conceived out of time cannot survive in time.

Time needs, therefore, to be introduced to the various stages of architectural representation. The key lies in drawing a line in the sand between the stages of architectural production (most particularly that of creative communication and that of technical production), and applying different approaches on either side. This will break the hold of specific techniques

Time, Space, and Lo-Fi Architecture

(the perspective, grids, computer-generated form) on the process as a whole, and allow techniques appropriate to each stage to be evolved. In terms of drawing time, the first requirement is to recognize the difference between drawings as communicative devices, there to work out and express ideas and their latent spatial possibilities, and drawings as instruments used in the production of architecture as built form. The latter role of representation is necessarily an abstraction, a process outside the temporal and social aspects of architecture as lived, and should be acknowledged as such. The drawing as instrument of production is a secondary means to an end, not the primary end that it has become in so much contemporary architecture.

The aspiration, therefore, is to inscribe time in the communicative stages of architectural production—communicative, that is, both to the architects themselves and also to an external audience. However, time in all its complexity cannot be summoned up in a single system of representation, so one has to resort to multiple modes of communication: drawn, made, photographed, told, enumerated, enacted. The tendency is to concentrate on one mode of representation, and so on one temporal condition. Thus the architectural model alone shunts the architectural object into a cul-de-sac of frozen form, but a model combined with, say, a narrative allows the participants to project occupation into the spatial frame. Thus numbers alone are reductive: while the contemporary fashion for datascapes (in which the final form is a response to, or fully determined by, a collection of data) might purport to capture the temporal aspects of, say, human flow through space, the conversion of these data into form inevitably sacrifices the actual flux.[58] But the combination of social data with mappings of place will begin to lead to a spatial understanding of the social dynamics of place. Elsewhere, Dalibor Vesely and his students have developed a form of drawing that combines the representational with the phenomenal in a rich depiction of the human occupation and understanding of space.[59]

Even the photograph holds promise as a means of engaging with the forces of time, but only if we relinquish the static hold that it casts over its subject. As Roger Connah convincingly argues, there are a number of "contested grounds" in photography that challenge the aestheticization and scenography that is the default mode for so much architectural photography. Pointing in particular to Roland Barthes and John Berger, Connah finds opportunities in these contested grounds that would reestablish the architectural photograph as a "memento from a time being lived."[60] Barthes's identification of the *punctum,* the moment in a photograph that disturbs the whole, and Berger's notion of radiality, "in which a photograph is seen in terms simultaneously personal and political, everyday and historic,"[61] both reveal the contingent. What Connah suggests is a new attitude to the architectural photograph which accepts the temporal and the social, but most importantly an attitude in which photography can be productively used as a site of (re)production, accepting all the stains that time can throw at it, even—especially—people. As Walter Benjamin notes in *A Small History of Photography*, "no matter how artful the photographer, no matter how carefully poised his subject, the beholder feels an irresistible urge to search a picture for the tiny spark of contingency, of the Here and Now, with which reality has so to speak seared the subject." This upsets the notion of "homogeneous, empty, time" that he finds as the normal description of photography.[62] The challenge here is to allow the architectural photograph to admit time on purpose, and in so doing to reformulate the priorities on which architecture may be constructed.

Of all the modes of communication that could be used in architectural production, that of storytelling is the probably the least used but potentially the most productive. All of us have stories within us, be they descriptive of the past or fictional for the future, anecdotal or practical. Stories have within them elements that are both personal and social; they become a means of describing one's place in the world, of locating the individual within shared spaces. Stories are the place where the imagination finds lines of flight. Importantly, stories collapse the barriers between expert architect and nonexpert client and user. "The very act of storytelling," writes Kristin Ross, "an act that presumes in its interlocutor an equality of intelligence rather than an inequality of knowledge, posits equality, just as the act of explication posits inequality."[63] The authoritative positivist explanation of the expert ("You should have your front door here because it is closest to the road") is replaced by the suggestive and imaginative storyline of the potential dweller (". . . we ran through the back door, steaming bodies into air dense with chip fat"). If one starts an architectural process through a "what if?" question, and then develops the answers through the forms of stories, two things happen. First, the stories arise out of experience of the world, and thus have a grounding in reality; secondly, the "what if?" allows stories to imagine and to project new spatial visions. Stories thus become conduits for the temporalization of architecture, but because of their founding in everyday experience those futures are not impossibly idealistic. The role of the architect becomes to understand and draw out the spatial implications of the urban storytelling. This role requires both knowledge and imagination, but in both cases these attributes are externalized and shared rather

Time, Space, and Lo-Fi Architecture

than being internalized and exclusive, as happens in the self-referential world of normal architectural representation and communication. Dalibor Vesely talks of the "participatory" role of architectural representation, in which drawings and other media are seen not as remote abstractions but as the place for the exchange of ideas, information, and inspiration open to all participants in the architectural process.[64] In order to fully draw out time, I would add to his methods of representation that of stories.

It is 1994. Sarah and I have just bought a site on which we are to build our home. Designing one's first building is a complex and pressured enough enterprise; add to this the fact that it is two architects with sometimes shared, sometimes conflicting, views and this is to be their own house and office, and the self-imposed stress seems even higher. We discuss how to start designing. Normatively this would be through drawing, but Sarah draws much better than I do (she was one of those whose 0.13mm pens always seemed to work with no splutters). It is in the nature of drawing that it is hard to shift far from the first mark made. Since Sarah's mark would always be more elegant, and thus more eloquent, than mine, the building would from the start be more hers than mine. To avoid this—in order to share—we therefore agree not to draw, but to tease the building out through words. We tell each other stories, often on walks through the back streets of London away from the frontal and the special. They are stories that compact the extraordinary in the everyday. We tell each other of climbing up a tower through walls of books, of wardrobes like Narnia, of wild strawberries on the roof, of swaddling the office, of walls of sandbags protecting glass walls during the Blitz, of trains passing through our living room. We tell stories of our memories, we project stories of our future; stories that fill the soon-to-be house with time. And since those stories are fluid and negotiable, the "design" of the house gradually evolves and is shared, so by the time the first drawing is done—by Sarah, on a scrap of paper, napkinlike, in a conference, sitting next to me—there is a sense of it innately settling those narratives into a structure we both feel comfortable with. It is only later that we do the drawings of time that have been reproduced so often that they have taken on a life of their own.[65] These drawings trace the course of a dinner party from the perfect order of the initial place setting (a condition undisturbed by time and occupation, which is how architects would like to view the world), through a period of hectic activity, to a plan of the table at the end of the meal, laden with the detritus of plates, food, and drink. This final plan became a metaphor for the plan of the house, a seemingly disordered collection of objects set on a plane—but in fact a collection that allows the passage of time and domestic life to pass through it in a relaxed manner. But the looseness of the house, its ability to—as one critic noted—accept the vicissitudes of everyday life, comes not from these drawings but from the stories that inspired them.

From Noun to Verb

We started this discussion of time with pictures of buildings out of time and have now traveled to a place where, it is hoped, buildings can be seen to be conceived in time. We have moved from seeing architecture as a fixed and controlling frame to understanding it as an open framework that can accommodate the multiple actions of time. The intention of the journey has been to release architecture from the clutches of abstract thought and allow it to be shaped by the contingent forces of temporal flux. It is a shift from noun to verb: from "the plan" as an authoritative fix on form and function, to "to plan" (vb.) as an open-ended description of the multiple actions that go into the architectural process. From "plot" as a demarcated territory into which architecture is inserted, to "to plot" (vb.) as the devising of a sequence of events. From "building" (noun) as a lump of stuff, to "building" (vb.) as the ongoing process through which architects, clients, builders, and users all contribute to the making and remaking of stuff.

But maybe all this is too intangible. Time, as Joyce reminds us, tends to disperse the moment one tries to pin it down ("like holding water in your hand"). The problem is one of separating time from its philosophical and phenomenological partner, space. In discussing time as a separate entity for so long, it appears that I may have joined countless others on the dangerous ground of considering time and space as separate categories.[66] And so, in order to avoid this artificial separation, it is necessary now to introduce time to space. Time and Space. Space and Time. Inescapably dependent, and so when divided each is wanting—wanting, that is, each other.

7   Slack Space

Making Space

Space and Time. Time and Space. Inescapably dependent. It is only in their intertwining that we can understand the world around us. Inevitably, given the dynamics of time, the relation between the two is unstable; indeed, for some commentators it is exactly their changing relationship that is the defining feature of the various states of modernity. Thus Anthony Giddens contrasts the premodern era, "in which 'when' was almost universally connected with either 'where' or identified with regular natural occurrences," with the modern era, in which time and space are routinely disconnected. The result is that the very dynamism of modernity derives from the uncoupling of time and space from their previously stable relationship and their recombination into various new forms, most obviously the ability to make connections between global and local networks that were simply unavailable in traditional societies.[1]

But one does not need to be guided by great philosophers or sociologists to understand the interaction of space and time. Just open your eyes and look around to see that the active occupation of architecture inevitably conjoins space and time. And so, if the connection of space to time is so obvious, why have architects so insistently separated them? The answer lies in the previous chapters, with the terror of time and all the unbearable forces and dependencies that it unleashes. Better, then, to think of space in isolation, there more easily to be controlled. Le Corbusier, again, stands for more than just himself when he speaks, in relation to a timeless architecture, of "a boundless depth opening up . . . contingent presences are put to flight, and the miracle of inexpressible space is achieved."[2] It is indeed miraculous that space so conceived could act as some kind of force field, repelling the occupation of those uncontrollable aspects of life and time that architects fear, but the miracle needs to happen if architects are going to claim space as their own. Expelled from time, space becomes a completely different matter—matter here being the operative word. In the hands and minds of architects, space is generally emptied, and with this is made available as something that can be directly manipulated as some kind of stuff. Listen:

"Architecture is the thoughtful making of spaces" (Louis Kahn).

"We separate, limit and bring into a human scale a part of unlimited space" (Gerrit Rietveld).

"I AM SPACE" (the wonderfully immodest Theo van Doesburg).

"Boundaries become fluid; space is conceived as flowing" (László Moholy-Nagy).

"The purpose of architecture is to create space" (Hendrik Petrus Berlage).[3]

All these voices, and many more, belong to an architectural chorus that makes out that architects *produce* space. It is a belief that is encouraged by the nineteenth-century German theorist August Schmarsow, who defined architecture as the "creatress of space."[4] As Adrian Forty notes in his brilliant etymology of the word *space* in architecture, this presumed production conflates two aspects of space: first space as a "physical property of dimension and extent," and second space as a "mental construct through which the mind knows the world."[5] One only needs to listen in on a review in any school of architecture to see this conflation played out loud. Students will describe their schemes in a myriad of spatial terms: folded space, negative space, positive space, layered space, free space. Space will be pushed around so that it "flows," "extends," or "multiplies." Lines will be drawn around areas to clearly demarcate "public space" from "private space." Sometimes these terms confuse physical description with conceptual analogy, so one is not sure whether the words are describing actual spatial conditions or just their metaphorical intent. Either way, it does not take long to find fault with these terms as portrayals of either physical or mental space. How does one fold space—like a shirt? If space can flow, does it assume some ectoplasmic presence? Isn't it one of the commonplaces of late modernity that the boundaries of private and public are continually blurred?

And yet despite this intellectual fault line, the use of terms that suggest the "making" of space persists in both architectural education and practice. One reason is the instrumental nature of the architectural drawing. Lines are drawn; these represent potential form. What is left over on the paper, the white stuff; that represents space. The architectural drawing ties form to space in a symbiotic relationship. Thicker lines: more form, less space. Curvy lines: free form, flowing space. Straight lines: simple form; pure space. Overlapping lines: complex form, layered space. The architectural drawing thus provides compelling evidence that architects do indeed "make" space. The drawing of lines sets in train a production line out of the end of which comes space. "Look," says the student, pointing at the white stuff, "there is the public space." And then touches the drawing, just to reinforce the reality of that space.

We are in the Guggenheim in Bilbao, in the central atrium where the sun bounces down across the seething glass surfaces of the staircases and out onto the surrounding water. It is hard to think of a space since the late Baroque churches of Bavaria or Piedmont that can match this one for sheer visual exuberance, but the experience is completely flattened by the aural accompaniment issuing from the headsets that everyone is plugged into. One wants to lie back and let all this light and sparkle wash over like a shower, but a voice in the background intrudes: "I just keep going until somehow I know it has come," says Frank O. Gehry about his sketching process. And so on, and on, Gehry's contributions intercut with one of those posh and patronizing voices that populate cultural audio guides. Just as we are admiring the trick of raising the river walk up on piers so that the artificial pond visually merges with the water of the River Nervión, Frank starts on his formal inspirations. And I think: "Don't mention the fish, Frank, please not the fish." But he does. "My grandmother kept carp when I was a child." Simple as that. Childhood fish morph into adult building, scales of titanium and all. He has made fishy space. If a second-year student said it, you would snigger dismissively, but this is the world's greatest architect unhindered by self-doubt, assured that the force of his creative being alone can effect the miraculously direct transformation of sketch to form to space. I want to shout: "Yes, and my grandmother kept Pekingese dogs," but don't for fear of being seen as infantile or eccentric, and also for fear that people might think all my designs are dogs.

Hard Space

It is a very particular kind of space that emerges from this production line. Because its genesis lies in the production of form, the space "made" retains physical associations. Architectural space may not be physical in the scientific sense of the word, but as long as it is conceived in the shadow of form, the objectlike qualities will stick around space. Such an understanding of space aligns precisely with the Cartesian view of the world. Descartes insistently relates space to matter;[6] in his version the world "out there" is defined by the relationship between *res corporea* (inert bodies); space is the stuff between these objects. The defining feature of these objects is that they appear *in extenso* (literally, "in extension"). "Indeed," Descartes argues, "extension in length, breadth and thickness constitutes the nature of corporeal substance."[7] By implication, if the objects of the world have these qualities, then so does the space in between them. While the common understanding of Cartesian space refers to its three-dimensionality, and thus its geometrical properties, the real sense of Cartesian extension implies a physical conception of space, in which it is subject to all the characteristics of *extensio*—it can be measured, divided, shaped, and moved.[8]

At one level the measurement of space is a benign, and useful, activity; it is necessary to know the area of a room so that, say, one can understand roughly how many people can occupy it. But the measure of space has a nasty way of becoming the dominant criterion of space. The clearest indication of the reduction of space to the rule of measure is in the priority given to various architectural handbooks that set the dimensions of space in relation to various activities, from Ernst Neufert's *Architects' Data* to the *Metric Handbook* first published by the Architects' Journal.[9] One of the strictest of these manuals is *Space in the Home,* in which a series of "typical" living situations are transformed into prescriptive formal layouts.[10] First furniture of a specific size is assigned to the activity (eating, sleeping, watching TV, and so on); the furniture is then laid out according to key dimensions, circulation space is defined around the furniture, and finally walls are drawn to contain that circulation space. There is a disarming simplicity to the whole process—so much so that one does not feel the need to disturb the apparent logic of the system. But scratch beneath the surface, and less benign characteristics become apparent. First, the user is inevitably treated as an abstraction. People are drawn with lines round them, as police chalk round cadavers; drained of their phenomenal or social presences, these bodies assume the equivalent status to the furniture, objects there solely for their ability to be moved and to behave in measured and universal ways. Second is the normalizing thrust of the whole process, in which everything from social behavior to family configuration to the sizes of chairs and people is marshalled into standardized descriptions. Dad is shown in his slippers watching television while Mum washes the dishes. There is no place for difference or deviation in these homes, let alone a feminist deconstruction of the gendered bias of the spatial configurations. Third is the mirroring

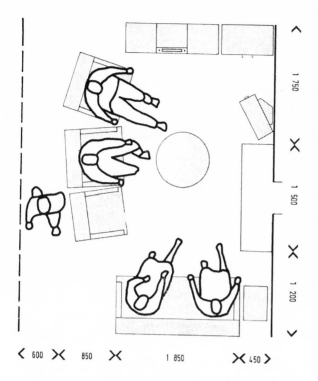

nature of the logic: the determinations on use lead to typical furniture lay-outs, which in turn prescribe the size and shape of the rooms, which when built fix the patterns of use as initially proposed. The designs as built thus play back the founding assumptions, and in this pass the test of fulfill-ing the brief. The establishment of self-reflective systems is a symptom of positivist thinking, and the production of space in this context assumes the same ordering tendencies that are associated with the rule of reason.[11]

It might be easy to dismiss *Space in the Home* as an extreme, and fairly marginal, manifestation of spatial control, but this would be to overlook the fact that it is an official government document used extensively by housing architects at the time. One might here begin to get a bit twitchy about the apparent extension of political control into the domestic arena, especially when it is associated with the three characteristics of abstraction, normal-ization, and ordering. The good intent of the document in the name of social betterment in public housing design masks a normalizing predispo-sition that, as William Connolly has so acutely identified, is symptomatic of all "liberal" democracies. It is a predisposition in which, he argues, "the desire to establish the appearance of harmony in actual democracies, or the possibility of it in ideal democracies, suppresses the ambiguity of democracy itself."[12]

Here we are back in the territory of architecture assuming an appearance of neutrality; after all, who could argue with the rule of measure, especially when it is associated with the virtues of the efficient use of space? This calm front stifles the background of contingent presences, including the political connotations of space—politics here being not just Connolly's public suppression of ambiguity but also the personal politics of the occupation of space. The supposed neutrality of metric space provides a comfort zone in which dimensions can be shared as uncontested values, but it does so at the expense of suppressing other aspects of the human occupation of space whose social dynamics are less easy to deal with and accommodate. As Bauman notes, physical space can be arrived at only "through phenomenological reduction of daily experience to pure quantity, during which distance is 'depopulated' and 'extemporalised'—that is systematically cleansed of all contingent and transitory traits."[13]

This contrasting of physical, static, metric space with social, dynamic, accommodating space is not new, nor is the argument about the reductive character of physical space: Heidegger in his unraveling of Cartesian space as the first move in his formulation of human spatiality;[14] Lefebvre in his devastating critique of abstract space and its replacement with the "lived" space of the social and political world;[15] Bauman with his identification of social space as "a complex interaction of three interwoven, yet distinct processes—those of cognitive, aesthetic and moral spacings—and their respective products."[16] All these three, in their very particular ways, and many others not only provide a challenge to the uncritical acceptance of metric space, but also suggest compelling alternatives. Why then has "physical" space so dominated architectural discourse, and why does it still persist?[17] (While the writhings of contemporary surface might deflect attention from the substance of the enclosed matter, their formal excesses in fact just reinforce a reading of space being brought along as the accessory of form.)

The answer to this question lies in the argument of this book: the perpetuation of physical space as an architectural paradigm is about the denial, and subsequent ridding, of those dependencies and presences that lie outside the direct control of the architect. However, the specific treatment of space in this context suggests that this denial is not a trivial matter of pushing aside inconveniences, but part of a rather more grave charge that can be brought against architects. The chief prosecutor is Henri Lefebvre, who argues that treating space as an abstract entity is hardly the benign act that the "neutral" tramlines of objective thought would have us believe. "This space has nothing innocent about it: it answers to particular strategies and tactics; it is, quite simply, the space of the dominant mode of production, and hence the space of capitalism."[18] These are tough words, implicating as they do architects in the wider systems of power and control that have dominated the modern era. Lefebvre implies that the way architects intellectually conceive of space inculpates them along with wider oppressive forces that are associated with abstract space—notably, in David Harvey's words, "the political absolutism that flows from absolute conceptions of space [and] the oppressions visited upon the world by a rationalised, bureaucratised, technocratically, and capitalistically defined spatiality."[19] Although their mental formulation of space as matter, and the subsequent attitude to space in practice, might mean that architects become the servants of the market, it is perfectly possible for them to argue that this happens unwittingly and in a manner beyond their direct control, rather than through explicit political intent. Few architects would open up a description of a project with an explanation of their connivance in the processes of power and domination through the manipulation of abstract space. However, Lefebvre's charge sticks because the qualities of hard space that dominate architectural production allow that space to be easily appropriated by the market. Voided of explicit political or social content, hard space is reduced to those aspects of architecture that are easy to commodify (aesthetics and technique) or those aspects of space that are to do with control (efficiency and visibility). In this way the architects of hard space are indeed complicit in providing a velvet glove of seductive surface to cover the hard fist of economic expediency. The issue is exacerbated, as we will see in chapter 10, by the codes of conduct under which architects operate being dominated by the terms of providing a service to the client (and not the users); by implication the architect can fulfill their professional obligations by answering the demands of the client, which in turn are often driven by the efficiencies of the market and short-term opportunism.

One of the problems of Lefebvre's critique, however, is that it potentially leads to an impasse as to what actions architects should take. On the one hand, why deal with a problem (the intentional production of capitalist space) when one does not identify with it? On the other hand, the intractable identification of architectural production with the forces of capitalist production leads to a certain feeling of helplessness: why bother to resist the inevitable? It is to this latter question that we shall return in the final chapter. But this potential impasse should not deflect us from the importance of Lefebvre's argument. If architects may not be guilty by clear intent of the misuse of abstract space, then they certainly are by default. Whether they like or not, they are in the thick of political space. Architecture is political. Full Stop. Not political in the party political sense of the term, but political in the original sense of the word in that it affects the lives of citizens. It is not enough for architects to deny the political consequences of their actions by retreating to the high ground of the "neutrality" of abstract space. Instead, we need to understand that the more insistently the flag of ideological or political neutrality is waved, the more the winds of spatial control are generated beneath it. The prioritizing of physical space over social space allows a certain reading of space to develop by default: emptied, simplified, and thus more manipulable. The space of measure leads to the assumption of space that can be divided, contained, and controlled. In the recourse to the justificatory support of "hard" science, the space that emerges is indeed hard. Not physically hard (how could it be?) but socially hard, because hard space is tied in with the drawing of boundaries that separate out the actions of life into neat functional and then spatial categories. It is this aspect of spatial manipulation and segregation that Bauman finds so unsettling in his connection of design to the ordering character of the modern era. In *Modernity and Ambivalence,* he argues that "modern mastery is the power to divide, classify and allocate," and, crucially, this is accomplished "in thought, in practice, in the practice of thought and in the thought of practice."[20] Hard space is one of the tools deployed in this mastery, and with Bauman's insistent connection of thought to practice, the responsibility for the social effects of their spatial conceptions should become all the more apparent to architects. In facing up to this responsibility it becomes necessary to find alternatives to the hard social consequences of hard space.

It is the final stages of judging an architectural competition. The jury are split. On the one hand there is a scheme, colorful and blobby and empty. On the other side there is a scheme in which the drawings are full of activity, where the architecture acts as a setting. Let's call them *blob* and *setting.*

"But I can't see the architecture," says a critic of *setting,* "the drawings are so busy with people! What are they giving us? What would I tell my colleagues we have actually got?"

"But that, that . . . thing. It's just vacant form. Where's the content?" replies the critic of *blob.*

"At least I can see it. And what I see looks really exciting."

"But it is just eye candy. You are falling into the trap of being seduced by image. It is just another clever architect playing the commodity game."

"Oh, for Christ's sake, don't give me that political bullshit."

"Look, anyone can draw people," another supporter of *blob* interjects, "making beautiful form is much more difficult."

"They aren't just drawing people. Of course there is stuff there, it is just that it is background. Kind of modest," says the second advocate for *setting*.

"Oh, that is so dull. So damn worthy. At least these guys are giving us something interesting and new. Something luscious, something soft."

"Come on, that isn't soft. Just because it has curves doesn't mean it's soft. Look at those plans. Pure, hard functionalism masquerading as cuddly space."

"Stop it," says the jury chair, "this isn't getting anywhere. We had better vote."

Hands go up. Still split, so the chair puts in her casting vote.

blob wins.

Asked afterward why she had tilted toward *blob*, the chair says she sort of liked the color.

Social Space

"(Social) space is a (social) product."[21] If I could choose just one slogan to hang over the entrance to the House of Architecture, this one of Lefebvre's would be it. It is a sentence whose apparent simplicity belies the complexity of its implications. It is the brackets that do it. Try it without them, or with bold, and the effect is just not the same:

Social space is a social product—too bland
Social space is a **social** product—too insistent
Social **space** is a social **product**—wrong message; too unrelentingly commodifying
(Social) space is a (social) product—just right

The brackets gently savage one of the founding assumptions of an Enlightenment understanding of space, namely that space is made, and that in the case of architectural space, the maker is the individual architect. The brackets let us read this claim—space is a product—at the same time as exposing its poverty. They draw attention to the repeated word *social,* giving it a pervasive presence without crudely emphasizing it.

The importance of Lefebvre's message is twofold. First, by introducing the social it banishes any notion that space could be treated as an abstract matter, devoid of any social content, or sundered from any social context. Second, it once and for all scotches the myth that space is produced by a single person. The central argument of *The Production of Space* is that space is "produced" through a complex set of overlapping societal agencies: the representational, the economic, the phenomenological, the conceptual, the spatial practice of the individual, the collective practices of the political, and so on. Lefebvre marshals these agencies into a spatial "triad"—the perceived, the conceived, and the lived aspects of life; the point is not so much as to whether this triad is "correct" but that as soon as it is posited one has to acknowledge that there are multiple and conflicting force fields which affect spatial production, of which architectural practice is but one small part. It also opens space up to political consequences because, as Lefebvre says, "there is a politics of space because space is political."[22] In this, questions of space are seen as inherently political, and by implication the playing out and manifestation of politics is inherently spatial.[23]

Once Lefebvre has said it—(social) space is a (social) product—one can never again see the world as a place set apart, or reduce architecture to a set of abstract forms. One has to stand and face this spatial force field, to be buffeted by winds that come from every which way. There is a feeling of exposure out there, which makes retreat to the sanctuary of the architectural drawing, and its suggestion of spatial control, all too understandable. But this, as should now be apparent, is a false sanctuary. Best then, as an architect, to get out there, to stare one's own fragility in the face. To be human. Remember who you were before you were branded an architect. Remember that you too inhabit this world. Remember that you too use buildings, occupy space. And remember that users, you included, are more than abstractions or ideals; they are imperfect, multiple, political, and all the better for it.

I was the bright, youngish, thing on the block. Or so I thought. Always at the front of lectures, always the first to put up his hand. I even did it with Rem Koolhaas, in front of 400 others. A question about his ethical ambivalence, which he knocked back hard with withering brilliance. No more questions followed; no one else was prepared to have skin pulled back in public. I should have learnt my lesson, but didn't. This time it was a lecture at the Bartlett in the mid-1990s, just in the period that Lefebvre was beginning to seep into the cracks left in the shiny surfaces. Ed Soja was lecturing on

"Thirdspace," his homage to and development of the Lefebvrian triad. At the end my hand went up. "Whilst geographers only speculate and comment on space, architects actually produce it . . . ," I started. At which, pulling himself up to his not inconsiderable full height, Soja cut in and thundered: "WE ALL PRODUCE SPACE."

I am not sure that I have ever been quite the same since.

Inauthentic Space

"Space is not in the subject, nor is the world in space."[24] That would be the second slogan to put up in the House of Architecture. This aphorism from Heidegger is more difficult, summarizing and deconstructing as it does the whole tradition of Western spatial metaphysics in a single sentence.

"Space is not in the subject" refers to the Kantian notion of space as "an *a priori* representation which underlies all our outer intuitions."[25] Space in the Kantian model is a "subjective condition of sensibility" and develops from within the subject so, as Heidegger disparagingly notes, it is as if the Kantian subject "emits a space out of itself."[26] Space for Kant is not "out there," it is "not an empirical concept that has been derived from outer experiences."[27] This is a challenging concept, because it goes against the grain of understanding the world on the basis of lived experience and replaces it with the very abstract idea of a wordless subject for whom space is a pure form of intuition. However, it is possible to make a crude connection between this abstracted notion of space and the space of architects (especially the capitalized claim of Van Doesburg: "I AM SPACE").

The other half of Heidegger's dismissal—"nor is the world in space"— refers to the Cartesian view of space that we have already encountered: objects set apart in a fixed, unifying space. In his deconstruction of the Cartesian worldview, Heidegger challenges the idea that our experience of space is one that can be measured and quantified. What is important here is not the philosophical niceties of Heidegger's critique—I once spent two years and 20,000 painful words on that one sentence, and would hardly inflict that experience on others—but rather what he suggests as a replacement. He follows up the sentence by arguing that "space is not to be found within the subject . . . but the 'subject' (Dasein) if well understood ontologically, is spatial."[28] Magda King is astute in outlining the implications of the term *spatial*, translating it as "space-ish": "The existential characters of man have an 'active' form . . . man is 'space-ish,' i.e. in an active way *discloses* space."[29] This disclosure of space is founded on man's spatiality. The language that Heidegger uses to establish his argument is not always easy, but some of the examples are more directly understandable. A key characteristic of man's spatiality is, for Heidegger, that of "de-distancing,"[30] a word that undermines the authority of measure as the definitive description of the relationship of things in space. Instead of subjecting space to the ruler, he introduces an existential understanding of space, arguing, for example, that what is "closest" is not what is the physically smallest distance from us, but what is of most "concern" to us. As an example, Heidegger notes that when "a man wears a pair of spectacles which are so close to him distancially that they 'are sitting on his nose,' they are environmentally more remote from him than the picture on the opposite wall."[31] The glasses, as mere tools, are of no real concern to us, whereas the picture as the object of our attention is revealed as spatially closer. The look across the room between two lovers collapses the distance that separates them. "De-distancing" thus actively breaks the hold of objective measure over distance and replaces it with an engagement with the world that is determined through familiarity and concern. A "good walk" and a "stone's throw" are, for Heidegger, examples of expressions that may sound vague, but are in fact a "truer" measure of the world than could ever be ascertained through physical measurement.

It is Heidegger's assertion that our understanding of space is founded on our spatiality that most clearly establishes the possibility of a new and active understanding of space; it might be called a phenomenology of space. After Heidegger, space can no longer be seen as an abstract and geometric category intuited by the worldless subject, but has to be understood through our lived engagement with the world as spatial, "space-ish," humans. So, if my call for architects to remember their humanity is to go heeded, then in relation to space this means starting with that essential human spatiality. Design in this context requires the imagining of one's own spatiality within the architecture being designed, understanding that certain aspects of human spatiality are common to all: lightness versus darkness, top versus bottom, directionality, constricted versus open, and so on. Architectural design here becomes a matter not of pushing bits of space around as abstract stuff, but of spatiality as a shared cultural and human condition, with an awareness that what we make physically affects that condition spatially. The architect becomes one among others, working from within as someone able to project spatial possibilities, rather than from without as the manipulator of hard space.

Unfortunately, such a commonly understandable version of spatial perception is too often hijacked in the name of discovering more fundamental

Time, Space, and Lo-Fi Architecture

aspects of the human condition. A later text by Heidegger, "Building, Dwelling, Thinking,"[32] leads architectural theorists into believing that there are "authentic" aspects to dwelling that can in turn be reflected in "authentic" approaches to the design of architectural space. Authenticity here becomes another method of ironing out the spatial flux that confronts the architect, a flux that fills him or her with anxiety. In the common version of spatiality there is an uncertainty, because one person's spatiality can never be exactly the same as another's insofar as, using Heidegger's terms alone, levels and priorities of concern and familiarity will differ from person to person. In turn, then, space will be disclosed in somewhat different ways to different people. There is a tendency among the architectural followers of Heidegger to even out this uncertainty by suggesting that there are archetypal spatial conditions: the horizon, the cellar, the attic, the hearth. Edward Casey makes the argument that the sheer possibilities of space induce an unease in Heidegger who, anxious at "the immensely threatening possibilities opened up by the ontological problem of space . . . shrinks back from the uncanny vision of radically other possible modes of space."[33] "Authentic" space can thus be seen as another form of retreat from the vicissitudes of everyday life. What becomes clear is that too many phenomenologists of space fall into the trap of replacing one privileged view of space (the Cartesian) with another privileged version based around the elevated values of the authentic and best apprehended by the virtuous solipsist. Heidegger's drive toward a fundamental ontology based around notions of authenticity is too often reflected in architectural obsessions with vague notions of poetics, the authentic situation, the rectitude of tectonics, and the retreat from everyday living into idealized notions of dwelling. In all of these we see a privileging of fundamental belief systems, which can be developed only in denial of the contingencies of the everyday world. As Hilde Heynen notes, any notions of the authenticity of dwelling are difficult to sustain in the face of modernity, and so "dwelling is . . . obliged to retreat into a realm of its own."[34]

This denial is reinforced by another tendency of authentic phenomenologists, which is to supplement their Heidegger (who absents the body from his understanding of space)[35] with Merleau-Ponty, with his brilliantly persuasive argument that "our body is not primarily *in* space" (because that would reduce it to just another object); rather, "it is *of* it . . . there would be no space at all for me if I had no body."[36] In this version of authentic phenomenology it is the body that is privileged in the understanding and design of spatial conditions but, importantly, it is the body phenomenal (alert to its senses) rather than the body politic (alert to the social effects of space).[37]

Now, I am as susceptible to sensual delight as anyone and so, like thousands of others, have made the pilgrimage to the temple of architecture and the body, Peter Zumthor's Thermal Baths at Vals in deepest Switzerland. It is indeed an extraordinary place. Stuttering down too-shallow stairs; pricked by light at one minute, washed in it another; invaded by resinous steam that dissolves bodily boundaries; scorched then chilled; foot slipping and then saved by the roughness of stone. No other place makes one so acutely aware of one's phenomenal body. But such intensity can be achieved only in a state of removal. This is much more than a programmatic retreat—a spa, after all, being all about escape; it is a definitively spatial removal that Zumthor

Time, Space, and Lo-Fi Architecture

choreographs, in a sequence that gradually strips us of all the vestiges of our ordinary selves (sunlight, accessories, clothes, modesty). Only once cleansed can we encounter the extra-ordinary, descending into the dark. And only once we have been imbued with the essences of the interior are we allowed to drift outside to be presented with views of nature, carefully framed to exclude anything average from demeaning this sublime vision.

It is a move from the inauthentic world to the authentic, a move that is consistent with Heidegger, of whom Zumthor is a reader, albeit by his own admission a sometimes confused one.[38] It is exactly the project of *Being and Time* to clear aside the inauthenticity of the everyday in order to reveal what has thus far been concealed, namely the essential character of Being. But this pushing aside comes at a price. In the central sections of *Being and Time,* Heidegger overcomes the inauthenticity of "the 'they'" (effectively the great mass of humanity) by exposing the way that, in their "averageness," "everything that is primordial gets glossed over."[39] Heidegger's three symptoms of inauthentic averageness—idle talk, curiosity, ambiguity—appear quite mild but are, he argues, enough to distract from an understanding of one's primal condition. These apparently trivial symptoms of the ordinary reveal the real problem with the notion of authenticity, namely that it is an all-or-nothing condition. One is not allowed to be just a bit authentic. In a manner that is startlingly self-fulfilling, authenticity throws an invincible barrier around itself: you are either in or you are out. Who I am to criticize it? If I do, I must be limited by the symptoms that stop me seeing to the depth of my inner self. Ergo my arguments have no credibility. It is just the same self-reflecting tactic used by the positivists to dismiss contingency because it does not accord with their own inner logic.[40] Here the authentics suffer exactly the same fate as the positivists—their arguments can be sustained only from a position of distance. As Adorno so scathingly argues, with their "jargon of authenticity," the authentics can achieve their movement into the radical inwardness of their primal Being only by blocking out the social context.[41]

Architectural investigations in authenticity are therefore generally conducted in rarefied conditions, but nonetheless have a disproportionate influence on architectural culture. Thus single-family houses—in which one can play out the myths of idealized dwelling—occupy many more pages of architectural books and magazines than they deserve in relation to their wider cultural or social significance. The same is true of the reverence in which matters of the tectonic are held. The correct making of buildings is accorded an importance by critics like Kenneth Frampton that then allows architects to believe that this making alone is sufficient as cultural activity.[42] Holding to the hope of redemption through tectonics is tenable only under a regime which posits that "the primary principle of the autonomy of architecture resides in the tectonic."[43]

Personally I enjoy those moments of the "they" that Heidegger dismisses as inauthentic. Idle talk (hence my anecdotes); curiosity (surely indispensable for any architect worth their salt); ambiguity (hence my insistence on contingency as the defining feature of architecture). I learn as much about the world through snatches of conversations in lunch queues as I do in the leather seats of British Library Reading Room Two. I am right with Foucault when he dreams of "a new age of curiosity."[44] And ambiguity—that is the condition that keeps me open and responsible, because if there were none, choices would be made for me under a regime of determinist control.

Personally, I am an inauthentic phenomenologist, even if in stating this I run the risk of being a contradiction in terms. This means on the one hand fostering a phenomenological understanding of space, but on the other hand dumping all the baggage of authenticity and Being that phenomenology sometimes brings along. If, as Bruno Latour laconically notes, "Being cannot reside in ordinary beings,"[45] then being an inauthentic phenomenologist means being ordinary. An inauthentic phenomenological reading of space understands space in all its lived sense, engaging in it as sensate, bodily beings alert to touch, to light, to scale, to smell, to softness, to heaviness—to all those aspects of space that exceed objective measure. In fact it is so direct, so commonsensical, a reading of space that one does not need a long word like phenomenology to get in the way of its understanding. But rejecting the jargon of authenticity also means opening up to the multiple and conflicting aspects of social space, so that the body phenomenal is understood at the same time as a body politic. Such bodies, that both experience space and are also part of the experience of space, are perceived not as things there to be measured and moved, but as social beings occupying social space.

I am at a review in a School of Architecture in North America. The students have all been reading "Building, Dwelling, Thinking," and are clearly as confused by Heidegger's elliptical text as am I. Words such as poetics, techne, ethics are sprinkled with alarming ease into the descriptions of the projects. After the third dwelling/retreat for a blind person/poet set on a cliff/in the woods I am beginning to get twitchy.

Time, Space, and Lo-Fi Architecture

"Look outside," I suggest, "look at the dynamics of the world out there. What happens to the sanctuary of the blind poet when the pizza delivery man drops a cardboard box onto the stone hearth?"

They look at me as if I am a bit dirty, a barbarian in their midst.

"Look up yourself," says one, gently but firmly.

I do. The blinds of the studio are drawn, blocking out the fallen world beyond.

Slack Space

In the unraveling of hard space through the twin agents of social space and (inauthentic) phenomenology, a new kind of space emerges. It is by implication a space that is "softer" than what it has replaced, insofar as it is not founded on the principles of abstraction, normalization, and order that underpin hard space. It does not presume to control or divide in the same way that hard space does. It is no longer possible, with an awareness of the bodies that will perceive and occupy this space, to abrogate responsibility for their phenomenal and political presences, or to ignore their potential vulnerability. It would make sense to call such a space "Soft Space" in recognition of its opposition to hard space, but the danger in this is that the social implications of the term are overtaken by its physical connotations, and thus that the associated architecture comes out all curvy.[46] So instead I turn to the concept of slackness as outlined in the political theory of William Connolly. In his critique of the normalizing tendency of liberal democracies (in which ambiguity is suppressed), Connolly calls for more slack to be allowed in the system. "Since the self is not 'designed' to fit perfectly into any way of life . . . we should therefore endorse the idea of slack as part of our conception of the good life. . . . Slack in the order enables a broader range of behavior merely to be. . . . Slack at once reduces the space virtue must cover and enhances the prospects for civic virtue within the space appropriate to it."[47] What is important in Connolly's formulation is that he does not dismiss out of hand the need for common ground, but argues that any common ground should not be overdetermined by regulation or order. It is not an argument for an anarchic "anything goes," but instead suggests that space must be left in politics for difference and ambiguity to flourish within a shared background.

These principles can be understood in a more architectural sense to provide a sense of slack space.[48] Most obviously, slack space has to be seen in time. In this it is open to changing use—not in terms of a literal flexibility of moving parts and sliding gizmos, but in terms of providing a frame for life to unfold within. It is space that something will happen in, but exactly what that something might be is not determinedly programmed. Slack space operates more as a robust background than a refined foreground. This, as we have seen with Hertzberger, takes just as much design skill, but that skill is deployed quietly in setting a social scene rather than noisily in constructing a visual scenography. Slack space is thus manifestly designed, but probably not overdesigned. It allows the user to make choices within its frame, and in this asks eventually who the designer of space is—in effect, it asks architects to share their design with the designs of others that evolve in the course of occupation, an argument made persuasively by Jonathan Hill in his *Actions of Architecture*.[49]

If slack space is to be seen in time, it means that it has to take what time throws at it, welcoming life into its interstices and not expelling it from shiny surfaces. This suggests a new type of architecture, perhaps a lo-fi architecture as developed in the next chapter.

8   Lo-Fi Architecture

Elvis Lives

I first saw Elvis Costello when I was an undergraduate student at Cambridge University in 1978. It was at a May Ball, a captive audience of drunken gilded youth on which to vent his bitter pills. Costello stood over us, spitting words; his anger hit like waves. It was only later that I realized his bile was directed not to us personally but to the situation that the country was moving toward, a situation in which a bunch of privileged and complacent students in black ties and gauche ball dresses epitomized one half of the divided society that Margaret Thatcher was to exploit so ruthlessly. Drunk though I was, it was mesmerizing.

I was happy to grow older with Elvis, and his songs became the soundtrack for my graduate student days in London. I needed Costello on the night that the HMS *Sheffield* was sunk in that meaningless war in the Falklands that she—Thatcher—had instigated to preserve an absurd notion of empire, a war that she shamelessly, shamefully, used to launch an election campaign. Later Costello wrote the lyrics to a song, *Shipbuilding*, which "evoked the numb waste of war and the destruction of traditional British industries under Thatcher's government."[1] Robert Wyatt's voice translated the anger we all felt into a lament, with Costello's words at their most precise, but in that control still more damning of the consequences of Thatcher's imperial games.[2] I played the record endlessly; the cover fell apart.

About the same time as *Shipbuilding* came out, I was working late. It was the final year of my studies, and I had adopted the absurd life pattern that is the ritual of graduation year for architectural students. Long days (not really that much work). Long nights (too tired to work). An inefficient and self-imposed form of boot camp which one feels one needs to endure in order to become a "proper" Architect. It was early morning, the time when one clings to the radio as a connection to the outside world. An interview with Costello was being repeated. "After recording a song, I get the engineers to play it back through a cheap radio. I need to hear how it sounds in real life. How it sounds over the noise of a breakfast table."[3]

That interview has always stayed with me. There he would be, in a recording studio cut off from light and life, engulfed in black speakers, polishing the nuances of the twenty-four tracks on a mixing desk with the technical complexity of an aircraft cockpit. Perfected sound. But what really counted for Costello was the sound coming out of the cheap little transistor radio on the kitchen table to accompany the crunch of cornflakes. Lo-fi sound.

The analogy is direct. The architect in the studio, cut off from the world. Creating hi-fi architecture on high-end equipment, fiddling with keystrokes and mice, dreaming of that perfected delivery in the polished aura of blue skies and happy people. When in fact they should be dealing with the cheap radio end of things, imagining the moments of occupation, of cornflakes showering crumbs onto the shining floor, of maybe sad people. Lo-fi architecture.

This is not the first time a radio has been invoked to support an architectural argument. In *Towards a New Architecture* Le Corbusier advocates the experience of listening to music on a radio over going to a concert hall: "the wireless will give you exact interpretations of first-rate music, and you avoid catching cold in the concert hall and the frenzy of the virtuoso."[4] However, the message of Le Corbusier's radio is very different from mine. He privileges the purity and exactitude of the mechanical reproduction, which would surely have been hi-fi if such a thing had existed in the 1920s, precisely to be rid of the annoying interventions of the outside world (the "contingent presences" we have seen him rail against before). "Catching cold" says everything about his fear of contamination, be it aural, architectural, or personal. My interpretation of the radio is not about the equipment per se, but the context in which it is situated. It is not the single man locked up in front of his stereo speakers, but the family for whom the transistor radio is the background soundtrack for everyday life.

Lo-fi might sound disparaging, a lowly form of production that demeans the high ideals of the profession; but this would be to misunderstand the purpose of Costello's breakfast table radio. The writing and production of the song is handled with all the attention and detail of a great artist. It is in the intent of its playing out that Costello makes the shift from the normal criteria of "high" art. He recognizes that he has to give up control over the final reception of his work, and adjusts the parameters of the making of the work accordingly. The painter or sculptor knows that the prime context for the appreciation (in both the aesthetic and economic sense of the word) of their work will be the gallery, and therefore aims specifically at this controlled and rarefied environment. But the songwriter does not have this luxury of knowing the precise circumstances under which their work will be received. Nor does the architect, which is one among many reasons why the close identification of architecture with art is such a misconception. However, just because the conditions in which architecture and popular music eventually find themselves are not culturally elevated in the received version of the elite, this does not mean that they are by implication lowly or should be treated in a dismissive manner. Quite the opposite. The lo-fi architect has to be just as precise and just as creative as Costello in the assembling of their work, but also just as prescient about where and how that work will be played out. Costello's artistic ambition is as high as that of the aspirational architect; it is just that he is more real about the means of its transmission and reception, as well as combining it with a political ambition. Lo-fi architecture thus asks the architect to design to their highest ability and, at the same time, be acutely conscious of the conditions which that design will finally encounter.

Exploding into Reality

In opening this chapter with Elvis Costello, I am flirting with the danger of being dismissed on the twin counts of vulgar populism and complete irrelevance. Isn't there something embarrassing in middle-aged professors attempting to show off their street credentials through resorting to quoting their teenage heroes, and what has this got to do with architecture anyway? These charges, however, stick only if they are thrown from within the sanctuary of "high" culture, within whose walls architecture too often places itself for protection. My brief excursion into Elvis Costello is to weave another warp into the weft of architecture. In using a "popular" source, this warp brings to architecture a necessary sense of the everyday, but also with Costello a necessary sense of the political. As the American academic Michael Bérubé notes (in an article called "The Elvis Costello Problem," but that is no more than a convenient coincidence), to ignore popular culture is to ignore the complexity and contradictory nature of contemporary culture.[5] This is especially the case with architecture; most buildings are inescapably embedded in the everyday world, and therefore need to take into account that context and the way it is engaged with, bodily, materially, spatially, and symbolically. Unfortunately, the production of architectural culture is dominated by those building types that are more or less removed from the everyday: history books full of the sacred; magazines dominated by one-off houses, museums, and theaters; award systems that favor the extraordinary program and budget over the ordinary ones.[6] That gap again between how architecture reflects itself and how it is experienced in the reality of the everyday.

This gap is founded on the unnecessary tension that is set up between architecture and the everyday, which in turn is sustained by wrongly perpetuating the binary of high and low, Cathedral and bicycle shed. Never was this more clearly shown than in the seminal exercise in architecture and the everyday, Robert Venturi and Denise Scott Brown's *Learning from Las Vegas*. The title alone suggests an active intention for the high to engage productively with the low, notwithstanding the fact that Las Vegas is not quite normal in the first instance. What happened was that the imagery of the Las Vegas Strip was seized for its aesthetic and formal substance; what had previously been denounced as beneath architectural dignity was championed as a rich source of visual and symbolic content. The project has good intentions of serving "a social need for architectural high art to learn from and relate to folk and pop traditions if it is to serve its real clients and do no further harm in the city."[7] But in the end the process is one of reification, both in the original sense of the word—turning something into matter—but also in the Marxist interpretation—that this procedure is also one of commodification. The everyday is raided for its visual stimulus, which in the case of Las Vegas is already conveniently excessive, but the social content of the life within is ignored. The high codes of the visual are refreshed, leaving the low still low. The commodification comes when Venturi and Scott Brown's brilliant rhetoric is transformed into the architectural capital of postmodernism. As we saw in chapter 7, those newly fresh, popular forms are appropriated by the market as velvet gloves for the iron fist of corporate capital, wrapping hard space in a quasi-familiar image, most obviously in places like Disneyworld, more insidiously in business parks and housing estates throughout the world.[8]

Lefebvre sounds the warning of collapsing into trite populism; the danger lies in "magnifying the life of the proletariat" to such an extent that one loses its human content, "of people who knew how to enjoy themselves, how to get involved, take risks, talk about what they felt and did."[9] His response is to enact a reciprocal transaction that dissolves the borders between high and low: "for we must be careful neither to abandon the

(acquired or potential) wealth of the content, of the 'human raw material'; nor to lose whatever is achieved in the highest, most intense moments. The problem is therefore to define the reciprocal relation of these activities and realities: the simple moments and the highest moments of life."[10] In this way the everyday is not "abandoned to vulgarity" because that would "grant art, science, ethics and philosophy the inordinate privilege of constituting superhuman—and therefore inhuman—'worlds.'"[11] It is also a transaction that rescues the everyday from being the site of pure alienation and banality. Lefebvre is acutely aware that the condition of the everyday is at the same time as full of transformative potential as it is full of potential oppression, and it was to counter the latter that he championed the former.[12]

In terms of lo-fi architecture, Lefebvre's critique of everyday life has important implications. If, returning to the Costello analogy, architecture is to be played out around the equivalent of the breakfast table, then it has to take the conditions of the everyday into account if it is to remain relevant. To put it simply, an architecture that ignores the everyday will be ignored every day.[13] But this does not mean a collapse into the everyday as a mere repetition of the architectural dross that is already there. Nor does it mean a sardonic display of popular motives in the patronizing hope that this will meet the demands of the everyday populace. What Lefebvre essentially does is to banish the fear that the everyday is merely ordinary; rather, it is the site that contains the extraordinary within the ordinary, *if one is prepared to look,* the place where "creative energy is stored in readiness for new creations."[14] There is an understandable urge among architects and architecture students to escape the ordinary—after all, why just repeat what is already there, in all its dreariness?—and therefore to look upward for inspiration: to the gods, to the specialized, to the rational, to the high minds of philosophers, to the extraordinary. And then turn from looking upward to looking inward, to one's internal stock of formal and linguistic tools, in order to display that invention. This upward and inward movement is the operation, and ultimately the autonomous fate, of the avant-garde in their failure to engage with the reality of the lived world.[15] But what if that original content does not always lie beyond the everyday but within it? Then to discover it one also has to look outward and downward, and not forget "the earth beneath, which has a secret life and richness of its own."[16] Only then can architects meet Tafuri's challenge to get out of their boudoir and effect the "explosion of architecture out towards reality."[17] And only then can we understand that lo-fi architecture is not lowly at all, because it has moved beyond the opposition of high and low.[18]

In moving beyond this separation of high and low, lo-fi architecture is necessarily transgressive not just of these categories but of others as well. Stallybrass and White open their classic work on transgression with the contention that "cultural categories of high and low, social and aesthetic . . . but also those of the physical body and geographical space, are never entirely separable."[19] This set of transgressions presents a complex context for anyone to operate in; not only do they mix the four domains (the social, the aesthetic, the bodily, and the spatial) but they also deny the comfort of separating them out into neat hierarchies of low/high, good/bad. We have already seen in chapter 2 how the tendency of architects when confronted with this jumble is, maybe understandably, to separate out and then classify these categories, so as to order and then control them more easily. One idea in a single category, rigorously carried through from large scale to the detail, is often seen to be enough. Mature architecture is identified by a consistency of approach, with clarity in the parts. Mature architecture is seen to fit into a genealogy of architectural progress, from which awkward moments, inconsistencies, and hybridity are edited. Architectural critics establish these genealogies through their writings, defining neat packages of styles, method, techniques, and taste. If you fit into one of these categories, you are an architect. If you define one of these packages, you are a great architect. Seminal buildings are those that establish a new category, be it Le Corbusier's early villas, Foster's Willis Faber Dumas, Michael Graves's

Portland Public Service Building, or Frank Gehry's Guggenheim. But if you transgress these packages, these categories, you are dismissed as wayward, immature, self-indulgent, maybe even not a proper architect.

It is 1997, an era before climate change had made the move from scientific journals to front-page news. Our building is still rumbling, half-designed, around our heads when the call comes. It is from the organizers of Inter-build, the largest trade show for building materials in the United Kingdom. They want us to build a section of our house on the main exhibition stand, in a display called "Façades of the Future." We are both flattered and gently amused at the idea of sneaking in a straw wall as an example of a pioneer-ing future. A hairy Trojan horse. But we waver. We have not even designed, let alone detailed, the wall yet, and the exhibition is to open in five weeks' time. What eventually sways us is the promise that our exhibit is to be placed next to a section of the Lords Media Centre by Future Systems, described to us over the phone as seven meters long and shiny. The temptation of jux-taposing our hairy agricultural wall with the smoothness of their nautically inspired technology is too much to resist.

We suspect we have been called in as the token eco-people: straw = hairy = handholding = female = amateur = crude = nonrational. This is a concatena-tion of lowly elements, which by association devalues the sustainable mes-sage that we have set out to deliver, particularly when set against the clarity and single-mindedness of Future Systems' progressive cant.

Five weeks later we arrive, three amateurs (two of them women) with a self-drive van in a hall full of trucks and big, skilled men. We have three days to erect a wall that will be seen by over 100,000 people using a method never previously used. The lack of any technological precedent is scary (we have to research everything from scratch and improvise where necessary), but also consoling since there is nothing to judge it against; our method is neither right nor wrong, it is just there. But this does not stop endless big-bellied men coming over, curious and judgmental, waiting to see something they can shake their heads over in the time-honored construction industry tradition:

"You're doing it wrong, mate."

"But there is no wrong."

We have the final laugh when three days later our not wrong, but maybe improper, wall is completed on time and according to plan, defeating the collective skepticism. This is in contrast to the promised seven meters of the Lords Media Centre which, when it arrives, has shrunk to a sample one meter square. Something about a "problem with production." Our exhibit

even looks "good," and becomes the inspiration for the part of our future house where the straw is displayed in all its agricultural and golden glory. The display certainly delivers the provocation that we intended. The reason is that we have added a twist to our detailing: to wrap the straw in a transparent polycarbonate screen sourced from an Italian DIY catalog, so that the straw is exposed to view. It is a transgression of material, technical, and ideological classifications. Hairy meets slick; natural, nonnatural. The eco-people are offended by the polycarbonate (plastics are not wholesome). The technocrats are put off by having to confront the natural stuff. A surveyor comes up and smugly tells us that he makes money out of people like us whose buildings fail. A man shouts into his mobile phone: "I am standing in front of a fooking haystack and they are calling it the future." A bathroom tiles rep asks if it is an art project. That is a lot of contraventions in one wall.

Monstrous Hybrids

What happens when a great architect appears to transgress and move from one category to another? A collective outpouring of anguish, that's what happens, or at least it did when Le Corbusier was seen to switch from one package, rational modernism, to another, organic rawness. The British architect James Stirling led the attack in two articles, one comparing one of Le Corbusier's early white villas, the Villa Garches of 1927, to the brick and concrete Maisons Jaoul of 1952; the other discussing the chapel at Ronchamp in terms of a "crisis of rationalism."[20] Three interrelated issues appear to be at stake. The first is a break in continuity: "More than any other architect of this century," writes Stirling, "Le Corbusier's buildings present a continuous architectural development which, however, has not recently been supplemented."[21] In breaking that continuity, Le Corbusier is transgressing categories. The second is the issue of logic, Stirling insinuating in the very title of the second essay that Le Corbusier's recent work was tainted by dint of it being "irrational" in comparison to the rationality of the previous work.[22] Third is the sense that in admitting elements of folk art and popular culture, Le Corbusier is somehow demeaning the sanctity of architecture. Stirling notes how Ronchamp appears to have been a hit with ordinary people simply because of its visual appeal. "This entirely visual appeal and the lack of participation demanded from the public may partly account for its easy acceptance by the local population," he writes sniffily.[23] The implication is that normal people just like the look of things and are not capable of reaching the heights of architectural thought. Not only is this a strange interpretation of Ronchamp, which is both intensely cerebral and deeply phenomenal as an experience, but it is also breathtaking in its dismissiveness of "the they," drawing up clear lines between us architects and them unwashed.

The outrage, however, is misplaced. Le Corbusier may have changed his spots, but underneath the consistency of a great architect's hand is still in place, doubly so because he has the brilliance to define two categories in the space of a lifetime. Perhaps the most telling words of all in Stirling's essays are when he writes: "As homes the Jaoul houses are almost cosy and could be inhabited by any civilized family, urban or rural. They are built by and intended for the status quo"[24] This is not a compliment, contrasted as it is in the next sentence with the utopian and progressive stance of the earlier houses to which "all architects must aspire if modern architecture is to retain its vitality." So the real symptom of Le Corbusier's transgression is that he has flirted with the ordinary: the houses could be lived in by anyone! *Quelle parodie!* "Almost cosy" becomes a term of derision for the "proper" architect, whereas for the lo-fi architect it might be an aspiration. The real project of modernism for Stirling is to retain the vitality and purity of architecture in its own right, and if the normative needs of users, the imperfections of popular art, or any other aspects of the status quo presume to intervene, then they need to be expelled from the House of Architecture.

Presented with these multiple transgressions (of styles, of the contamination of the rational with the irrational, of pure architecture with popular art, and so on), Stirling's unease and subsequent dismissal is archetypally modern; "the horror of mixing," says Bauman, "reflects the obsession with separating."[25] The two are but two sides of the same modernist coin. As Bruno Latour clearly identifies: "moderns . . . refuse to conceptualize quasi-objects as such. In their eyes hybrids present the horror that must be avoided at all costs by a ceaseless, even maniacal, purification." But this cleansing comes at a cost: a mushrooming of a certain type of idealized object "expelled from the social world, attributed to a transcendent world that is, however, not divine."[26] As we have seen, however, this task of purification is an impossible one, because the more one turns upward to construct artificial worlds of purity and transcendence, the more one has to turn one's back on the social construction of the world, and in this turn a blind eye to the mixing of things with people. The mixing takes place anyway, wherever one's eyes are cast, and so "the proliferation of hybrids has saturated the framework of the moderns."[27]

Latour's response to this false hope of the moderns is to come up with a "non-modern" constitution, one of whose guarantees is "to replace the clandestine proliferation of hybrids by their regulated and commonly agreed upon production."[28] This is not, absolutely not, about the formal construction of aesthetic hybrids by mixing up two pure forms to make a third one, but about the social construction of hybrids rubbing together things and people, architecture and life. The formal production of hybrids has been underway in architecture for the past forty-odd years. In their own ways, and for their own reasons, postmodernist and deconstructivist architects disturbed the purity of modernist form by combining formal elements to create new hybrids. However, with both the historical collages of the former and the geometric distortions of the latter the hybrid game is played out on a strictly visual field, and one that privileges the internal obsessions of the architect in its exploitation of the aesthetic excess of the hybrid. Latour's production of hybrids takes into account far more than the visual, acknowledging as it does the relationship of the nonhuman to the human—of things to their social context, of objects to subjects, of nature to politics, and so on. And, crucially, "the production of hybrids by becoming explicit and collective becomes the object of an enlarged democracy . . . a democracy extended to things themselves."[29] What Latour suggests here has direct implications for architecture: the production should be at the same time intentional *and* participative, and all in the name of contributing to an expanded political field. Hybrids are here released from their previous identification as something horrific to be rid of, and instead revealed as something remarkable to be employed positively. So when I talk about monstrous hybrids, it is not in the derogatory sense of the English word but in the prodigious, fantastic sense of the Italian word: *mostruoso*.[30]

All this begins to fill out the sketch of lo-fi architecture, if we are to treat it as a hybrid in Latour's sense of the term. First is the sense that it is much more than an aesthetic issue alone, but brings in the social and the ethical. Attention is thus displaced from architecture as object and into the negotiating of a much more complex set of relationships. Second is the sense that its production is collective and thus dependent on far more than the guiding hand of the single architect. The intentionality of the production is thus a matter of negotiation, not of imposition, and the tenor of that intent is laying the ground for possible consequences rather than the positivist expectation of certain ends. Third, lo-fi architecture, as an intentional hybrid, transgresses conventional boundaries, both in terms of content and in terms of cultural categories. It is neither precisely high nor determinedly low, but can accommodate the highest and lowest moments. Fourth, lo-fi architecture is always alert to the context, physical and social, in which it will be played out. Generalized or abstracted solutions will be quickly unraveled by the particulars of those contexts, which means that the lo-fi architect has to work with and within them.

This all chimes with the idea of situated knowledge which, as we saw at the end of chapter 3, forms a good basis for making the choices that the contingent world presents us with. In this, learning from situated knowledge, the lo-fi architect is full of vision and optimism, but modest and grounded enough not to turn these into false hopes that will flounder in the face of the particular. Although lo-fi architecture must deal with the particular, this does not imply that it is wholly local. Much is written about the tension between the local and the global but, as Latour suggests, this straightforward binary is no longer sustainable. Instead, confronted with the confusion of the contemporary labyrinth, he says there is "an Ariadne's thread that would allow us to pass with continuity from the local to the global, from the human to the nonhuman. It is the thread of networks of practices and instruments, of documents and translations . . . the two extremes, local and global, are much less interesting than the intermediary arrangements that we are calling networks."[31] The important term here is networks, which suggests a set of negotiations between the extremes. This is different from the now commonplace term the "glocal," which implies an uncritical and inevitable combination of the two. The rallying call of the glocal ("think global, act local") is in the end despairing in its ordering of its terms, in which the intellectual and social conditions of the global overwhelm the simple action of the local. Latour's networks imply that there is such a thing as local knowledge,[32] but that this needs to be played out in a context in which strict modernist categories are dissolved into more hybrid conditions. The beauty of lo-fi architecture is that because it asks the architect to project the potentially autonomous activities of the design studio out through the equivalent of the cheap radio, the architect necessarily has to address all those cross-breedings; the contingent studio is, to push the Costello analogy just once more, a veritable mixing desk.

How They'll Tell if Your Building Is Gay

So, I hear you say, what does this lo-fi architecture actually *look* like? How can you write a book about architecture and not show pictures of what you mean? Aren't we, after all, a visual profession? To the last of which my answer is yes, and overly so. If I showed you pictures it would shut down what is meant to be an open argument. You would say: "So it looks like Lina Bo Bardi / Geoffrey Bawa / Neave Browne / Herman Hertzberger / William Lim / Sambo Mockbee / Jo Noero / Cedric Price / Jean Renaudie / Kenzo Tange / Sarah Wigglesworth / Shadrach Woods / . . ." and then maybe try to compile a list of common visual features, and conclude: "So he likes the *dirty* stuff," and suddenly my carefully assembled warp and weft of arguments would be smothered under a misplaced aesthetic. Already, in that teasing list of names, I have given away too much. But who knows, it may be a false trail, insofar as it is just the names of individual architects (and all those men in an argument that owes much of its genesis to feminism), when in fact my visual curiosity is equally stimulated by anonymous places, the interstices of buildings and things beyond architecture. The main issue, however, is that my argument is founded not on architecture as object, in which the visual presence often overwhelms critical thought, but rather on architecture as agency. It is to this agency that we now turn, to excavate its operation and find its potential, not to display its good or bad looks.

It is 1995. I am in the office at the top of the house. Sarah, Duncan, and Katerina are out in London putting in place the final arrangements for Desiring Practices, their mammoth and selfless enterprise in bringing gender theory into the center of architectural discourse (they are purposely holding the main conference at the headquarters of the RIBA, an organization that is "the central locus for the production and control of the patrimony of architecture").[33] I am manning the phones, selling tickets, and handling press queries, most of the latter of which can barely disguise their skepticism of the premise of an assorted bunch of feminists, queer theorists, historians, ecologists, and artists storming the bastion of architecture. Particularly insistent, and particularly sneering, is someone from *The Daily Telegraph*, the Conservative broadsheet. My hackles are already up: the *Telegraph* will want the story only so as the better to set it up for a fall. The scorn in the voice makes it clear that talking to a minor academic ("Kingston *Polytechnic*, did you say?") is beneath the dignity of someone more used to passing on the platitudes of Tory grandees.

"But what does this women's stuff look like?" he presses.

"It is not the way it looks that matters," I say, "it is about the ideas behind it."

"How about the gay stuff then? Do they like it bendy, if you see what I mean?"

"I am not sure that I do" (not rising to the bait).

"OK, then tell me where I can go and see this *gender* architecture," he says, twisting gender into a term between hilarity and mockery.

Worn down by the cross-examination, I relent and tell him about Jane Rendell's piece on the Burlington Arcade.[34] He has got what he wants, the promise of visual evidence, and puts the phone down.

Sure enough he goes off to Piccadilly, and sure enough he mangles Jane's interpretation in with lots of other stuff, and sure enough he comes back with a piece that manages to knock architects, feminists, gays, and lefty theorists into one risible hat, killing off many birds with one slightly jokey stone.

The headline is: "How They'll Tell if Your Building Is Gay."

III   ARCHITECTURE : A DEPENDENT PROFESSION

Part III deals with architecture. Where Giedion's focus is on architecture as final object, I am more interested in the processes that go toward creating that object. Architecture is thus discussed as agency. The introduction of dependency as a defining feature of architectural practice, and in particular the introduction of others into the processes and products of that practice, brings with it political and ethical dimensions. This in turn suggests a reformulation of aspects of practice: a move from the idea of architect as expert problem-solver to that of architect as citizen sense-maker; a move from a reliance on the impulsive imagination of the lone genius to that of the collaborative ethical imagination; from clinging to notions of total control to a relaxed acceptance of letting go.

Chapter 10, on ethics, states that the architect's ethical duty is solely in terms of a responsibility to others: the users and recipients of future buildings. The book ends with an outline of how such architects, in their role as transformative agents, may be involved in the construction of hope. Architecture's dependency is finally seen as an opportunity and not a threat, with the architect working out from the contingencies of the given situation and using their embedded knowledge, skills, and imagination in an open and curious way in order to contribute to the making of new spatial possibilities.

9 Architectural Agency

Lost in Action

I recently conducted a very bad piece of research. It was at a party full of architects, at the headquarters of the RIBA. I asked six of these architects at random what the letters RIBA stood for. Three said *Royal Institute of British Architects.* Two said *Royal Institute of British Architecture.* One spluttered *Right Ignorant Bunch of Assholes,* but he was drunk and so sadly must be excluded from my unscientific sample. The other five reflected a confusion common among architects, and within the RIBA itself. The Royal Charter, granted in 1837, sets out the objectives of the institution as: "The advancement of architecture and the promotion of the acquirement of the knowledge of the various arts and sciences connected therewith." It would be logical, therefore, to assume that the "A" stands for "Architecture," but in fact it stands for "Architects." The Royal Institute of British Architects.

The very founding of the RIBA reflects this confusion. In the first place it was an act of self-protectionism. The defining feature of any profession is to distinguish itself from the ordinary; professions inscribe territories in order to better control them, and thereby give themselves status and economic power.[1] But such naked self-interest is not what one receives Royal charters for, and so the foundation of the RIBA is publicly marked in the charter by a statement not about architects but about architecture, with the implication that the advancement of the subject is in some way for the greater public good. The fact that this responsibility is vested in the Institute of Architects (and not Architecture) only goes to confirm that it is architects alone who control this patch of knowledge called architecture. Under the worthy cloak of the charter, the whole operation is essentially self-serving: in a circular logic, the knowledge as to what constitutes architecture is defined by architects, who in turn are therefore deemed to be the only people capable of delivering that self-defined architecture. The RIBA is not alone in this; nearly all the national architectural bodies have the word *architect* in their titles.[2] The implications are clear: architecture is defined by architects. Further control is exerted by allowing the term *architecture* to have a dual meaning; it refers both to the professional activity and also to the outputs of that activity, the stuff out there that elevates itself above mere building. Architects thus presume to define, and so control, the whole field of architecture from its internal processes to its external products.

The founding address of the Institute of British Architects makes this system of closure, and its obvious benefits to the profession, very clear. The second paragraph states that the Institute "must be obviously advantageous to the country at large, from its responsibility to public opinion for the direction and maintenance of the national character for taste, and from its affording a body to whom Individuals may have recourse for its opinion upon professional matters."[3] Only we, architects, can define taste, and it is for your convenience, ordinary people, that we have grouped together to better advise you. There is a barefaced cheek in hiding the expediency of private gain behind the mask of public good. Many, especially the ordinary many, would argue that things have not moved on much since this self-satisfied opening to the very first transactions of British architecture in 1836.

This degree of self-satisfaction is really possible only under a belief system that conflates architect (as expert) with architecture (as profession) with architecture (as practice) with architecture (as product), because it is assumed that a chain is set up which passes the accepted virtues of the expert—the source of the self-satisfaction—down through to the products, the buildings. Historically the RIBA has perpetuated this conflation. At times a learned body there to promote the knowledge of its experts through lectures and reports, to regulate that knowledge through its educational influence, and to protect that knowledge in its library. At times a trade union there to protect the interests of the profession against the marauding hordes of surveyors and engineers, and to counter the insatiable claims of clients and contractors. At times supporting the practice of architecture through legal advice and best practice prescriptions. At times displaying and advocating the products through exhibitions and awards systems.[4] Small wonder, then, that the President of the RIBA, as with other international architectural figureheads, wears his various hats rather uncomfortably. What exactly is he (and it always has been a he) representing at any one time? Put on the feathered hat of the award-giver, and all the outsider sees is

Architecture : A Dependent Profession

the cloth cap of the self-protectionist. Wear the mortarboard of the learned leader, and the members demand the bowler hat of the businessman. So many costume changes that the profession gets lost in the action.

This conflation of incompatible elements does the profession of architecture no real favors, but it is clung to in the belief that there is a direct and virtuous set of links along the line expert-profession-practice-product. However, the assertion of the direct transmission of values along this line is difficult to maintain: it is a chain that successively unravels as one moves down it, the architect gradually losing authority within the increasing contingency of each link. The weakest link is the last one, in which buildings, as the products, are finally exposed to forces way beyond the architect's direct control. This exposure can be seen as the profession's Achilles heel. No "strong" profession is so closely associated with things as opposed to knowledge; law is the exercise of codified knowledge, medicine is defined through procedures guided by expert knowledge. In this, the two professions can protect themselves from the outside by always asserting control over their particular knowledge base. The profession of architecture in its close association with things, in all their dependencies and flux, cannot claim this authority.[5]

The only way to avoid the apparent loss of professional authority as one moves along the line from expert to building is to reel in that final link in the chain, that of the exposed building, and to situate it in a closed loop: the expert defines the profession which orders practice which produces buildings which in turn define the knowledge of the expert. The means of achieving this closure is to limit the architectural knowledge to those aspects that are controllable by architects. Which brings us back to Vitruvius, that monkey on the back of architecture, and to the modern version of his triad: function, tectonics, and aesthetics. These are areas in which architects feel they can exercise their expert knowledge: function as an abstraction of the complexities of use, tectonics as a codification of the vagaries of construction, and aesthetics as the "maintenance of taste" through various theories of form and composition. This circumscribing entails a severe editing of those social and political aspects deemed beyond architectural control, and with this architecture becomes limited in the conditions that it addresses.

With the assumed controlling of knowledge, professional closure is effected. The key aspect of this operation is its very circularity, because in this closed loop autonomy is founded. Part I of this book attempted to show the fallibility of such an assertion of autonomy. As Garry Stevens notes in his acute analysis of the profession, architecture "like other cultural fields . . . strives to increase its autonomy," but at the same time no other discipline is less autonomous in terms of its relationship with other cultural fields.[6] This creates an intolerable tension between the will to separate in order to maintain professional power, and the inevitability of being conjoined with societal forces. He argues that to look at architecture as an art, science, or profession alone has no utility: "these are all simply inadequate concepts to apply to such a complex entity." Instead one must understand "that architects are but one part of a much wider social system."[7] This includes the social construction of notions of expertise, from which so many of the values of the profession flow. In order to intervene in the circle of influence from expert knowledge round to buildings and back again, and the way that those values are pushed around it, it is necessary to unpack some of the underlying assumptions of being an expert as the first step in challenging the false autonomy of the profession, before moving on to proposing alternatives.

I have ordered the original 1837 charter of the Royal Institute of British Architects from the British Library. I am curious about any evidence that there might be around the edges: who the printer was, what the introduction was like, how it was laid out, pencil marks. It is also good just to hold and sniff these old things. (I remember trembling as we were handed original Borromini drawings in the Albertina in Vienna; we had bluffed our way in and now felt overwhelmed by the fragility of the pencil marks—what if we sneezed?)

It was disappointing, therefore, when the woman at the issue desk told me that the charter was "missing." She looked sad on my behalf; they knew me by now.

"But if it's missing from here, the citadel of knowledge, what does that mean for British architecture—is it lost too?" I mumble, half to myself. "What happened, does it say?"

"The docket just notes: 'Lost in World War 2,'" she replies. "Looks like they got your profession as well as your buildings. Lost in action. Didn't anyone ever tell you?"

Self-Control

When Zygmunt Bauman states baldly that "expertise creates and enhances the need of itself,"[8] one is quickly made to rethink the basis on which any profession operates. Being an expert suggests a positive activity, helping society solve its problems through the application of expert knowledge. It is on the basis of this affirmative contribution to the common good that professions assert not just their economic worth but also their moral authority.

Architecture : A Dependent Profession

It is not just a matter of needing experts (and thus needing to pay them) but also a loftier mission of meeting collective aspirations: for society to build better, be healthier, have better jurisdiction. The word *vocation* is telling as a description of a profession, since it operates between the poles of straightforward service provision and a higher calling.

What Bauman and others point to is that expertise is not quite as benign as it is often assumed to be. The self-serving nature of the establishment of the architectural profession in the UK is indicative of a wider pincer movement that has been well documented by the historians of the professions. Thus Randall Collins notes how the skills of professionals are often "answers to self-created problems; the skill is intrinsic to the professional structure and does not exist without it."[9] In this light the development of the expertise of any given profession, far from being mainly for the general good, can actually be seen as a means of self-legitimation, and so self-perpetuation. Take the example of quantity surveying, the profession that defines costs in the UK construction industry; as a profession it does not exist in every country, and so elsewhere its particular area of knowledge is dispersed and, some would say, less restrictive. But in the UK it is an established profession, and therefore needs vehicles to show off its expertise. One such is the Bill of Quantities, an archaic practice of reducing a building in all its constructional complexities down to a list of its constituent elements, there the better to be quantified and so costed. In large parts of the world—notably the USA, where Quantity Surveying does not exist as a profession—Bills of Quantities are not deemed necessary, but in the UK they remain as a very narrow conduit through which some building projects are still forced to flow, the moment where control is seized from the architect and placed firmly in the hands of another set of professionals.

UK architects attempt to exert the same control over their unruly practices in many ways, one of which is by constricting them to the linear procedures of the "RIBA Plan of Work," a document that divides the briefing, design, and construction of buildings into neat stages. The outline document cleverly manages to combine on a single page the setting of problems associated with each stage together with the tasks needed to find solutions to each problem. In the final column the people involved are identified; in all but one of the twelve stages architects are required. Well, one might say, they would be: it is they who have set the tasks.

It was really the first building that I had ever designed, a small block of apartments for a social housing provider on a nondescript back street in London.

Nothing special, but nonetheless I was immensely proud of it and fought for every corner. This was in the early days of design-and-build contracts, and we had been working for a contractor from the early days of the process. Working drawings had been done, costs had now been agreed, contracts signed, and the site cleared. Foundations were just about to go in. At this stage the development officer from the housing association rings.

"Where's the Bill of Quantities? We can't start without one."

"But the cost is agreed, signed off, as are all the drawings," I reply. "We know where we stand. Why bother with a Bill? It's too late for that now."

"But we need one, to know where we are."

"What are you," I ask, "some kind of surveyor?"

"Oh you clever-clog, smarty-pant architects. All the same."

And of course he was a surveyor, and of course in the end he got his own way; he was, after all, the client. He insisted on a Bill of Quantities being drawn up, in all its redundancy. For him as an ex-Quantity Surveyor the building did not exist except as a Bill of Quantities. For me it did not exist, then, except as a set of drawings.

I still remember the absurdist conversations with the quantity surveyor appointed to draw up this document that no one else but he and the development officer would ever look at.

"What about the tiles round the basin?"

Tiles are a particular obsession for some QS's; they come in all shapes, sizes, colors, edge tiles, corner tiles. Lots of stuff to quantify.

"Do them as the drawing," I respond.

"But is that edge tile a special?"

"Yes," I say, "and it's purple. And the special corner ones are yellow, and the ones in the middle are like a Battenberg cake, spotted yellow and purple in a checkerboard pattern. Absolutely no cutting, and it is important to start with the spotted yellow at the top left of that central section. And, oh yes, the grout is black." I was young then, and these things meant a lot.

This was all grist to the QS mill; the more problems, the more he could exercise his skill. One square meter of tiling ended up as over a page of description. The contractor, probably sensibly, ignored us both and put in what he could get down the local merchants where he had an account; a car crash of splattered colors and cut ends. It was painful for me to see. Not that it mattered in the long run: I recently went back to see the building to check my memory. It had been demolished to make way for something much grander, the nondescript street having been levered into desirability by the machinations of the London property market.

Left Brain, Right Brain

There are countless other examples of professions self-defining in order to self-perpetuate: the voracious spiraling effect of more lawyers leading to more litigation leading to more lawyers is probably the most striking, particularly in the USA. All point to the truth in Bauman's analysis that "expertise becomes its own cause (rather than its own purpose)."[10] It is significant that these words come from Bauman's masterpiece, *Modernity and Ambivalence*. Bauman sees the expert as one of the key agents in modernity's war on ambivalence and the consequent overriding of contingency with the presumed virtues of certainty. Experts, endowed with the authority of professional knowledge, legislate what is the right or wrong way to deal with issues. If this operation assumes the status of a battle with the forces of uncertainty and disorder, then this just serves to reinforce the heroic status of the professional. It appears that Vitruvius, that monkey on my back, was mindful of this when he opened his treatise with a set of military metaphors. The well-educated architect, "fully armed" with the knowledge of both theory and practice, will reach his goal "speedily and with authority." As Indra McEwen notes, "swift attack appears to be the watchword here," and the ultimate goal is that of order.[11]

If the trust of the nonexpert is to be gained, it is important that the professional's decisions are founded on certain principles rather than open interpretation. Trust, as Anthony Giddens notes, is a necessary if sometimes uncomfortable part of dealing with the juggernaut of modernity.[12] In the face of all the increasing complexities of the modern world, one has to place one's trust in experts, and to do this one has to be reassured that their systems are reliable. As Bauman says, "expert knowledge caters for another crucial need of the individual, that of rationality . . . lay desire to be rational lubricates the flywheel of expertise."[13] Rules are acceptable, hunches are not. However, this placing of trust comes with reservations. "Lay attitudes to science and technical knowledge," says Giddens, "generally are typically ambivalent . . . this is an ambivalence that lies at the core of all trust relations . . . for trust is only demanded where there is ignorance. Yet ignorance always provides grounds for scepticism or at least caution."[14] The nonexpert needs the expert to take in hand their ignorance, but at the same time feels resentful of this passing over of control. The result is that people "make a 'bargain with modernity,' in terms of the trust they vest in symbolic tokens and expert systems. The nature of the bargain is governed by specific admixtures of deference and scepticism, comfort and fear."[15] The layperson is unwillingly exposed in their ignorance, hence the skepticism and fear, but cannot survive in ignorance, hence the deference and need for comfort. They are pairings that play beautifully into the hands of the expert; for example, the plumber who moves quickly from establishing fear to demanding deference with the inevitable opening line: "Oh dear, oh dear. Some fathead hashed this one right up; this is going to take some sorting," or the mystifying jargon of the computer expert that sets up fear of the unknown and at the same time comfort that only the geek can deal with it.

Architects have been good enough at exploiting these tensions: expediently swapping the hats of scientist and artist, they have two cards to play. Through recourse to codes, techniques, and typologies, the profession attempts to provide itself with a strong knowledge base founded on rational principles and their associated methods, which only architects have the skill and knowledge to manipulate. A quote from Peter Eisenman gives explicit illustration of this action of professional legitimation: "When one denies the importance of function, programme, meaning, technology and the client—constraints traditionally used to justify and in a way support form-making—the *rationality* of process and the *logic* inherent in form become almost the last 'security' or legitimation available."[16] What he is intimating is that the issues of use, meaning, and clients are too diffuse to pin down with any authority, and so one has to find more rational parameters to describe architecture as both process and product. This provides the comfort, at least to the left side of the brain, which processes the rational. The deference is obtained when the objective ground of reason is overlaid with the mystique of the artist-genius whereby the architect alone can, in an almost magical way, give aesthetic form to the rational principles. The idea of architect as artist plays an important part in establishing architectural culture to the outside world. The uncanny thing about architectural creativity is that, despite many attempts, it resists complete explanation; it is exactly this enigmatic quality that raises its value on the external market. It also affects the internal economy of the profession, with the "star" architects underpaying their staff, but offering an osmotic relationship with artistry in return. With the left-brain, right-brain, double punch of objective reason and subjective genius, professional closure is effected. The most successful architects are those who deliver these punches in quick succession.

I once had a very talented student who went to work for a very famous architect. This student had a remarkable facility to draw quick but cogent sketches. The famous architect recognized this talent, and would take the

Architecture : A Dependent Profession

student to initial client meetings. While the client and architect discussed the problems of function, site, and cost, the student would sit quietly at the back picking up hints that the architect was subtly dropping—"it would be most efficient to have the entrance on the lake." "The sun angle gives a curve here as the optimum solution." "The plot ratio says go high."—turning them into suggestive sketches. At the end of the meeting the architect would present these drawings. You could knock the client over with a feather. It was normally a done deal.

Remember I'm the Bloody Architect

Of the six people I questioned about the meaning of RIBA it was disappointing, but maybe not surprising, that not one referred to the nickname by which it is known to others in the construction industry: "Remember I'm the Bloody Architect." It is a phrase that is at the same time sad and desperate, speaking of a lost authority. The reason for this loss may be that the knowledge that is needed to define the profession is different from the knowledge needed to effect architectural practice. The profession of architecture and the practice of architecture are clearly different but often treated as if they are the same. The profession of architecture is internally defined and necessarily self-contained; the practice of architecture is a set of external networks, and necessarily dependent. The knowledge that is developed to meet the internal needs is of a very particular kind, and not at all the same as that required to deal with those external contingencies.

Professionals, as Burton Bledstein argues, attempt to "define a total coherent system of knowledge within a precise territory."[17] If that knowledge is to be totalizing, then it has to lift itself above particular conditions, and so is developed away from particular tasks. Professional knowledge thus tends toward the development of common principles and set methods arising from them, all underwritten by the mandate of reason. It is this combination of detachment and rationality that is typical of professional knowledge, combining two clichés: the calm voice of reason is delivered by the remote figure of authority. The problem comes when the principles and methods that are needed to define the profession are instrumentally transferred across to become the rules and procedures of practice. In medicine and engineering we would be deeply concerned if the knowledge base of the profession was *not* directly played out in practice; without this instrumental application people would die, buildings would fall down. There are good hearts and bad hearts; knowledge of how good hearts operate allows doctors to deal with the specifics of the bad heart. This does not mean, as Ivan Illich so clearly shows, that the medical profession does not define the limits of that knowledge base and, through its institutionalization, control it, but it takes someone as intellectually and personally brave as Illich to completely desist from that knowledge.[18]

In architecture, however, the knowledge is being transferred from the apparent security and stability of the self-defined domain of the profession into a much less stable and predictable set of conditions. Bringing the paradigm of certainty to the world of uncertainty is foredoomed. The more typologies, codes of conducts, plans of works, schedules, and specifications are sharpened into categories and systems in order to control those unruly conditions, the more they will be blunted by them. The "RIBA Plan of Work" is not intrinsically a useless document, but it is if one trusts it as a true description of an unfettered linear sequence: every single project will loop back and forward to revisit or accelerate stages as costs, briefs, clients, and other conditions change. It is professional insecurity in the face of such potential unraveling that reinforces the quest for certainty, but the result is an endless chasing of one's own impossibly beautiful tail in that internalized loop. One symptom of this is the exercising of architectural knowledge less on the fluid practices and more on the static objects. Analyses of design processes, reflections on the profession or discussions of social occupation, are overwhelmed by attention to the building as aesthetic and tectonic object. Taking Bryan Lawson's useful model of the processes, products, and performance of architecture as a description of the various stages of architectural design and occupation,[19] the normal focus is on the stable middle of the product rather than on the more open-ended outlying terms. The result is a false sense of detachment; products can be treated as neutral objects of contemplation, removed from their political and social ramifications.

Professions are quick to engage with politics when it directly affects their professional status in terms of protection of title or funding for their area, but much less quick to acknowledge the political constitution of their actual practices or the wider consequences of their products. Architects are no different in this. The twin poles of objective reason and creative artistry are both seen to rise above the political world. But just saying that something is not political does not mean that it actually isn't. Quite the opposite: the assumed innocence makes it more vulnerable to appropriation. Objective reason is commandeered in the guise of greater functional efficiency and control, and creative artistry in the guise of aesthetic commodification. As

Architecture : A Dependent Profession

we have seen, architects are complicit in this appropriation of professional values by the market. Yet they prefer not to acknowledge this raid on their professional capital, and instead focus on the pursuit of the higher ideals, using the smokescreens of perfection and beauty to disguise any dealings with dirty reality.[20]

At this point I was going to tell a story, of life before architects and life with architects, the latter's ideals built on the lofty shoulders of philosophers, but then I found that the Roman author Seneca had beaten me to it by two thousand years, and says it better. Listen:

That philosophy discovered the arts of which life makes use in its daily round I refuse to admit. Believe me, that was a happy age, before the days of architects, before the days of builders! All this sort of thing was born when luxury was being born; this matter of cutting timbers square and cleaving a beam with unerring hand as the saw made its way over the marked-out line. The primal man with wedges split his wood. On another point also I differ from Posidonius, when he holds that mechanical tools were the invention of wise men. . . . It was man's ingenuity, not his wisdom, that discovered all these devices . . . invented by some man whose mind was nimble and keen, but not great or exalted; and the same holds true of any other discovery which can only be made by means of a bent body and of a mind whose gaze is upon the ground.[21]

The Crucible

"That was a happy age, before the days of architects." This is a severe view, and hardly one that as an educator and architect I can subscribe to without severe hypocrisy. But I can subscribe to the general sentiment that to deal with issues in the "daily round," a different kind of thinking is required: full of ingenuity, keen, nimble, eyes to the ground rather than raised up with pretensions to detached greatness. The disjunction between the type of knowledge that the profession needs to legitimate itself and the form of thinking that practice requires is best summarized in Bauman's distinction between legislators and interpreters. Legislators are the thinkers of the modern era, granted authority by access to "superior (objective) knowledge." It is a form of knowledge that reflects the modern view of the world as "essentially an ordered totality" that can be the object of control.[22] In its objectivity and authority the knowledge of the legislator aligns with that of the professional. Interpreters, on the other hand, are the thinkers of the postmodern, in the sense of a condition which accepts uncertainty and lack of order as inescapable features of life and thought. The interpreter attempts to make sense of this more fluid landscape, working from within the context of a particular issue rather than observing it from without.

Faced with conflicting demands, as any architect inevitably is, the legislator will attempt to smother them through imposition while the interpreter negotiates with them. While professional knowledge is predicated on the efficacy of set ways of doing, what practice really needs is nimble ways of thinking. That gap, again, thus opens up between what the profession thinks it should do and what practice actually requires it to do. To overcome this gap demands, in Bauman's terms, "the replacement of the dream of the legislator with the practice of the interpreter,"[23] the significant word here being *dream,* because the longer the profession holds to its false dreams the longer it will fail in its responsibilities to others, and the more it will be moved to the margins.

Interpretation clearly demands different ways of thinking that do not assume there is a perfect answer. Hermeneutics, as that branch of knowledge that invokes interpretation, "pits itself against the notion that human affairs can finally be formalized into explicit rules which can or should function as a decision-procedure."[24] Importantly, hermeneutics works with rather than against contingency; indeed, it needs the very openness that the contingent field provides for any interpretations to be made free from preconceptions. As the philosopher Nicholas Smith argues, "the recognition of contingency serves to define the theoretical outlook and practical momentum of hermeneutics . . . in opposition to the idea that the correct grasp of a matter can be gained by following neutral methodological or procedural rules, hermeneutics insists that what counts as a sound understanding cannot be fixed in advance of the contingencies of real engagement."[25] The interpreter thus not only needs but relishes the engagement with contingency; the variables and potential conflicts are not something to be smothered but become the crucible for exchange between a mix of interpreters: professionals, amateurs, dreamers, pragmatists.[26] The crucible is the setting of the almost miraculous transformation of coarse, incompatible elements into something miraculous—or at least, that is how it is seen in my backyard, Sheffield, the birthplace of crucible steel. It is in this light, the brilliant light of the crucible, that architecture's dependency, far from being its weakness, becomes its opportunity, with the architect acting as open-minded listener and fleet-footed interpreter, collaborating in the realization of other people's unpolished visions.

This model of the architect as interpretive agent, and thus of architecture (as profession, practice, and product) as transformative agency, is dependent on a revised version of professional values, asking them to come down from their detached heights and instead engage as one set of informed principles among many. It does not—and this is important—ask that architectural knowledge should be disbanded, but does ask that it should be reconsidered away from any notions of authority and certainty. The disavowal of knowledge in the name of dissolving the authority of the expert is only to throw the baby out with the bathwater. This was exactly the predicament of the community architecture movement in the 1970s and 1980s. In the name of political rectitude, power was passed from architect to community; in the enforced relinquishment of power, the expert professionals also relinquished their knowledge (because, in the well-worn formulation reduced from Foucault, knowledge is power). As mere technical facilitators the architects were not able to use their embedded knowledge transformatively; rather, their skills were just used instrumentally. The Brazilian social theorist Roberto Mangabeira Unger makes much the same point in the construction of his idea of the transformative vocation, without a commitment to which a professional "soon finds himself driven down to the instrumental conception of work."[27] The technical know-how of the expert is not enough to enable others to expand on their nascent but unarticulated desires, and so these remain at the level of the lowest common denominator. The philosopher Gillian Rose, in her brilliant critique of community architecture, captures it perfectly in the memorable phrase: "the architect is demoted; the people do not accede to power."[28]

However, maybe all this talk of promoting and demoting, detached and engaged, is in fact a distraction if, along with Lefebvre, we understand that "superior, differentiated and highly specialised activities have never been separate from everyday practice, [but] have only appeared to be so."[29] What this suggests is that professional knowledge needs to be seen as part of a network that weaves together human and nonhuman, specialized knowledge with everyday insights, rules with instincts, the social sciences with the social.[30] It asks the profession to be part of the networks of others, and in this confronts it with its very worst fear, that of being normal. If a professional is deemed to be like any other person, they lose everything, hence their insistence on being different. This, however, is to misinterpret these networks and their hybrid use of knowledge. Instincts and everyday insights are not random impulses; they are developed from within the context of embedded experience (which is where the professional can claim a distinctive understanding) but are delivered in a context that is shared with others (which is where the professional engages). In fact, as Unger argues, the institutional ideas of a profession "have to be realised by collective action. They remain unpersuasive and dreamlike until we have complemented them with a view of the social activities that might establish them."[31] This notion that professional knowledge is actually dependent on others for its development and transformative enaction usefully punctures that balloon of self-aggrandizement in which the original members of the RIBA lifted off. Those early professionals persuaded themselves that they "were obviously advantageous to the country at large," but the reality is that we are all mutually reliant—not just in terms of economic exchange, but also in the context of intellectual exchange.

All this reinforces the argument made at the end of chapter 3 that architectural knowledge, as situated knowledge, should not be applied as an abstraction from the outside, but developed from within the context of the given situation. This calls for a new type of knowing. The profession is traditionally predicated on a knowing "that" and a knowing "how." Architects deploy their knowledge either in the form of a set of facts or theoretical principles (knowing "that") or else as a set of technical and instrumental skills: drawing, detailing, planning (knowing "how"). John Shotter argues that these types of knowledge are "decontextualised." Instead Shotter calls for a knowing "from within," a developmental knowledge that adjusts to, and grows out of, the social-cultural surroundings in which it is situated. In Shotter's terms, this is "knowing of the third kind," unlike the first two (knowing "how" and "that").[32]

The Problem of the Problem

In order to move away from the model of knowing "how" and knowing "that," architects are going to have to abandon the paradigm of problem-solving; this assertion might come as a shock, because problem-solving is often seen as the defining characteristic of the architect's role. In education, the architectural studio is held up as an exemplar of problem-based learning, the space where students are set a "problem" and, through the creative, and reflective, act of design, come to a "solution." In architectural practice, the "problem" is what gives the profession something to act upon in a specialized manner. As Reyner Banham notes, "a professional is a man with an interest, a continuing interest, in the existence of problems."[33] Solving problems is how the profession legitimates itself; setting problems is how it perpetuates itself. It is no surprise that buildings are offered as the only solution to architecturally defined problems, since it is architects who are professionally legitimated to deliver buildings. Problem-solving is also the symptom and cause of the wider professionalization of the built environment in which, as Habraken notes, "what used to remain unquestioned has been taken up as a design problem to be solved: nothing may be taken for granted. . . . Built environment, the ubiquitous, stable, ordinary background for architectural innovation, is now itself being reinvented by professionals, bit by bit, time after time."[34]

It is difficult to reconcile the notion of transformative agency with that of problem-solving. Problems look determinedly backward, while agency looks hopefully forward. The negative connotation of the term *problem* casts a gloomy pall over the design process, implying that the best we can expect from the solution is to make the world a slightly less bad place, as opposed to transformative agency which is founded on a mutual aspiration to make the world a better place. John Chris Jones gets it just right when he says: "to think of designing as 'problem-solving' is to use a rather dead metaphor for a lively process and to forget that design is not so much a matter of adjusting to the status quo as of realizing new possibilities and discovering our reactions to them."[35] In this light, problem-solving is revealed as an inherently conservative act of incrementally shifting around what is already there in a manner directed by preconceived ideologies.

If one problem with the problem is the way it closes down the potential for new possibilities, the other is that the framing and solving of the problem is an exclusionary act, and thus inappropriate for the terms of transformative agency involving the voices and networks of others. Problems require a certain type of professional, expert knowledge to solve them. The identification of the problem thus inevitably privileges the expert over the nonexpert, limiting the possibility of the architectural agency as a shared enterprise.

Of all the challenges to the strictures of the architectural problem, the most direct and devastating is Cedric Price's dictum that the best solution to an architectural problem is not necessarily a building.[36] It is devastating because it so clearly exposes the fallibility of the closed loop of the expert (the one in which the expert defines the profession which orders practice which produces buildings which in turn define the knowledge of the expert). If buildings are removed as the only solution, then what is left to the profession or, worse, *of* the profession? As Price's own oeuvre indicates, a lot, but to find this expansive field the profession needs to shift the application of architectural attention from objects to agency.

This entails the exercising of architectural intelligence rather than the imposition of architectural knowledge. Architectural intelligence is the application of flexible thinking; this is different from architectural knowledge, which is predicated on the search for stable foundations, a search that Jonathan Hill likens to pouring water into a colander.[37] Architectural intelligence, when freed from the shackles of attempting certainty and fixity, is far more febrile than the intelligence of other professions. Architectural education, when not obsessed with the production of visual imagery, exposes students to an extraordinarily broad range of intellectual activity, from poststructuralism to the structure of posts. This provides the potential for the development of exactly the kind of flexible thinking that is required to cope with the contingencies of architectural practice. The stumbling block is that the professional validation process, to which nearly all architectural education is subjected, finds it difficult to legislate architectural intelligence and the judgments that arise out of it, and so stifles them under demands for the acquisition of skills and knowledge, thus privileging the outputs of problem-solving exercises.

We therefore need to find an alternative paradigm to problem-solving as the basis of the architectural practice. In an eloquent paper, the planning theorist John Forester suggests that we should replace the normative metaphor of design as the search for a solution with the idea of design as "sense-making." "Sense-making is not simply a matter of instrumental problem-solving, it is a matter of altering, respecting, acknowledging, and shaping people's lived worlds."[38] Central to Forester's argument is that such a move from the problem to sense-making necessarily brings with it an acknowledgment of the contested social situation in which the design process is first initiated, and of the contingent social world in which buildings and their users will eventually be situated. "If form giving is understood more deeply as an activity of making sense together, designing may then be situated in a social world where meaning, though often multiple, ambiguous and conflicting is nevertheless a perpetual practical accomplishment."[39] Where problem-solving, predicated as it is on positivist thinking, tends to either abstract or exclude the social and the political, sense-making inevitably engages with them and, in so doing, accords with a model of architectural agency in which social and political issues are brought to the fore and then negotiated through spatial discussions.

In order to gain the full force of making sense, one has to address the complete range of conditions with which design, as the application of architectural intelligence, might be involved. It is normally assumed that the most creative part of design is concerned with the building as object, hence the fixation with formal innovation, but it may be argued that the most

Architecture : A Dependent Profession

important, and most creative, part of the process is the formulation of the brief. The brief is often seen simply as an instrument of rationality: how one can most efficiently get functions into rooms. Often written by the client, with the assistance of surveyors and project managers, briefs reduce architecture to abstract quantity, and are swiftly translated into deadening room data sheets.[40] These reductions are then passed as fait accompli to the architect, who is left with little more to do than turn these systems of flows and efficiencies into plans (a mainly technical act) and then disguise the deficiencies of the process (and their own marginality within it) through dressing the building up in various skins (a merely aesthetic act). Worst of all, the defining of briefs in abstract terms suppresses their social content under a set of conservative norms. The shift from the design of the object to the design of the brief, on the other hand, inevitably brings the social to the surface. The creative brief is about negotiating a new set of social relations, it is about juxtapositions of actions and activities, it is about the possibility to think outside the norm, in order to project new spatial, and hence social, conditions. This process of evolving a brief may not provide the immediate rush of visual stimulation that is associated with the creative design of an object—a rush which has proved addictive to architects over the ages—but it does have a much longer-term and profound effect.

Letting Go

One of the reasons that the design of the object is so privileged over aspects such as briefing is that it is one aspect of the whole process where the architect still retains nominal control. Even if this design control is highly mediated by the actions and demands of others (clients, cost managers, builders, and so on), the architect in the detachment of their studio can still dream of the hi-fi reproduction of their design ideals. It is under these conditions that the production of objects is attached to the power that Nietzsche accuses the architect being "under the spell of"; he associates the power with object-making ("architecture is a kind of eloquence of power in forms") in a way that results in the power "reposing in itself, fatalistically, a law among laws." In this isolated world the self-interest of the professional leads to a certain blindness to the state of others.[41] However, with the shift from object-making as a form of problem-solving to the idea of architectural agency, the execution of this detached power is not ethically sustainable. Briefing is but one of many architectural activities that involves others, and in their role as interpreters architects have to assume a stance of modesty.

"The thought of flux . . . makes us wary of power . . . hermeneutics is a lesson in humility; it comes away chastened from its struggle with the flux," writes John Caputo. "It understands the power of the flux to wash away the best-laid schemes of metaphysics. It takes the constructs of metaphysics to be the temporary cloud formations which, from a distance, create the appearance of shape and substance, but which pass through our fingers upon contact."[42] Faced with the storm of forces that constitute the architectural scene, one can but be humble; the modest acceptance of making best sense as opposed to the imperious assertion of "truth" is the only realistic option if architecture is not to be another of those evanescent clouds. This means letting go of the traditional values of authority and passing over some of the associated control to others, while retaining and exercising the febrile architectural intelligence that defines the profession. But most of all it means acknowledging that in this architects are not acting for themselves but on behalf of others, and this means acting ethically. It is to ethics that we now turn.

Architecture : A Dependent Profession

10 Imperfect Ethics

Bad Ethics

I am sometimes asked if I like architecture. This question usually comes at the end of a lecture when I have rhetorically bashed away at some of the holy cows of the discipline. Maybe you are feeling the same way by now.

My answer is always the same. I love architecture for its potential, but despair of architects for too often throwing away that potential in their stubborn attachment to a certain set of values. I know that even this might read as a generalization. I know that there are of course architects operating out there who do not fit my—at times—cussed characterization. My issue is not with these individuals, but with the collective and the culture that sustains it. If this critique comes across as intemperate, then it is meant to be no more than tough love, a small call to save the profession from itself, from its distracting addictions. This chapter, however, is not tough love, it is just plain tough. No jokes, no stories; the evidence will speak for itself. It is tough because it is about ethics, a notion that is used all too freely and vaguely in architecture, and in this way is misappropriated as a convenient smokescreen under whose cover unethical values are allowed to perpetuate.

There is something about the inclusion of the words *ethics* and *morals* in architecture writing that too often makes me see red. When a book sanctimoniously opens with a critique of "the ethics of statics" and replaces it with a vague notion of "the ethics of motion," and then gives us vacuous pictures of blobs floating in empty space.[1] When a distinguished philosopher writes a lucid book on the ethical function of architecture and ends up with a picture of the US Capitol to illustrate the argument.[2] When architects conflate professional codes of conduct with an ethical stance. When another distinguished philosopher mutters about the way "aesthetic principles (of twists, curves and color) are coded in ways that carry significant ethical and social weight."[3] When organizers of an architectural conference string poetics, ethics, and reconciliation together in the title, and then wistfully hope that each term will virtuously rub off against the other.[4] When architects burble on about the ethics of construction as if "honesty" in structure and detail somehow fulfills a moral purpose. When another philosopher argues that a well-made brick wall shows that the maker cared, and in this caring there is some kind of moral stance.[5] When Le Corbusier shouts: "Whitewash is extremely moral."[6] When beauty alone is seen to have a redemptive ethical purpose . . . I could go on, but you get the point: these things make me see red, and if in this one paragraph I have stepped on every type of architectural and intellectual toe, then maybe that is as much a reflection of the extent of the problem as it is of the extent of my irascibility, something that maybe I share with Manfredo Tafuri when he talks of the "pathetic 'ethical' relaunchings of modern architecture."[7]

Then there is the biggest architectural moralist of all, Mies van de Rohe. He said (or is said to have said): "God lies in the details."[8] But what happens when you place this pious bead on the architectural rosary against Mies's opportunist entanglement with the Nazis?[9] What happens then to that insistent morality? It should collapse under its own hubris, that's what should happen. I once pointed this out in a review of a Mies exhibition, in which the curators, in a paean to his rigor and artistic genius, had dramatically underplayed his political expediency. A letter came back: "Doesn't the eccentric professor realize that (a) Mies was driven out by the Nazis (b) Mies was a great architect," or words to that effect. *Don't mess with Mies* was the message. However, it is necessary to mess with Mies as a good starting point in the untangling of the tortured relation between architecture and ethics.

That letter says so much. It is factually incorrect (Mies was hardly cast out of Germany, but went to America on the invitation of a number of suitors) but the repetition of a commonplace mistruth conveniently casts him as a victim, thereby accentuating his heroic status as "great" architect, a status in which he is elevated up above the political foibles of mere mortals. So in one line the letter manages to establish the myth that architecture is a world unto itself, and in this separation operates under its own moral laws. Franz Schulze, in his "critical biography" of Mies, says as much when he observes: "politically Mies was a passive soul; his active moral energies were turned toward his art and away from practically all else."[10] No one could remain politically "passive" in the face of the rise of National Socialism, but maybe, just maybe, they could trick themselves into believing in a parallel universe, a retreat to a higher plane of consciousness in which morality is associated not with other people but with the rectitude of architecture as the rigorous discipline of fine, godly detailing and strict aesthetics. Only in such a parallel universe, presided over by the gods of architecture, could one believe that "there is an ethical project that is carried out precisely in the work."[11]

Here, perhaps, I should be feeling pity at these delusions, but I still see red at the abuse, and conflation, of the terms *ethics* and *morals*. To explain why, it is first necessary to define what I understand by "ethics." There are four common usages of the word, all rather different. The first is the association with ethos, the originary sense of how human beings exist in the world according to commonly agreed, and virtuous, custom; for Karsten Harries, the ethical function of architecture is "its task to help articulate a common ethos."[12] Second is the meaning derived from Aristotle, in which ethics is associated primarily with the development of the good self in the pursuit of good conduct. Third is the sense developed by Kant, in which a universal code of morals is seen as part of the wider project of reason. Finally there is the utilitarian interpretation of ethics being the deployment of knowledge to bring about the greatest benefit for the greatest number of people. As will become apparent, none of these understandings of ethics suits my purpose, because all in one way or another tie ethics to the broader assumption that there are definitively right and proper ways of doing things. To execute ethics under any of these guises is therefore to smother exactly the contingency and otherness of the world which, I have argued, should be allowed to flourish.

My understanding of ethics is informed by Zygmunt Bauman, who in turn acknowledges "the greatest ethical philosopher of the twentieth century," Emmanuel Levinas, for whom ethics is defined simply and directly as "being-for the Other." To assume an ethical stance means to "assume responsibility for the Other."[13] It is this, and this alone, that should guide the ethics of architecture. The "other" here is the diverse mix of builders, users, occupiers, and observers of architecture, people whose political and phenomenal lives will be affected by the construction of a building and its subsequent occupation. A number of implications arise out of this ethical dimension. First, because architecture is engaged primarily as a spatial experience, it follows that the focus of ethical attention should be on the dynamics of social space, not on the statics of vision. Second, the desires and needs of the "Other" are different from those of clients, which means that any ethical stance must be clearly separated from the codes of professional service, the latter of which are concerned primarily with meeting the demands of the client. Third, the spatial and social conditions of contemporary life, in all their flux, need to be met with new kind of ethics, not with the restitution of a previous form of originary ethics. Finally, the "Other" is inevitably diverse and unpredictable, and so an ethical stance must accept this difference rather than attempt to muffle it under a blanket of universal morals. The rest of this chapter attempts to flesh out what such an ethics might mean to architects.

Phony Ethics

The 2000 Venice Architecture Biennale was launched with the challenge "Less Aesthetics, More Ethics," a provocation from the overall curator, Massimiliano Fuksas, for architects to address issues beyond the aesthetic. It was a well-meant call, but fatally flawed because those four words still wedded aesthetics to ethics; they just asked for a rebalancing of the priorities. They suggest that if you just play down aesthetic excess, then ethics will emerge in the gaps that are left.

Fuksas is far from alone in linking aesthetics to ethics; it is a persistent strand in architectural thought, and the one most responsible for the delusions found in the parallel universe where morals are attached to objects. One can list a whole series of pronouncements from famous architects and theorists that build a picture of the insistent connection between aesthetics and ethics.

In the last resort great art will be distinguished from that which is merely aesthetically clever by a nobility that, in the final analysis, is moral; or, rather, the nobility in life, which we call 'moral', is itself aesthetic.
—Geoffrey Scott[14]

A building must be beautiful when seen from the outside if it reflects all these qualities. The architect who achieves this task becomes a creator of an ethical and social character.
—Bruno Taut[15]

We are an ethically confused but still morally strong and simple-hearted people, a people that will yet instinctively bring forth strong and healthy art when ethics and a true philosophy take hold.
—Frank Lloyd Wright[16]

Architecture : A Dependent Profession

We are aspiring to a new ethic. We are looking for a new aesthetic.
—Le Corbusier[17]

In a long life I have become increasingly aware of the fact that the creation and love of beauty not only enrich man with a great measure of happiness but also bring forth ethical powers.
—Walter Gropius[18]

The mass production house, healthy (and morally so) and beautiful in the same way that the working tools and instruments which accompany our existence are beautiful.
—Le Corbusier[19]

To us clarity means the definite expression of the purpose of a building and the sincere expression of its structure. One can regard this sincerity as a sort of moral duty.
—Marcel Breuer[20]

I was left with a deep conviction of the moral rightness of the new architecture.
—James Stirling[21]

The common message arising out of these voices is simple: that ethics and aesthetics are mutually dependent; good aesthetics, in the form of beauty, leads directly to a good life, in the form of an ethical society, and equally that ethical society is the necessary context for the context of good aesthetics. This closed loop is very consoling for architects, because it places them—as arbiters of aesthetics—as central figures in the ethical process. The iteration of this loop was precisely the response of most architects to Fuksas's provocation at the Venice Biennale; not less aesthetics but actually more, on the understanding that as long as aesthetics can be equated with ethics, more aesthetics results in more ethics. Thus in writing about David Chipperfield, one of the architects chosen to represent Britain at the Biennale, Jonathan Keates argues that: "while not setting himself up as a moralist, Chipperfield appears continually to enforce the moral dimension surrounding an architect's work, whether in sharpening our apprehensions of beauty . . . or through ennobling activity by allowing it sufficient breadth in which to achieve, or at least to aspire to, suitable proportions of dignity and grace."[22] It is sanctimonious (and, it must be said, vapid) sentiments such as these that allow architects to enter into a comfort zone in which they believe that they are doing good by doing what they do best, namely making beautiful things.

One can equally easily make a list of quotes that equate rectitude in construction with an ethical stance. From Ruskin's moralist admonitions about the "deceptions" that architects have played in terms of presenting structure, surface, and materials in a "dishonest" manner, through Pevsner's "sham materials and sham technique are immoral,"[23] to Kenneth Frampton's discussions on tectonics, introduced in an article with the title "Rappel à l'ordre."[24] Frampton's title is telling because it implies, just like Ruskin and Pevsner, that tectonics (described as "the activity that raises construction to an art form")[25] is a means of creating a visual order, which in turn is associated with a social order. But this argument can be sustained only in a rarefied and reified atmosphere.

It is rarefied because the values of tectonic order are so internalized. Others do not share the obsessions of architects with shadow gaps, "crisp" detailing, and articulate joints. It is an elite language spoken only by the few and sometimes misunderstood, more often ignored, by the many. The same is true of the upper echelons of aesthetic discourse and its presumed ethics. In both the aesthetic and the tectonic the ethical association is so far removed from the world of social dynamics, where ethics has to be situated, that it becomes a phony ethics. In both cases there is also a worrying coercion going on: you (the world beyond) can have access to these ethical standards, but only if you join us in our parallel universe. Ethics are thus detached from their essential condition of being worked out through shared negotiation and instead are situated in a very controlled environment that positions the architect as arbiter. This detachment explains the very different perception of how architects see themselves, and how others see them. Within the limited value system of aesthetics and tectonics, architects can assure themselves that they are indeed doing good, whereas from outside these values are seen as either marginal or impositional, and the architect is cast as a removed (and possibly reviled) figure of authority. An impasse is reached in the phony ethics of architectural discourse: no architect sets out to behave badly or to inflict unhappiness on the world; the problem is that their priorities as to what constitutes the good are so misplaced.

The underlying reason for the impasse may lie in the second feature of associating visual order with social order, namely its reification. In materializing ideas as objects, the reification of ethics as aesthetic form results in the abstraction of ethics, and in this the creation of something that is not ethics. Ethics, to go back to my understanding of it, is the responsibility for the other; it is, at its core, to do with social relations. For the architect to engage in the ethical field therefore means to engage with how these (social)

Architecture : A Dependent Profession

relations are played out in (social) space. The phony ethics of aesthetics and tectonics freeze that dynamic and place all the attention on the contemplation of the object beautiful and refined, a state of removal for both viewer and viewed that can be reached only away from the flux of everyday space. In this, any connection to ethics as played out through social, spatial, relations is broken.

To put it simply: a brick has no morals. The careful placing of two bricks together, Mies's definition of the starting point of architecture, is not an ethical act; it is in fact, as Beatriz Colomina pithily notes, "just about the dumbest definition of architecture that I have heard."[26] There is no redemption in shadow gaps. People are not elevated to a higher plane of virtue through the appreciation of beauty. Blobs do not possess an "ethics of motion"; they are, at best, just blobs, at worst, part of the commodification of architecture and thus part of an ethically reduced world.

Arguing that aesthetics do not equate to ethics does not imply that one should throw away attention to the way that things look and are made. The accusation may come that in dismissing the ethical function of aesthetics and tectonics, I am dismissing them altogether; that in effect I am arguing for ugly, shabby, thrown-together buildings. However, this accusation stands up only in the court of law which legislates that "people who wash their shirts, paint their houses, clean the glass in their windows have a different ethic from those who cultivate dust and filth."[27] It is a court of law that places bad aesthetics in the dock and charges them with bad morality. This is a shabby and simplistic allegation; the really pernicious side of the aesthetics = ethics coin is the reverse, namely that ugly, dirty architecture is both symptom and cause of ugly, dirty morals. It is so dangerous because it associates architecture deterministically with society, as if the cleansing of one will lead to the cleansing of the other. The *bad architecture = bad morals = bad behavior* argument was exploited to greatest effect by the sociologist Alice Coleman in her 1985 book *Utopia on Trial*.[28] Her argument was that that symptoms of bad social behavior, expressed through counts of litter, graffiti, vandalism, and feces, were directly related to the design failings of modernist housing estates. The depressed areas of London, exposed to mass unemployment at the time of her study, provided ample evidence to support her arguments. It is not surprising, but may be sobering, that Coleman's ideas were taken up by the Thatcherite government of the time, because not only did they disassociate these symptoms of urban decay from societal causes (poverty, social division, collapse of the public infrastructure) but they then tied them in with the failures of the era of state housing, and so by association with the failure of socialism. The ideas effectively and conveniently made urban decay someone else's problem, and certainly not the government's. By calling the book *Utopia on Trial*, and so firmly identifying these failed utopias with architectural rather than political conditions, Coleman was able to lay the blame firmly at the feet of design, thus absolving society from the responsibility. The trouble is that architects had set themselves up for this attack. By promoting the *good aesthetics = good ethics* line, they made it all too easy for critics such as Coleman to make the opposite charge of *bad aesthetics = bad ethics* when things start to go wrong.

The *aesthetic = ethics* equation is flawed for the simple reason that far from society being dependent on architecture, the reverse is true. *Architecture Depends.* To argue that there is not a direct, causal link between aesthetics and ethics is not to argue for the dismissal of the role of aesthetics and tectonics, but to more realistically understand the role they play in the context of the much wider set of social dynamics to which architecture contributes. This effectively relieves the pressure on the design of the perfected object beautiful, and of its reception as the be-all and end-all of architectural culture. By all means craft the building, compose the elevation, worry over the detail, but at the same time see these as just some tasks in service to another. The key ethical responsibility of the architect lies not in the refinement of the object as static visual product, but as contributor to the creation of empowering spatial, and hence social, relationships in the name of others.

Social Scales

One way to reconsider the role of the architect is to look again at the use of scale in architectural design.[29] The scale drawing is the foundation of architectural production, insofar as it is the site of both technical and cultural evaluation; builders can build from it, surveyors cost from it, other architects form comparisons with it, and clients make a stab at understanding it. The classic architectural scale is 1:100. Throughout the world, architectural students are exhorted to draw up their schemes at 1:100. Plans, sections, and elevations. It is a scale that is detailed enough to give a semblance of reality, but not so detailed that one has to confront the actuality of spatial occupation in all its mess and uncertainty. In its removal and abstraction, 1:100 is a comfort zone in which architects can twiddle with compositional niceties and play aesthetic tricks. What if, instead of being a scale of abstracted metrics, 1:100 is first considered as a social scale? *1 to 100: one architect to one*

Architecture : A Dependent Profession

hundred citizens. What does one do when faced with one hundred different characters? In this light, 1:100 as a social scale assumes an ethical dimension, facing up to one's responsibility for others.

The same move from the metric to the social can be applied across other scales. 1:1, the scale at which real obsession with the aesthetics and technics of the architectural detail is exercised, becomes the scale of the personal, the intimate, the human. *1 to 1: more than just a detail.*

1:10,000, the scale at which cities are pushed around on the end of a felt-tip pen, lining up streets empty of life. One thinks one can understand the city at this scale, squinting down from on high through fingers of abstract patterns, and dreaming of ordering all that complexity with the sweep of a mouse or the streak of a pencil. But, as Michel de Certeau put it, to be "lifted to the summit is . . . to be lifted out of the city's grasp." 1:10,000 is a large scale, but is maybe best understood as an accumulation of the smaller scales, "one's body grasped by the streets . . . by the rumble of so many differences."[30] And so to see better, it is necessary to surrender the view and claim the experience, to come down from on high, both literally and metaphorically, and to listen to the voices coming up. *1 to 10,000: these are stories, not streets.*

In all these scales, and in ones in between and beyond, the social assumes priority: the metric scales of aesthetic and technical composition remain, but are in service to something beyond their normally self-referential realms. It is this idea of service to, and responsibility for, something beyond the autonomous walls of the profession that should be the irreducible core of an ethics of architecture.

Codes of Misconduct

One of the most commonly made mistakes is to confuse professional propriety with an ethical position, as if acting in accordance with the codes of professional conduct will ensure ethical behavior. It is a confusion encouraged by the ARB (Architects Registration Board), the registration body for architects in the UK. The introduction to their code of conduct states: "the code should be central to the life of an architect, not only as a *source of ethical guidance* but also as a commonsense indicator to the principles of good practice."[31] However, this high-minded intent is simply not delivered in the detail of the code. There are twelve standards that must be followed by anyone using the title architect. Just listing keywords from the heading of each standard is enough to show the ethical paucity of the ARB code. *Acting with integrity · Adequate professional, financial, and technical resources · Truthful and responsible promotion and advertising · Conscientious execution of work · Regard to users · Maintain professional and technical competence · Security of client's monies · Adequate indemnity cover · Manage own finances prudently · Promote the standards of the code · Organise work responsibly and with regard to clients · Deal with complaints promptly and appropriately.* I reckon my hairdresser could meet those standards. In fact, I reckon he exceeds them, having turned down the business of a certain well-known architect who had behaved badly just once too often. The point, as Tom Spector notes, is that these standards are aimed at "clarifying the architect's responsibilities to the client," and nothing more.[32] Even the one standard—*Regard to users*—that gives one hope that there is a responsibility beyond meeting the immediate demands of the client is significantly compromised in the detail. In the headline it states: "In carrying out or agreeing to carry out professional work, Architects should pay due regard to the interests of anyone who may reasonably be expected to use or enjoy the products of their own work." In an apparent admission that this goes too far away from serving the client, the headline is immediately qualified: "Whilst Architects' primary responsibility is to their clients, they should nevertheless have due regard to their wider responsibility to conserve and enhance the quality of the environment and its natural resources." "Nevertheless," a word that says so much about the ethical deficiency of the code. The client is seen as primary, and the responsibility for anything beyond framed as a secondary environmental, not social, issue. The user is suppressed.

It is consistent with ARB's statutory role that their codes are so focused on the service to the client. ARB's regulatory power concerns "the protection of the consumer," the consumer here being the person who procures the services of the architect, not the people who live out their lives within or around the buildings of the architect. The problem lies in the assertion that the codes provide "ethical guidance"; they do not, often quite the opposite. A client's demands, particularly in the private sector, are often short-term, opportunist, and potentially exploitative. It takes an enlightened client to understand the long-term benefits of user well-being or environmental responsibility, mainly because the market is geared toward the maximizing of development value in the short term. Serving the client through fulfilling the code of conduct is not only likely to be incommensurable with the wishes and needs of the future users, but may actually work against them. It may, in fact, be unethical on my terms.

Architecture : A Dependent Profession

The RIBA promises more, but delivers still less. Although the claim in the introduction to the recent RIBA Code of Professional Conduct is one of being more "outward looking than its predecessor," with a focus on "the consumer and society at large," the detail suggests something quite different. The first two sections on integrity and competence more or less repeat and expand on the ARB statements. The third section on "Relationships" states clearly in its headline: "Members should respect the beliefs and opinions of other people, recognise social diversity and treat everyone fairly. They should also have a proper concern and due regard for the effect that their work may have on its users and the local community." This sounds promising. However, in the guidance notes all this good intent is thrown away with a series of statements relating to other professionals: *Duties to other architects · Supplanting other architects · Verifying offers of work (in relation to other architects) · Taking over someone else's work · Acknowledging the contribution of others · Commenting on the work of others*. No mention, again, of the user, so that one is only left to assume that the real other in the headline "members shall respect the relevant rights and interests of other people" is the other architect. Once again the interests of the wider public come up against those of professional self-protection, and it appears the former are steamrollered by the latter. The tragedy is that the driver of the steamroller is wearing a hat called "professional ethics," and therefore believes that there is something acceptable going on beneath.

I could extend this argument: the American Institute of Architects (AIA) slams all the terms together in its "Code of Ethics and Professional Conduct," a document that also asserts the "obligations" to clients, architects, and colleagues over that of the obligation to the public, in relation to the latter of which the Code basically says: "stay within the law." The point, whether in the ARB, RIBA, or AIA Code, is the same: behaving according to professional "ethics" is not the same as behaving ethically. Indeed, they might actually be Codes of Misconduct.

The only way out of this apparent conundrum is clearly and insistently to separate the two spheres. There are ways of acting professionally and there are ways of acting ethically; the two operate according to different parameters. The former, professional, life is prescribed by the various codes. These codes are overseen not by a sense of duty to society at large, but by service to the client and employer. These have no aspirations; they are there merely to draw a line across minimum, extremely basic, standards.[33] As minimum standards they are reasonably easy to fulfill; the problem is that they are often taken as the complete description of an architect's duties. Meeting the demands of these codes is a necessary, but not sufficient, part of an architect's role. It is not sufficient because they do not address the wider responsibility of the architect.

A client may argue that they are not paying for an architect to address these broader ethics, and an architect may say that the whole idea of wider responsibilities smacks of idealism. But the point is that issues of social ethics are inherent in the design of any building, and just to ignore them does not mean that they will go away. Better then to face up to them, and in this deal with the tension between the values and priorities attached to the professional codes and those implicit in social ethics. The former are framed by a short-term transaction between architect and client, and thus tend to focus on short-term delivery in which architecture is reduced to a commodity; the latter operate beyond these fiscal exchanges and in the long term. The negotiation between the brute reality of immediate demands and the long-term vision of how to relieve the pressures arising out of short-term expediency is, as we shall see in the final chapter, at the heart of the architect's role. As Unger argues, the visions have to arise out of an engagement with the realities.[34] In this light, not to engage with the dirty reality of short-term demands is as much a form of escape as the positing of utopian proposals of a harmonious ethic.

In both engaging and envisioning, one inevitably enters the arena of conflicting demands. It is easy to be overwhelmed by the quantitative claims of cost, efficiency, and speed, and in this to neglect the social needs of the long-term future. Never has this tension been more acute than with the issue of the environment. Designing to address the cause and effect of climate change is necessarily a long-term issue. One cannot justify it within the limited value system of the market-driven production of the built environment, which is why much of the early "sustainable" design played no more than lip service to the word *sustainability* through expedient technological fixes. As many have noted, to frame sustainability in technological terms is only to try to solve the problem with exactly the same tools that created it, setting up a self-defeating circle.[35] If, however, the environmental crisis is seen in sociological rather than technical terms, then it immediately becomes an ethical issue, insofar as a concern for others is directly understood as a concern for the future well-being of others and how they will be able, and enabled, to live their lives in an environmentally degraded world. As an ethical issue, the architectural approach to sustainability becomes much more than short-term technical fixes: it has to take on the wider interactions between nature and society, humans and nonhumans.

The architect has the opportunity and means to deal with the tensions between short-term demands and long-term visions, in environmental issues and many others, more than anyone involved in the process of construction. The reason is that (social) space escapes the reduction to the rule of quantity alone. Because of the complexity of architectural production, there is no one right and proper solution that can be systematically evaluated, only a range of options that are open to multiple interpretations. It is exactly this openness and inexactitude that the architect should seize and use as an opportunity to enable and empower others. It is here that architecture's very dependency becomes the means of finding its independency, paradoxical though that might sound. In the external force field nothing is fully controllable or capable of exact replication. One can thus tell the client, perfectly truthfully and with no duplicity, a set of good reasons why things should be like that and at the same time get on and deliver the real reason.

Equally, there is no one way to behave professionally. There are always opportunities in spatial design that exceed the basic demands summarized in the professional codes; indeed, it is precisely the limited nature of these codes that allows and encourages one to go beyond them while at the same time satisfying them. The important thing is for the architect to be alert to these other potentials, always in the service of the other. This does not mean that one purposely compromises the demands of the client, but is a recognition that there is no one absolutely right way of meeting those demands in the name of short-term efficiency, and therefore there is always the potential to wring the most phenomenal, environmental, and social advantage out of the various spatial alternatives. Architects have at their disposal a whole range of elements that affect the social occupation and perception of space: the placing of doors and windows, the proportion of rooms, the width of circulation, the admittance of light, the material characteristics, and so on. Equally importantly, the creative briefing process allows different social relations to emerge, both in terms of the way that uses are arranged and also in the ability to adapt these over time. In the phony ethics of aesthetics and tectonics, all these elements are exploited in the name of visual or constructional display; in the social ethic the elements and relations are deployed in the name of the other through the formation of empowering spatial contexts.

The Ethics of Responsibility

The question remains: on what basis should these decisions be made? The answer has to come from an understanding of "the other." In the traditional versions of ethics, the divergent voices of the other are often subsumed under a uniform moral code. First, in the Aristotelian version, one gets communitarian philosophers such as Alasdair Macintyre proposing local communities of individuals all "situated" in a common good. Macintyre talks of the "new dark ages which are already upon us . . . the barbarians are not waiting beyond the frontiers; they have already been governing us for quite some time,"[36] and in reaction proposes a revival of Aristotelian virtue. The problem with this solution, as many critics have observed, is that for these arguments to succeed one has to assume a closed and static system in which communal norms become stable and coherent.[37] However, as Barbara Herrnstein Smith argues, "no community can be immured from interactions with a changing environment, nor can the heterogeneity of its members be altogether eradicated and their potential conflicts altogether prevented. Where difference continuously emerges it must be either continuously negotiated or continuously suppressed, the latter always at somebody's cost and often enough, it appears in the long run, at considerable communal cost."[38] This means that any ethics has to take into account this diversity, and negotiate within it.

Macintyre's version of ethics is at heart one of a revival of a state of prelapsarian virtue; pre, that is, the lapse into the amorality of the modern world. It is a version that resonates with those who call for the return to some form of primordial, originary ethics.[39] John Caputo, in his critique of originary ethics, knocks both Heidegger and Macintyre into the same hat: "although they are otherwise unlikely bedfellows, [they] agree in all the essentials: the great beginning in the Greeks, the terrible decline in modernity, the hope in a new beginning; nostalgia, anti-modernism. They both look to antiquity for light and a time of original solidarity."[40] It is a similar version of originary ethics that is implied, but not explicitly demarcated, in the most influential recent work on architectural ethics, Karsten Harries's *The Ethical Function of Architecture*. The book is a cogent argument for the reestablishment of an architecture that takes into account that human dimension of dwelling which has been suppressed by the forces of modernity. But one looks hard for a precise definition of what is meant by ethics beyond "its task to help articulate a common ethos." The establishment of an ethical function is wrapped up in a critique of the dangers of modernism, the distractions

Architecture : A Dependent Profession

of postmodernity, the false hope of aesthetics, and the autonomous back-waters of architectural language. The ethics are then assumed to arise out of an attention to the authentic dimensions of dwelling. When, toward the end of the book, Harries finally states clearly what the ethical function of architecture is, the message is very telling in its call to something beyond: "Architecture has an ethical function in that it calls us out of the everyday, recalls us to the values presiding over our lives as members of a society, it beckons us toward a better life, a bit closer to the ideal."[41] The implications are that an ethical life can be found only in a state of removal from the everyday, with "dreams of another and better world."[42]

The problem with this kind of originary ethics is that it finds the ethical solution outside of the realities of the everyday world rather than within them, turning its back on Macintyre's barbarians rather than engaging with them. Its retreat provides hope of a new dawn, but one that allows the "forces of oppression [to] ravage the land" that is left behind.[43] The Achilles heel both of this form of originary ethics and of the Enlightenment notion of universal morals is that they believe a version of the common good can be found. The flux of the contemporary world presents a disturbing vision of irreconcilable difference, and this, by these two accounts, must be amoral inasmuch as no shared vision can be found. The reaction on the one hand is to walk away from the mess, on the other to order it through the imposition of "objective" moral systems. Zygmunt Bauman's solution to the apparent problem of finding an ethical stance in what might appear an irreconcilable condition is one of his most brilliant intellectual maneuvers. He suggests that "ethical choice and moral responsibility assume under the postmodern condition a totally new and long forgotten significance; an importance of which modernity tried hard, and with considerable success, to divest them, moving as it did toward replacement of ethical discourse with the discourse of the objective, translocal and impersonal truth."[44] Modernity divested the individual of the responsibility to make ethical decisions, passing that task to the higher authority of reason and totalizing moral systems. In the post-modern condition, however, these moral truths are dispersed in the storm of forces and differences, which means that "the ethical paradox of the post-modern condition is that it restores to agents the fullness of moral choice and responsibility while simultaneously depriving them of the comfort of the universal guidance that modern self-confidence once promised."[45] The brilliance of Bauman's move lies in his insistence that postmodern condi-tions do not lead to a form of moral relativism in which anything goes, nor should we think that the extraordinary openness of the postmodern field absolves us from the need for an ethical stance.[46] Instead, in the face of uncertainty, the individual is thrown back to their irreducible ethical core and is asked to make choices; not certain choices or perfect choices, but the best possible choices in the name of others. "If in doubt consult your conscience," writes Bauman at the end of his *Postmodern Ethics;* "moral responsibility is unconditional and infinite, and it manifests itself in the constant anguish of not manifesting itself enough."[47]

Bauman's approach effectively gives us what we need: a new ethics for a new era. It is not reliant on the restitution of previous models, nor does it have any pretensions to foundations or absolute correctness. Instead, it works from *within* each situation rather than imposing an abstract set of moral codes from without. This ethics thus has to work with the contingencies of each context and not attempt to stifle them. Contingency here, far from being a threat to the establishment of firm rules, becomes the necessary context for the development of an ethical position. John Caputo's version, which he calls the "ethics of dissemination," "offers not overall strategies, not total schemes or masterplans, but only local strategies for local action."[48] In all this particularity, worked out in response to the concrete conditions of the specific context, the resultant ethical sense is inevitably partial—both incomplete and on the side of the other. In this it does not meet the standards of providing for the common good by which previous ethics have measured themselves. But these standards have been found wanting in the face of uncertainty, and so if the new ethics is imperfect according to the values of the previous models, then it wears that badge with pride. This is because an imperfect ethical solution is a realistic recognition that the diverse points of view in any situation can be resolved only in as best a manner as possible and not as perfected a manner as possible. Imperfect ethics is not a contradiction in terms but an aspiration, because right at the heart of that term is a responsibility for the other and the appreciation of the differences of the other. As Hans Jonas puts it, "the starry-eyed ethics of perfectibility has to give way to the sterner one of responsibility."[49]

It may feel lonely for the architect out there, exposed to conflicting demands, with a responsibility for others but no moral codes or rules of reason to fall back on. But the new ethics relieves the pressure of the creation of generalized perfection; it works modestly and realistically, and because it works with and through others, loneliness is dispersed. For the feminist theorist Carol Gilligan, an ethics of responsibility emerges "from the experience of connectedness, compassion and sensitivity to context,"[50] words that are the antithesis to the social indifference and autonomy of the phony ethics of aesthetics and tectonics. They are words that will grate with the macho construction of the architect as legislator, but in their challenge to the distant voice of authority to come down and listen carefully to the stories of others,[51] they begin to sketch a figure of the architect as an agent of hope, an idea that will be developed in the final chapter. Roberto Mangabeira Unger, our guide to that chapter, says it far better than I ever could: "the architect at his best must make forms enabling people as individuals and as groups to express themselves by changing their situations. In this manner he becomes like the lover for whom the fulfilment of the beloved's life plan is part of his own life project. He lives out his transformative vocation by assisting someone else's. Then, we can forgive him his signature on his buildings. We can forgive him because he makes pieces of stone serve hearts of flesh."[52]

11   Hope against Hope

Gymnasts in the Prison Yard

In the last chapter of *Architecture and Utopia,* Manfredo Tafuri writes of the impossible position of the architect: caught within the structures of capitalism, the architect has lost any means of resistance. Tafuri's most devastating argument is that architecture has deluded itself into believing that the production of form alone can intervene productively in the social world, and that this delusion has hidden the real state of affairs in which fresh form has been appropriated by the very forces of capital that it presumes to escape. The final sentence of the book talks of "impotent and ineffectual myths, which so often serve as illusions that permit the survival of anachronistic 'hopes in design.'"[1] Tafuri's trenchant argument—he talks of being "'uselessly painful' because it is useless to struggle for escape when completely enclosed and confined without an exit,"[2]—leaves no apparent way out of the conundrum, and so led his critics to talk of the death of architecture. Answering this charge, Tafuri sees "architecture obliged to return to *pure architecture,* to form without utopia; in the best cases to sublime uselessness."[3] It is too easy to take these words at face value, to escape from the pressures and just fiddle with form while the world burns. But that sentence is surely not a prescription but a provocation, with all its caustic sarcasm meant to shake the profession out of its slumber. In another book Tafuri talks of "how ineffectual are the brilliant gymnastics carried out in the yard of the model prison, in which architects are left free to move about on temporary reprieve."[4] It is a prison yard of architecture's own making, doubtless well-designed but all the more ensnaring in its distracting beauty. This final chapter attempts to escape Tafuri's trap, hoping against those anachronistic "hopes of design," in order that architecture's gymnasts are not damned to permanent imprisonment.

The Flight to Utopia

How could architects ever propose utopia? U-topia. Not-place. It is a contradiction in architectural terms. Architecture needs place if it is to be real; anything else is pure fantasy. Despite this, the flight to some form of utopia has a powerful attraction. "In the midst of the present—messy, fetid, rambling and chaotic, and thus deserving of the death sentence," writes Bauman, "utopian thought was a bridgehead of future orderly perfection and perfect order."[5] Hope is here founded in new futures, untainted by the scars of history and unfettered by uncertainty. "Let's drive away the agony of the unknown," shouts Le Corbusier, again exposing his fear of the uncontrollable, "let's reconstruct everything: the roads, the ports, the cities, the institutions."[6] Here Le Corbusier conflates the spatial (cities) with the social (institutions), but as an architect the spatial aspects come first, hoping to set the ground for social transformation. The geographer David Harvey's analysis of utopia in his book *Spaces of Hope* is acute in identifying two prevalent forms. First the utopias of process, those which rethink the social structures of the world, "usually expressed in temporal terms . . . they are literally bound to no place whatsoever."[7] Second the utopias of spatial form, which expel time in their pursuit of idealized formal solutions. Harvey notes that both approaches are flawed. Utopianism of process "inevitably gets upset by its manner of spatialization," while utopias of spatial form "get perverted from their noble objectives by having to compromise with the social processes they are meant to control."[8]

In denying on the one hand space, and on the other time, these two forms of utopia inevitably fail. Harvey's solution is to propose an "explicitly spatiotemporal" utopianism, or what he calls dialectical utopianism.[9] In proposing this utopianism Harvey is very aware of the dangers of flight and fantasy, and sees the challenge as one of working out a spatial and social language that is "materially grounded in social and ecological conditions but which nevertheless emphasizes possibilities and alternatives for human action through the will to create."[10] Harvey's spaces of hope thus arise out of a transformation of what is given, rather than as inventions torn from spatial and temporal contexts. The figure that David Harvey uses in fleshing out his argument around spaces of hope is that of the architect; not, he stresses, the architect as a professional person but the architect as a figure who "struggles to open spaces for new possibilities."[11] It is the architect, effectively, who can still maintain a hope against hope, turning away from flights to utopia and toward a critical engagement with the world as found.

Formative Contexts

For the given to be seen as a place of potential, one has to rid it of the negative connotations of mess and chaos. The only way to do this is by understanding the contingency of the given, in its very uncertainty and openness toward establishing something else, as an opportunity and not a threat: to see that freedom is to be found in the recognition of contingency and not outside of it. Of all the people who have made sense out of this apparent riddle—of finding hope within the conflictual ground of reality—the writing of Roberto Mangabeira Unger stands out. *False Necessity,* the title of the centerpiece of his magnum opus *Politics,* is clear in setting an intent of working against the idea that there are necessary and inevitable patterns in the development of society. In relation to how progress might be made, Unger takes issue with two positions. The first is that which takes existing conditions and moves the bits around without essentially transforming them, a paralyzing condition in which "people treat a plan as realistic when it approximates to what already exists." He calls this latter "reformist tinkering."[12] The second is that of the utopist: he describes the utopian proposal as "little more than the inverted image of current reality,"[13] and that mirroring leaves reality unscathed.

It may be argued that architecture takes up each of these positions. On the one hand the uncritical perpetuation of social conditions that constitutes a lot of architectural production, all the stuff that falls below the radar of the academy or the media, but equally all the stuff that most profoundly affects the environmental quality of the world and the lives of its citizens. On the other hand the flight to the iconic buildings of prize ceremonies and the media that both sustains architectural culture and masks the reality of the production of the dross. However, the argument is much more than one of form and aesthetics; Unger's thesis is based on the premise that "everything is society is politics," and so to understand its implications for architecture, we have to understand architectural production in its political context.

Unger's central theme in *False Necessity* is that of formative contexts, the structures and frameworks of social life. This is a term that has negative traits, insofar as the formative contexts "circumscribe our routine practical or discursive activities and conflicts . . . and resist their destabilising effects."[14] It is only through an awareness and understanding of these restrictive features of formative contexts that one can break through them transformatively. Unger's essential contribution is to see that in every formative context there is the potential for change; these contexts might be shaped by existing frameworks of social and economic life, "but they are not shaped completely."[15] He argues that even the most entrenched context has the potential for change, or rather, that the most entrenched context demands change.[16]

The key agent in this transformation is that of imagination, because it is only through the exercise of imaginative vision that one can see the potential for change in what otherwise might appear restrictive. Social or architectural reality, if viewed as a set of determinate rules and procedures, tends to shut down the imagination, because the apparent certainty leaves no gaps for vision to open up. However, the contingent, with its multiple but uncertain potentials, allows the imagination room to project new futures. Here it is worth quoting Unger at some length:

The visionary imagination of our age has been both liberated and disoriented. It has been liberated by its discovery that social worlds are contingent in a more radical sense than people had supposed; liberated to disengage the ideas of community and objectivity from any fixed structure of dependence and dominion or even from the determinate shape of social life. It has also, however, been disoriented by a demoralising oscillation between a trumped-up sanctification of existing society and would-be utopian flight that finds in the land of its fantasies the inverted image of the circumstance it had wanted to escape.[17]

This imagination, therefore, is not the imagination of the detached dreamer; it grows out of the real, fueled by the very uncertainty that the rationalists and utopists found so threatening. It is an imaginative vision that both projects new futures and also embraces their imperfections.

Although Unger's work is generally concerned with formative contexts found in the constitution of governments, in economic organizations, and in local politics, it is possible to transfer the ideas to the architectural field without, I trust, demeaning the theory. Indeed, Unger himself hints at this transfer in his notion of the transformative vocation and his later association of this with the architect.[18] To view the setting of an architectural project as a formative context is to see the architect playing out the role of the imaginative interpreter, and because these contexts are by their very nature social,

Architecture : A Dependent Profession

that role is played out with and for others. The action of the architect is here not about the implementation of generic solutions to particular problems. It is not about the architect as the detached polisher of form and technique, but as the person who gathers the conflicting voices of a given situation and makes the best possible social and spatial sense of them. Hope is not discovered in the clouds of ideals that are blown away by the slightest breeze; hope is founded in the interstices of the given, and since it has a tough start in life, this hope is a survivor. Where Tafuri identifies the prison and then throws the keys away, constructing a seamless barrier of capital contra architecture that leaves the architect helpless, Unger allows us to see opportunities in the smallest gap. Even the seemingly most compromised and fixed condition offers some prospect of change. Unger's model is not about wholesale revolution from on high, but is one of engaging with existing structures and "establishing small-scale, fragmentary versions of the future."[19] Such hope has to be established first in the reconfiguration of the social, not in the false hopes of form and technique. If one accepts that social relations are embedded in spatial relations, then the architect has an important role to play in this reconfiguration, as long as the tenets of the transformative vocation are followed: work out from the given context, be both practical *and* imaginative, critical *and* visionary. In every case there is a formative context that can be transformed, and in every case there is a productive tension between realism and imagination, because "we must be realists in order to become visionaries and we need an understanding of social life to criticize and enlarge our view of social reality and social possibility."[20]

Finally, then, we can see how architecture's dependency is not just a truism but a positive condition. Remember Hegel's definition of contingency—the "unity of actuality and possibility"[21]—in which the openness of that possibility is too much for the philosopher of reason to tolerate, and so has to be suppressed. But what if, not in the name of irrationality but in the name of seizing the moment, we see the unity of actuality and possibility as an opportunity to celebrate? In the actual there is always the possible. It is too easy to think that the external forces are so overwhelming that there is no room for maneuver. But in casting a critical eye over those forces and then projecting an ethical imagination against them, gaps open up.[22] In any architectural situation there are freedoms and opportunities to be found, not in terms of wholesale changes but in terms of "fragmentary versions of the future." Perhaps the architectural project, if accepted in all its dependency, is the paradigm of the formative context, because in each project there is the chance for the construction of a small chunk of (social) spatial hope. And so architecture, finally, may show others how to struggle for, and find, their independence through depending.

Angels with Dirty Faces

I spoke earlier of the contingent researcher purposely crossing disciplinary boundaries, welcoming each new book with a sense of curiosity, finding their way through the networks guided by intent, and taking competing fragments and filtering them with that intent. The contingent researcher—and now, we see, the dependent and contingent architect—has to be light enough on his or her feet, and modest enough, to allow that intent to be shaped by other events and ideas, but at the same time purposeful enough not to be overwhelmed by them. For the contingent architect the book is replaced by the project as the site of curiosity, and the intent is guided by the aspirations to reform space in the name of others. It is a model for architects as Angels with Dirty Faces. The inspiration here is Wim Wenders's film *Wings of Desire*. The secular angels, in black and white, first look down observing and commentating but removed from the world. They then sweep down, colored and embodied, discursive and slightly grubby as they drink cheap coffee from street stalls. It is movement from on high to low and back again that is necessary for architectural angels if one is not going to get overwhelmed by the brute realities of the everyday world. This is why the philosopher Merleau-Ponty says that "one must be able to withdraw and gain distance in order to become fully engaged."[23] One needs to draw back and gain distance in order to have the space to speculate, but one needs to come back down in order that those speculations are not false dawns. Each informs the other in a symbiotic relationship; vision lifts and transforms the given, but the given feeds the vision with nuggets of reality, saving it from irrelevance, stopping it from floating free into implausibly pure zones.

One of Wenders's angels notes wearily:

I've stood outside long enough. I've been absent long enough. Let me enter the history of the world. I get tired of my spiritual existence . . . of forever hovering above. I wish I could grow a weight which would bind me to the earth. To guess for once instead of always knowing. To have a fever. To blacken my fingers reading the papers.

Maybe, just maybe, that angel then raises his stained fingers and absent-mindedly rubs his cheek. Angels with Dirty Faces. *Angels,* "able to pass through space, time and walls,"²⁴ *with dirty faces,* and then able to bring them all together. *Angels,* androgynous imaginers of possibility, *with dirty faces,* which is always engaged. *Angels,* the original messengers, *with dirty faces,* human and slightly flawed. Architects modestly bound to the earth but with the vision, environmental sense, and ethical imagination to project new (social) spatial futures on behalf of others.

I am at the stage in writing this book when the basic argument is in place but, in the paranoid manner of academics everywhere, I am worried about the loose intellectual ends that critics might delight in unraveling. I am there- fore, in the self-centered manner of academics everywhere, pleading with my publisher for a later deadline in order to give me time to tie up those ends. I realize that this is an impossible task and one that is incompatible with the tenor of the book, but it is still more important to me than getting into the Spring catalog. But I know my time is up when the email comes from Roger Conover, my editor at the MIT Press. I do not even have to read the message; the subject line is enough. It is to do with the placing of the comma, which is somehow both threatening and encouraging:

"final deadline, Jeremy Till"

And now that deadline is here, so that is it. Not an end, but a point on the way. My argument could never be complete anyway, because that would pre- sume to all the certainty and universality that this book has resisted. Archi- tecture, in all its dependency, has to remain open. I kind of hate this deadline because there is so much more to say. But then I actually need this deadline because by not saying more I retain some of that openness for myself and, I hope, for you.

Acknowledgments

I often start books by reading the acknowledgment pages. No book is written in a vacuum, and so it is interesting to see what air the author has breathed. In my case the route to this, my first sole-authored book, has been supported and stimulated by too many people to list, so I apologize to those not mentioned.

My intellectual journey has been forged in three academic settings. I was lucky to start teaching, and in effect learning, at Kingston Polytechnic in the 1980s, at which time the School of Architecture was an extraordinary training ground for academics. Three people were particularly influential during that time. Tim Bell first introduced me to teaching and then gave me space to develop. He was in many ways my mentor. Robin (Bob) Evans often came to reviews at Kingston and never failed to astound with his ability to see things from the side and to say critical things without making them hurt. Most of all, Kath Shonfield had a deep influence on her many friends and students; her combination of wit, wisdom, and passion has been an enduring lesson for me. That Tim, Bob, and Kath are no longer with us is a terrible tragedy. I miss them all. They represent a type of original and brave thinking, maybe peculiarly British, that is all too rare.

In the 1990s I was at the Bartlett, University College London in the early, and heady, days of Peter Cook and Christine Hawley's tenure, when Peter rightly cajoled us all to think very quickly. While I may have moved away from some of the pedagogical tenets, I am indebted to the intellectual milieu and energy of that period, in particular stimulated for me by Adrian Forty, Jonathan Hill, Kevin Rhowbotham, Neil Spiller, and Phil Tabor. I showed Adrian the very first draft of this book, and he said quietly: "Just be yourself, Jeremy." I took his advice and started again, for better or worse being more myself. I learned most of all in that period from my Bartlett teaching partner, Ro Spankie, in particular from her endless curiosity and brilliant ability to see something original in almost anything.

In the 2000s I moved to the University of Sheffield, where I found an intellectual home in the School of Architecture. To pick out only some of my colleagues is not quite right, because there is a genuine collective will in shaping a new educational agenda. However, I must mention some who in particular have helped with this book. Peter Blundell Jones laid an intellectual and political ground at Sheffield that I was more than happy to walk on. Prue Chiles pioneered many of the pedagogic initiatives that are now driving the School. Judith Jackson, the departmental administrator and my right hand, has taken the brunt of my absences to complete research with calmness and grace beyond the call of duty. Bryan Lawson was exceptionally generous in being there when I needed him, and not there when I didn't, at the time that I took over from him as Head of School. Ruth Morrow ran a seminal first-year program whose lasting influence is still felt. Doina Petrescu has provided a model of inventive and politicized architectural thought and action. Roger Plank, who took over from me as Head of School, has been incredibly supportive in providing me time for research. Tatjana Schneider has been selfless in driving our two joint research projects while I was preoccupied with first the 2006 Venice Architecture Biennale and then this book.

It is commonplace to thank one's students, but for architectural teachers this gratitude is of real importance. Often, maybe too often, tutors' ideas are played out through students' design work, in that they are revealed more quickly and more visibly than in any other discipline. It is easy to abuse this power and so live vicariously through other people's efforts; I apologize to any of my past students who feel that I have done so. I hope that I developed ideas with rather than through students, and in this I am grateful to them all for their patience and perseverance in grappling with sometimes unformed concepts.

I am indebted to Roger Conover at the MIT Press for having faith in me in the first instance and then supporting me through the whole process, to Gillian Beaumont for her subtle copyediting which often saved me from myself, and to Sharon Deacon Warne for her calm design. It is a wonderful privilege to have a publisher who still cares so intensely about books.

At a personal level Barry, Antonia, Nick, Lucy, and Emily Till have supported me more than they know with that mixture of love and blind faith which only families can provide. Finally, and most importantly of all, there is Sarah Wigglesworth. Her intellectual and personal presence is everywhere in the book, but more than this she never stopped believing in me even, especially, when I stopped myself. A book dedication is a small recompense for all this, but I give it with indescribable love.

Notes

1 Deluded Detachment

1. Tatjana Schneider, *This Building Should Have Some Sort of Distinctive Shape . . . : The Story of the Arts Tower in Sheffield* (Sheffield: PAR, 2007). This book, with its meticulous record of Committee meetings, is one of the best descriptions of architecture's dependency that I know. Also good is Peter Murray's warts-and-all version of the building of the Sydney Opera House, which is so upsetting of the idealized myth of Utzon's architectural genius that it is not sold in the Opera House bookshop. Peter Murray, *The Saga of Sydney Opera House: The Dramatic Story of the Design and Construction of the Icon of Modern Australia* (London: Spon Press, 2004).

2. Michel de Certeau, *The Practice of Everyday Life* (Berkeley: University of California Press, 1984), p. 92.

3. Reyner Banham, "A Black Box: The Secret Profession of Architecture," in Banham, *A Critic Writes,* ed. Mary Banham (Berkeley: University of California Press, 1996), p. 295.

4. Ibid., p. 297.

5. See Thomas A. Dutton, *Voices in Architectural Education: Cultural Politics and Pedagogy* (New York: Bergin and Garvey, 1991), p. 94. Dutton talks of the asymmetry of power apparent in the crit. See also Karen Anthony, *Design Juries on Trial* (New York: Van Nostrand Reinhold, 1991); Charles Doidge, Rachel Sara, and Rosie Parnell, *The Crit* (Oxford: Architectural Press, 2000).

6. Garry Stevens, *The Favored Circle: The Social Foundations of Architectural Distinction* (Cambridge, Mass.: MIT Press, 1998), p. 200.

7. Jacques Lucan, ed., *A Matter of Art: Contemporary Architecture in Switzerland* (Basel: Birkhäuser, 2001), p. 44.

8. Le Corbusier, *My Work,* trans. James Palmer (London: Architectural Press, 1960), p. 197.

9. As quoted in Richard Chafee, "The Teaching of Architecture at the École des Beaux-Arts," in *The Architecture of the École des Beaux-Arts,* ed. Arthur Drexler (London: Secker and Warburg, 1977), p. 69.

10. Ibid., p. 92.

11. Andrés Duany, "The Beaux Arts Model," in *Windsor Forum on Design Education: Toward an Ideal Curriculum to Reform Architectural Education,* ed. Dhiru Thadani (Miami: New Urban Press, 2004), p. 133.

12. Ibid., p. 137.

13. Stevens, *The Favored Circle,* p. 199.

14. Le Corbusier, *When the Cathedrals Were White: A Journey to the Country of Timid People,* trans. Francis Hyslop (London: Routledge, 1947; French edition 1937), p. 119. Emphasis in the original.

15. Ibid., p. 114.

16. Ibid., p. 118. Emphasis in the original.

17. Le Corbusier, *Precisions on the Present State of Architecture and City Planning,* trans. Edith Schreiber Aujame (Cambridge, Mass.: MIT Press, 1991), p. 32.

18. Le Corbusier, *When the Cathedrals Were White,* p. 116.

19. Ibid., p. 117.

20. Paulo Freire, *Pedagogy of the Oppressed,* trans. Myra Ramos (London: Penguin, 1996), p. 53.

21. Ibid., p. 52.

22. The charette is an exercise in which students are asked to complete a given task in a very limited time; the term charette comes, unsurprisingly, from the École des Beaux-Arts, where it referred to the cart that was used to transport the students' work to the final hand-in after a design exercise.

23. Roemer van Toorn, "Fresh Conservatism: Landscapes of Normality" (1997 [cited June 20, 2005]); available from <http://www.xs4all.nl/%7ervtoorn/fresh.html>.

24. Thus for Manfredo Tafuri, "the avant-garde entrenches itself all over again in nostalgia." Manfredo Tafuri, *The Sphere and the Labyrinth: Avant-Gardes and Architecture from Piranesi to the 1970s* (Cambridge, Mass.: MIT Press, 1987), p. 267.

25. The fashion was started at Harvard by Rem Koolhaas who, with his students, "copyrighted" certain terms (City Of Exacerbated Difference©, Scape©, Infrared©, etc.), and has been taken up by, among others, the Design Research Laboratory at the Architectural Association. For the former, see Rem Koolhaas, *Mutations: Rem Koolhaas, Harvard Project on the City et al.* (Barcelona: ACTAR, 2000). For the

latter, Brett Steele, "BrandSpace ™: Design ®esearch and Product Placement," *Archis* 1 (2001).

26. The point is well made by the American artist Robert Smithson, who compares the fruitless quest of the avant-garde to overtake the values of the bourgeois art world to Zeno's paradox of Achilles' race with the tortoise. Achilles will never overtake the tortoise because whenever he covers half the distance another half still remains to be covered, and no matter how small the interval becomes, it will never be completely closed. The point, as Gary Shapiro notes, is that both avant-garde and bourgeois art are framed by the same ideology, namely the production of form and taste. Gary Shapiro, *Earthwards: Robert Smithson and Art after Babel* (Berkeley: University of California Press, 1995), p. 36.

27. Magali Sarfatti Larson, "In the Matter of Experts and Professionals, or How Impossible It Is to Leave Nothing Unsaid," in *The Formation of Professions,* ed. Rolf Torstendahl and Michael Burrage (London: Sage, 1990), p. 31.

28. M. A. Wilson, "The Socialization of Architectural Preference," *Journal of Environmental Psychology* 16 (1996).

29. As quoted in Denis Hollier, *Against Architecture: The Writings of Georges Bataille,* trans. Betsy Wing (Cambridge, Mass.: MIT Press, 1989), pp. 46–47. In another section Bataille repeats the argument: "Thus great monuments rise up like levees, opposing the logic of majesty and authority to any confusion." Ibid., p. xi.

30. More people like Paul Oliver and his magisterial *Encyclopaedia of Vernacular Architecture,* which has more lessons in it than any other architecture book I know.

31. Roger Connah, *How Architecture Got Its Hump* (Cambridge, Mass.: MIT Press, 2001), p. 166.

32. As quoted in Zygmunt Bauman, *Modernity and Ambivalence* (Cambridge: Polity Press, 1991), p. 82.

33. As Miles Glendinning and Stefan Muthesius note, the combination of land control, costs, and required densities led to "production-dominated" housing in which designers were seen as little more than technical facilitators. See Miles Glendinning and Stefan Muthesius, *Tower Block: Modern Public Housing in England, Scotland, Wales, and Northern Ireland* (New Haven: Yale University Press, 1993), esp. chapters 8, 20, and 22 (the last is entitled "Quantity or 'Quality': Defeat of the Designers").

34. Ignasi de Solà-Morales, *Differences: Topographies of Contemporary Architecture,* trans. Graham Thompson (Cambridge, Mass.: MIT Press, 1997), p. 77.

35. Arthur Drexler, Colin Rowe, and Kenneth Frampton, eds., *Five Architects* (New York: Oxford University Press, 1975), p. 1. Emphasis in the original. In the same catalogue Colin Rowe writes: "It is an argument largely about the physique of building and only indirectly about its morale" (p. 7). Kenneth Frampton's analysis of

the projects is eventually purely formal—formalism being an identifying trait of autonomous architecture.

36. K. Michael Hays, "The Oppositions of Autonomy and History," in *Oppositions Reader*, ed. K. Michael Hays (New York: Princeton Architectural Press, 1998), p. ix. Hays's essay is an extremely good introduction to issues of autonomy in architecture. The complete Agrest quote reads: "Design, considered as both a practice and a product, is in effect a closed system—not only in relation to culture as a whole, but also in relation to other other cultural systems" (*Oppositions Reader*, p. 333).

37. Hays, "The Oppositions of Autonomy and History," p. xii.

38. Ibid., p. xiii.

39. Philip Johnson and Mark Wigley, *Deconstructivist Architecture* (Boston: Little, Brown, 1988), p. 11.

40. Ibid., p. 18.

41. See Peter Eisenman, *Eisenman Inside Out: Selected Writings 1963–1988* (New Haven: Yale University Press, 2004).

42. Drexler, Rowe, and Frampton, eds., *Five Architects*, p. 27. Eisenman was by no means alone in this elision of analysis and production. One can also see it in many other cultural spheres: for example in the 1970s, the work of the image-text photographers such as Victor Burgin and the filmmakers Laura Mulvey and Peter Wollin.

43. Aldo Rossi writes of his book *The Architecture of the City:* "This book is an architectural project." Aldo Rossi, *The Architecture of the City*, trans. Diane Ghirardo and Joan Ockman (Cambridge, Mass.: MIT Press, 1982), p. 179.

44. For an analysis of the difference between the modes of production encountered in drawing, building, and text, see Andrea Kahn, ed., *Drawing, Building, Text* (New York: Princeton Architectural Press, 1991), p. 6.

45. Suzanne Frank, *Peter Eisenman's House VI: The Client's Response* (New York: Whitney Library of Design, 1994), p. 23. For those worried about the meaning of the terms fulcrum and datum, worry not. I haven't a clue either.

46. Ibid., p. 60.

47. Rossi, *The Architecture of the City*, p. 7. As Peter Eisenman notes in his introduction: "The architecture of the book's title is now defined in two ways: as the ultimate and verifiable data within the real city, and as an autonomous structure" (p. 4).

48. Solà-Morales, *Differences*, p. 77.

49. Aldo Rossi, *A Scientific Autobiography*, trans. Lawrence Venuti (Cambridge, Mass.: MIT Press, 1981), p. 55.

50. Rossi defends himself against the charge of scenography in his work by explaining that other great architects have also used this technique: "A number of critics have stated that my works resemble stage designs, and I have responded that they do have this resemblance just like the architecture of Palladio, Shinkel, Borromini—just like all architecture." (Ibid., p. 74.) My point is that this just further entrenches his self-referentiality.

51. Vincent Scully, "Afterword," in ibid., p. 114.

2   A Semblance of Order

1. Arata Isozaki, introduction to Kojin Karatani, *Architecture as Metaphor: Language, Number, Money,* trans. Sabu Kohso (Cambridge, Mass.: MIT Press, 1995), p. ix.

2. "It is not surprising that over the years many have found solace in the prescription 'commodity, firmness, delight' as the clear account of what a building should incorporate, leaving it to experienced designers and builders to interpret this within the tacit assumptions of a supposedly shared culture." Steven Groák, *The Idea of Building: Thought and Action in the Design and Production of Buildings* (London: E. & F. N. Spon, 1992), p. 54.

3. The Vitruvius quotes are from the translations in Indra Kagis McEwen, *Vitruvius: Writing the Body of Architecture* (Cambridge, Mass.: MIT Press, 2003), pp. 17, 65. The sections in Vitruvius are Book 4, Preface, and Book 1, Section 1.2. *Ordinatio* means literally "a setting in order."

4. Ibid., p. 55.

5. Ibid., p. 38.

6. This is set out in the section "Phony Ethics" in chapter 10 below.

7. Jeremy Till, "Too Many Ideas," in *Research by Design,* ed. A. Langenhuizen, M. K. van Ouwerkerk, and H. J. Rosemann (Delft: DUP Satellite, 2001).

8. Vitruvius was by his own admission both an unsuccessful architect and a writer of no great merit. See McEwen, *Vitruvius,* p. 7.

9. Sigmund Freud, *Civilization and Its Discontents* (London: Penguin, 2002), p. 40.

10. See Mark Wigley's exhaustive survey of whiteness, fashion, and cleanliness in modern architecture. Mark Wigley, *White Walls, Designer Dresses: The Fashioning of Modern Architecture* (Cambridge, Mass.: MIT Press, 1995).

11. Plato, *The Republic,* trans. Desmond Lee (London: Penguin, 1974), section 501a, p. 237.

12. Le Corbusier, *The Decorative Art of Today,* trans. James Dunnett (London: Architectural Press, 1987), pp. 188, 92.

13. Peter Stallybrass and Allon White, *The Politics and Poetics of Transgression* (London: Methuen, 1986), p. 22.

14. Ibid.

15. Susan Sontag, *Illness as Metaphor* (London: Penguin, 1979), p. 76.

16. Ibid., p. 84.

17. Le Corbusier, *Precisions on the Present State of Architecture and City Planning*, trans. Edith Schreiber Aujame (Cambridge, Mass.: MIT Press, 1991), p. 68.

18. "The cancerous germ is coming up against the fine young, vigorous germ," he writes of decadent art. "In biology, it is a dreadful disease, cancer, which kills by strangling," of sensualists. "The dilemma is in the heart of the School . . . like cancer which establishes itself comfortably around the pylorus of the stomach, or around the heart. The cancer is in excellent health," of Beaux-Arts academies. See, respectively, Le Corbusier, *The Decorative Art of Today*, p. 207; Le Corbusier, *Precisions*, p. 32; Le Corbusier, *When the Cathedrals Were White: A Journey to the Country of Timid People*, trans. Francis Hyslop (London: Routledge, 1947), p. 116.

19. Le Corbusier, *When the Cathedrals Were White*, p. 50.

20. Le Corbusier, *Precisions*, p. 172.

21. Zygmunt Bauman, *Wasted Lives: Modernity and Its Outcasts* (Cambridge: Polity Press, 2004), p. 31.

22. All quotes from Martin Parr and Nicholas Barker, *Signs of the Times* (Manchester: Cornerhouse Publications, 1992).

23. One of the few contemporary architectural theorists to acknowledge Bauman is Kim Dovey, who employs Bauman's concept of liquid modernity in Kim Dovey, *Fluid Cities* (London: Routledge, 2005).

24. John Dewey, *The Quest for Certainty* (London: George Allen and Unwin, 1930), p. 268.

25. Some commentators have noted that Bauman's daughter, Irena, is an architect, and this may account for some of the architectural threads in his work. See Peter Beilharz, ed., *The Bauman Reader* (Oxford: Blackwell, 2001).

26. Zygmunt Bauman, *Modernity and Ambivalence* (Cambridge: Polity Press, 1991), p. 99.

27. Hilde Heynen's explanation of the difference between modernity (as a societal condition) and modernism (as an artistic and intellectual expression) is useful here: "Modernity here is used in reference to a condition of living imposed upon individuals by the socio-economic process of modernization. The experience of modernity involves a rupture with tradition and has a profound impact on ways of life and daily habits. The effects of this rupture are manifold. They are reflected in modern-

ism, the body of artistic and intellectual ideas and movements that deal with the process of modernization and with the experience of modernity." Hilde Heynen, *Architecture and Modernity: A Critique* (Cambridge, Mass.: MIT Press, 1999), p. 1. The terms are also explored in Berman's classic work on modernity: Marshall Berman, *All That Is Solid Melts into Air: The Experience of Modernity* (New York: Viking Penguin, 1988), p. 16.

28. Nikolaus Pevsner, *Pioneers of Modern Design, from William Morris to Walter Gropius* (London: Penguin, 1975).

29. Bauman, *Modernity and Ambivalence*, p. 4.

30. Ibid., p. 7.

31. Le Corbusier, *The Decorative Art of Today*, p. 192.

32. Zygmunt Bauman, *Globalization: The Human Consequences* (Cambridge: Polity Press, 1998), pp. 41–43.

33. Zygmunt Bauman, *Intimations of Postmodernity* (London: Routledge, 1992), p. xiii.

34. In Bauman, *Modernity and Ambivalence*, p. 30.

35. From Zola, "Les squares," as quoted in Denis Hollier, *Against Architecture: The Writings of Georges Bataille*, trans. Betsy Wing (Cambridge, Mass.: MIT Press, 1989), p. xv.

36. The first approach is broadly that of Foucault, the second that of Lefebvre.

37. Bauman, *Intimations of Postmodernity*, p. xi.

38. Bauman, *Modernity and Ambivalence*, p. 7.

39. Ibid.

40. Friedrich Nietzsche, "On Truth and Falsity in Their Extramoral Sense," in *Essays on Metaphor*, ed. W. Shibles (Whitewater: Language Press, 1972), p. 7.

41. Agnes Heller, "From Hermeneutics in Social Science toward a Hermeneutics of Social Science," *Theory and Society* 18 (1989): 291.

42. Ibid., p. 292.

43. Edmund Bacon, *Design of Cities* (London: Thames and Hudson, 1967), p. 137.

44. Le Corbusier, *When the Cathedrals Were White*, p. 16.

45. Le Corbusier, *The Modulor*, trans. Peter De Francia and Anna Bostock (London: Faber and Faber, 1961), p. 32.

46. Bauman, *Intimations of Postmodernity*, p. xii.

47. In Aristotle, *De interpretatione*, 22b11ff.

48. "In classical metaphysics contingency has always denoted a limitation of reason." George di Giovanni, "The Category of Contingency in Hegelian Logic," in *Selected Essays on G. W. F. Hegel,* ed. Lawrence S. Stepelevich (Atlantic Highlands, N.J.: Humanities Press, 1993), p. 42.

49. Ibid.

50. Jürgen Habermas, *Postmetaphysical Thinking: Philosophical Essays* (Cambridge, Mass.: MIT Press, 1992), p. 141.

51. Di Giovanni, "The Category of Contingency in Hegelian Logic," p. 46.

52. Issues of contingency are discussed in *Science of Logic,* vol. 1, Book 2, Section 3, Chapter 2A. The quote is from G. W. F. Hegel, *Science of Logic,* trans. A. V. Miller (London: George Allen and Unwin, 1969), p. 545.

53. "Hegel always demanded specificity or what he called concreteness.... Few philosophers have been so critical of the type of abstract claims that lack determinateness or specificity. This is the primary defect of knowledge that Hegel called understanding which is to be contrasted with the concreter determinate knowledge of reason (Verkunft)." Richard J. Bernstein, "Why Hegel Now?," in *Philosophical Profiles: Essays in a Pragmatic Mode* (Cambridge: Polity Press, 1986), pp. 157–158.

54. Di Giovanni, "The Category of Contingency in Hegelian Logic," p. 56.

55. Bauman, *Modernity and Ambivalence,* p. 3.

56. Zygmunt Bauman, *Modernity and the Holocaust* (Cambridge: Polity Press, 1989).

57. William E. Connolly, *Politics and Ambiguity* (Madison: University of Wisconsin Press, 1987), pp. 8–9.

58. *Rückschlag* means both misfire and backlash. With thanks to Florian Kossak and Tatjana Schneider for this formulation.

59. Philippe Boudon, *Lived-in Architecture,* trans. Gerald Onn (London: Lund Humphries, 1972), pp. i–ii. A visit in 2003 revealed that the changes documented by Boudon are now themselves being ripped out as the project is "restored" back to its original state. Inevitably, many of the new inhabitants appeared to be architects or designers.

60. Tom Spector, "Codes of Ethics and Coercion," in *Architecture and Its Ethical Dilemmas,* ed. Nicholas Ray (London: Routledge, 2005), p. 101.

61. I am attempting to use parody knowingly. I do not simply employ it in its negative conception as a mocking dismissal of ludicrous or outmoded rituals. For more on the various ways in which parody has been used, both negatively and positively, see Margaret Rose, *Parody: Ancient, Modern, and Postmodern* (Cambridge: Cambridge University Press, 1993), pp. 186–190. As she argues: "the restriction of par-

ody to the more negative term in some modern or late-modern theories and uses has now been superseded by a 'post-modern' understanding of both its complex meta-fictional and comic aspects (which) may mean that it will be given some even more complex and positive functions in the future."

62. For instance in the *Metaphysics*, Book III, Part 2, and the *Nicomachaean Ethics*, Book VI, Part 4.

63. Karatani, *Architecture as Metaphor*, p. 6.

64. Descartes, *Discourse*, Part II, Paragraph 1.

65. Descartes, *Meditations*, Meditation 1, Paragraph 1.

66. Martin Heidegger, *Kant and the Problem of Metaphysics* (Bloomington: Indiana University Press, 1990), p. 2.

67. Martin Heidegger, *An Introduction to Metaphysics* (New Haven: Yale University Press, 1959), p. 93.

68. Mark Wigley, *The Architecture of Deconstruction* (Cambridge, Mass.: MIT Press, 1995), p. 39.

69. Karatani, *Architecture as Metaphor*, p. xxxii.

70. Quoted in Franco Borsi, *Leon Battista Alberti*, trans. Rudolf Carpanini (Oxford: Phaidon, 1977), p. 13. Borsi goes on to note: "The nights of the fifteenth century were populated with images: Paolo di Dono lay awake at night thinking of 'sweet perspective' and Leonardo was to praise 'the straying of the imagination over the superficial features of forms when you lie in bed in the dark.'"

3 Coping with Contingency

Epigraph: William Rasch, *Niklas Luhmann's Modernity: The Paradoxes of Differentiation* (Stanford: Stanford University Press, 2000), p. 52.

1. Kojin Karatani, *Architecture as Metaphor: Language, Number, Money*, trans. Sabu Kohso (Cambridge, Mass.: MIT Press, 1995), p. xxxix.

2. Ibid.

3. Clifford Geertz, *Local Knowledge: Further Essays in Interpretive Anthropology* (London: Fontana, 1983), pp. 215–218.

4. For a useful summary of the constraints that architects face and the limits of design methodologies, see Bryan Lawson, *How Designers Think*, 2nd edn. (London: Butterworth Architecture, 1990), pp. 76–81.

5. Steven Groák identifies five forms of uncertainty in the building process: industrial uncertainty, uncertainty for the firm, project uncertainty, workplace uncertainty,

uncertainty of site organization. Steven Groák, *The Idea of Building: Thought and Action in the Design and Production of Buildings* (London: E. & F. N. Spon, 1992), p. 41.

6. Daniel Sherer, translator's introduction, in Manfredo Tafuri, *Interpreting the Renaissance*, trans. Daniel Sherer (New Haven: Yale University Press, 2006), p. xvi.

7. Karatani, *Architecture as Metaphor*, p. xl.

8. "Thus arose the great divide which was to become the trademark of modern living: one between reason and emotion." Zygmunt Bauman, *Alone Again: Ethics after Certainty* (London: Demos, 2000), p. 4.

9. See John Gray, "The World Is Round," *New York Review of Books*, August 11, 2005, for a cogent critique of Friedman's argument, which is set out in Thomas L. Friedman, *The World Is Flat* (New York: Farrar, Straus and Giroux, 2005).

10. Niklas Luhmann, *Observations on Modernity*, trans. William Whobrey (Stanford: Stanford University Press, 1998), p. 44.

11. Nicholas H. Smith, *Strong Hermeneutics: Contingency and Moral Identity* (London: Routledge, 1997), p. 3.

12. Anthony Giddens, *The Consequences of Modernity* (Cambridge: Polity Press, 1990), pp. 137–138, 3.

13. Rasch, *Niklas Luhmann's Modernity*, p. 10.

14. Zygmunt Bauman, *Modernity and Ambivalence* (Cambridge: Polity Press, 1991), p. 98. The idea of modernity without illusions is found in Zygmunt Bauman, *Postmodern Ethics* (Oxford: Blackwell, 1993), p. 3.

15. See Giddens, *The Consequences of Modernity*, p. 150, for a table summarizing the differences between postmodernity and radicalized modernity.

16. Bauman, *Modernity and Ambivalence*, p. 98.

17. Richard Rorty, *Contingency, Irony, and Solidarity* (Cambridge: Cambridge University Press, 1989). This book is a reworking of three lectures Rorty gave that were published in the *London Review of Books* in 1986 and which are more accessible in style. Richard Rorty, "The Contingency of Community," *London Review of Books*, July 24, 1986; Richard Rorty, "The Contingency of Language," *London Review of Books*, April 17, 1986; Richard Rorty, "The Contingency of Selfhood," *London Review of Books*, May 8, 1986.

18. For a brilliant and concise critique, see Richard J. Bernstein, "Rorty's Liberal Utopia," in Bernstein, *The New Constellation: The Ethical-Political Horizons of Modernity/Postmodernity* (Cambridge: Polity Press, 1991). Much of my argument in this section is reliant on Bernstein. See also C. J. Misak, *Truth, Politics, Morality: Pragmatism and Deliberation* (London: Routledge, 1999), pp. 16–18; Barbara Herrnstein

Smith, *Contingencies of Value: Alternative Perspectives for Critical Theory* (Cambridge, Mass.: Harvard University Press, 1988), pp. 166–172; and Nicholas Smith, *Strong Hermeneutics*, pp. 1–18.

19. An argument that Rorty famously deployed in Richard Rorty, *Philosophy and the Mirror of Nature* (Princeton: Princeton University Press, 1979).

20. Rorty, *Contingency, Irony, and Solidarity*, p. 91.

21. Ibid., p. 28.

22. Ibid., p. xv. Rorty later contrasts this notion of a liberal ironist with two prominent philosophers, Habermas and Foucault, the former of whom is "a liberal who is unwilling to be an ironist, and the latter of whom is an ironist who is unwilling to be a liberal" (ibid., p. 61).

23. Rorty, "The Contingency of Community," p. 11. In the book this reads: "Only poets, Nietzsche suspected, can truly appreciate contingency."

24. Ibid., p. 15. This passage, with all its naivety, is not included in the book.

25. Rorty, *Contingency, Irony, and Solidarity*, p. xiv. He says that he is "aware of the objection that I am treating democratic societies as existing for the sake of intellectuals," but his defense is hardly robust enough to get him out of the hole he has dug. "My initial reply to this objection is that there are fairly tight connections between the freedom of intellectuals and the diminution of cruelty on the other." Footnote in Rorty, "The Contingency of Community," p. 13.

26. Rorty, *Contingency, Irony, and Solidarity*, p. 28.

27. Ibid., p. 38. My emphasis.

28. Bernstein, "Rorty's Liberal Utopia," p. 287.

29. William E. Connolly, *Politics and Ambiguity* (Madison: University of Wisconsin Press, 1987), p. 22. In a later collection of essays Rorty will argue that the stability and rightness of Western liberal democracy is such that political resistance is not necessary. See Richard Rorty, *Philosophy and Social Hope* (London: Penguin, 1999). As Hodges and Lachs note, Rorty "suggests that there is little or nothing for philosophers to do after critical detachment has been achieved. Broadly speaking the institutions of Western civilization are in order as they are, and whatever changes might be necessary do not require the sort of thought that has characteristically been called 'philosophical.'" Michael Hodges and John Lachs, *Thinking in the Ruins: Wittgenstein and Santayana on Contingency* (Nashville: Vanderbilt University Press, 2000), p. 11.

30. Walter Gropius, *Apollo in the Democracy: The Cultural Obligation of the Architect* (New York: McGraw-Hill, 1968), p. 8.

31. Ibid., p. 18. Emphasis in the original.

32. Ibid., p. 10. My emphasis.

33. Hilary Putnam, *Realism and Reason* (Cambridge: Cambridge University Press, 1983), p. 181.

34. Agnes Heller, "From Hermeneutics in Social Science toward a Hermeneutics of Social Science," *Theory and Society* 18 (1989): 321.

35. Bauman, *Modernity and Ambivalence*, p. 234.

36. Zygmunt Bauman, *Intimations of Postmodernity* (London: Routledge, 1992), p. 134.

37. Heller, "From Hermeneutics in Social Science toward a Hermeneutics of Social Science," pp. 320–321.

38. Bauman, *Modernity and Ambivalence*, p. 245.

39. As quoted in Roger Connah, *How Architecture Got Its Hump* (Cambridge, Mass.: MIT Press, 2001), p. 120.

40. As quoted in Jason Read, "A Universal History of Contingency: Deleuze and Guattari on the History of Capitalism," *Borderlands* 2, no. 3 (2003).

41. Bruno Latour, *We Have Never Been Modern*, trans. Catherine Porter (New York: Harvester Wheatsheaf, 1993).

42. Ibid., p. 35.

43. Ibid., p. 119.

44. Ibid., p. 54.

45. Ibid., pp. 73–74.

46. Latour traces three reactions to the crisis of the modern constitution not being feasible in the face of the quasi-object: (a) the modernizing philosophers from Kant to Habermas who increase the gap between subjects and objects, nature and culture, until it is incommensurable; (b) the semiotic turn which deals with the middle ground of quasi-objects, but which can exist only as an autonomous discourse and thus cuts itself off from the world of objects on the one hand and the identity of the speaking subject on the other; (c) phenomenology: but the problem with phenomenologists is that their description of Being is so removed as to be not real, "Being cannot reside in ordinary beings." Ibid., pp. 56–67.

47. Ibid., p. 73.

48. Ibid., p. 46.

49. Ibid., p. 40.

50. Ibid., p. 71.

51. Barbara Herrnstein Smith, *Contingencies of Value*, p. 152. Smith's critique of objectivist thought and assertion of the inevitable contingency of judging value is trenchant and convincing. However, her insistent rejection of any overriding imperatives means that in the end her position is dangerously relativist. As Steven Connor notes, Smith's evaluative choices "seem either entirely determined by the product of their contingent circumstances or entirely spontaneous." Steven Connor, *Theory and Cultural Value* (Oxford: Blackwell, 1992), pp. 28–29.

52. Smith, *Contingencies of Value*, p. 156.

53. For example, in Jürgen Habermas, *Postmetaphysical Thinking: Philosophical Essays* (Cambridge, Mass.: MIT Press, 1992), pp. 126–130.

54. The charge is set out and then firmly rebuffed by William Rasch. His response to the charge goes: "If modernity is necessarily contingent and there is no escape from the vertigo of ever-shifting self-descriptions, then the description of this state of affairs is itself necessarily not contingent. . . . Contingency, then, cannot be merely the contingent condition of modernity; rather it is the necessary condition required for modernity's continued existence." See Rasch, *Niklas Luhmann's Modernity*, pp. 23–24.

55. Alberto Melucci, *The Playing Self: Person and Meaning in the Planetary Society* (Cambridge: Cambridge University Press, 1996), p. 45.

56. "The identification of freedom with 'freedom of will' locates contingency in the wrong place. Contingency of will would mean that uncertainty was uncertainly dealt with; it would resort to chance for a decision." John Dewey, *The Quest for Certainty* (1929; London: George Allen and Unwin, 1930), p. 238.

57. Donna Haraway, "Situated Knowledges: The Science Question in Feminism and the Privilege of Partial Perspective," in Haraway, *Simians, Cyborgs and Women* (London: Free Association Books, 1991).

58. Ibid., p. 190.

59. Ibid., p. 196.

60. Ibid., p. 192.

61. Apart from texts already mentioned in the first three chapters, the following have informed my argument: Rosi Braidotti, *Nomadic Subjects: Embodiment and Sexual Difference in Contemporary Feminist Theory* (New York: Columbia University Press, 1994); Alex Callinicos, *Making History: Agency, Structure, and Change in Social Theory* (Cambridge: Polity Press, 1987); John D. Caputo, *Radical Hermeneutics: Repetition, Deconstruction, and the Hermeneutic Project* (Bloomington: Indiana University Press, 1987); Mary Ann Doane, *The Emergence of Cinematic Time: Modernity, Contingency, the Archive* (Cambridge, Mass.: Harvard University Press, 2002); Roberto Mangabeira Unger, *False Necessity: Anti-Necessitarian Social Theory in the Service of Radical Democracy* (Cambridge: Cambridge University Press, 1987); Roberto

Mangabeira Unger, *Social Theory: Its Situation and Its Task* (Cambridge: Cambridge University Press, 1987); Albrecht Wellmer, "Truth, Contingency, and Modernity," in Wellmer, *Endgames: The Irreconcilable Nature of Modernity* (Cambridge, Mass.: MIT Press, 1998); and Gary Wihl, *The Contingency of Theory: Pragmatism, Expressivism, and Deconstruction* (New Haven: Yale University Press, 1994).

62. Dewey, *The Quest for Certainty*, p. 238.

Part II

1. Sigfried Giedion, *Space, Time and Architecture* (Cambridge, Mass.: Harvard University Press, 1946), p. 329. The first quote ("a supreme study . . . ") is from Frank Lloyd Wright, but Giedion does not give the source.

4 Time of Waste

1. In the UK, 24% (17.5 million tonnes) of all construction waste is designated officially as landfill, but a further 28% (20.3 million tonnes) is dumped on "registered exempt sites," and 13% (9.5 million tonnes) is "reused" in construction or engineering works, mainly to make up levels. This means that in total 65% (55 million tonnes) of construction waste ended up somewhere on the land in 1999–2000. See Symonds Group, *Construction and Demolition Waste Survey* (Swindon: Environment Agency, 2001). Guthrie's figures for the percentage of landfill which is construction waste are at the upper end of estimates.

2. See John Scanlan, *On Garbage* (London: Reaktion Books, 2005), p. 22.

3. Nancy Holt, ed., *The Writings of Robert Smithson* (New York: New York University Press, 1979), p. 83.

4. Le Corbusier, *When the Cathedrals Were White: A Journey to the Country of Timid People,* trans. Francis Hyslop (London: Routledge, 1947), p. 25.

5. Mary Douglas, *Purity and Danger: An Analysis of Concepts of Pollution and Taboo* (London: Routledge, 1966), p. 36.

6. Don DeLillo, *Underworld* (London: Picador, 1998), p. 121.

7. Ivan Klima, *Love and Garbage,* trans. Ewald Osers (London: Penguin, 1991), p. 6.

8. Michael Thompson, *Rubbish Theory: The Creation and Destruction of Value* (Oxford: Oxford University Press, 1979), p. 7.

9. "The rubbish to transient transfer is theoretically impossible for the following reason. Both the value and expected life-span of an item in the rubbish category are zero. In the transient category they are positive and decreasing. The transfer of rubbish to transience would involve a change from zero to a positive quantity which inevitably involves an increase and in consequence would exclude the item from

the transient category." Thompson does acknowledge that some fringe figures—the scrap merchant, the rag-and-bone man—do manage to effect this transition. Ibid., p. 106.

10. Richard Fardon, *Mary Douglas: An Intellectual Biography* (London: Routledge, 1999), p. 144. Thompson's later coauthored book introduced Douglas's approach to a wider audience. Michael Thompson, Richard Ellis, and Aaron Wildavsky, *Cultural Theory* (Boulder: Westview Press, 1990). The compliment was returned by Douglas in a letter to the *Times Literary Supplement* (January 2004), when she noted that Thompson's book had achieved the rare scholarly accolade of being classified as "durable."

11. Thompson, *Rubbish Theory*, p. 50.

12. Ibid., p. 48.

13. Ibid., p. 10.

14. Ibid., p. 37.

15. This is, almost unbelievably, a quote from the "urban design statement" submitted by the developers, Arsenal Football Club, in support of their application for planning permission.

16. Zygmunt Bauman, *Wasted Lives: Modernity and Its Outcasts* (Cambridge: Polity Press, 2004), p. 30.

17. DeLillo, *Underworld*, p. 184.

18. Scanlan, *On Garbage*, p. 16.

19. Thesis IX from Walter Benjamin, "On the Concept of History," in *Collected Writings*, ed. Howard Eiland and Michael Jennings (Cambridge, Mass.: Harvard University Press, 2003), p. 392.

20. As Gary Shapiro notes, Smithson "is deeply suspicious of progress and conscious of industrial devastation, decay, waste and the general tendency toward entropy. Rather than attempting to catch up with 'progress,' he regressively allows the waste and the ground to emerge in its wake." *Gary Shapiro, Earthwards: Robert Smithson and Art after Babel* (Berkeley: University of California Press, 1995), p. 36.

21. All quotes from Holt, ed., *The Writings of Robert Smithson*, pp. 111–113.

22. Scanlan, *On Garbage*, pp. 33–34.

23. This is what Rem Koolhaas does in his piece "Junkspace," a brilliant excoriation of the world of shopping malls, airports, and suburbs that now litter our environment. The trouble is that we are left smashed at the end of a twelve-page sneer with no room for maneuver. The sense of being unable to escape his dystopia is at the same time highly convincing and highly depressing. Rem Koolhaas, "Junkspace,"

in *Harvard Design School Guide to Shopping,* ed. Chuihua Judy Chung, Jeffrey Inaba, Rem Koolhaas, and Sze Tsung Leong (Cologne: Taschen, 2001).

5 Out of Time

1. See Beatriz Colomina, *Privacy and Publicity: Modern Architecture as Mass Media* (Cambridge, Mass.: MIT Press, 1994), p. 327.

2. Roger Connah, *How Architecture Got Its Hump* (Cambridge, Mass.: MIT Press, 2001), p. 44. I return to some of Connah's perceptive comments on architectural photography in chapter 6 below.

3. The most extensive and compelling analysis of the relation of photography to high modernism is that of Colomina; see note 1 above.

4. Karsten Harries, "Building and the Terror of Time," *Perspecta* 19 (1982): 65.

5. Aldo Rossi, *A Scientific Autobiography,* trans. Lawrence Venuti (Cambridge, Mass.: MIT Press, 1981), p. 2.

6. Harries, "Building and the Terror of Time," 65.

7. From *L'expérience intérieure,* as quoted in Denis Hollier, *Against Architecture: The Writings of Georges Bataille,* trans. Betsy Wing (Cambridge, Mass.: MIT Press, 1989), p. 46.

8. Walter Gropius, *Apollo in the Democracy: The Cultural Obligation of the Architect* (New York: McGraw-Hill, 1968), p. 123.

9. Michel Serres and Bruno Latour, *Conversations on Science, Culture, and Time,* trans. Roxanne Lapidus (Ann Arbor: University of Michigan Press, 1995), p. 50.

10. On the reaction of modernism to the new temporalities, see chapter 1, "The Nature of Time," in *Stephen Kern, The Culture of Time and Space 1880–1918,* 2nd edn. (Cambridge, Mass.: Harvard University Press, 2003). For the philosophical background, see chapter 1, "Modernity: A Different Time," in Peter Osborne, *The Politics of Time: Modernity and the Avant-Garde* (London: Verso, 1995). For the relationship of time to architecture in early modernism, see Sanford Kwinter, *Architectures of Time: Toward a Theory of the Event in Modernist Culture* (Cambridge, Mass.: MIT Press, 2001).

11. See Hilde Heynen, *Architecture and Modernity: A Critique* (Cambridge, Mass.: MIT Press, 1999), p. 11. Heynen identifies two concepts of modernity, the transitory and the programmatic. The former stresses the transient and momentary aspects of the modern world; the latter is characterized by "an irreversible emergence of autonomy."

12. As quoted in Peter Carter, "Mies van de Rohe," *Bauen und Wohnen* 16 (1961): 239.

13. Gropius, *Apollo in the Democracy*, p. 172.

14. Sigfried Giedion, *The Eternal Present: The Beginnings of Art* (London: Oxford University Press, 1962); Sigfried Giedion, *The Eternal Present: The Beginnings of Architecture* (London: Oxford University Press, 1964).

15. Osborne, *The Politics of Time*, p. 151.

16. Osborne applies the term eternal present to Hegelian philosophy, which "must always eternalise its own present if it is to offer the possibility of an absolute knowing. . . . The end of history, the eternalisation of the present, and the abolition of the past as past are the three temporal dimensions of a single method." Ibid., p. 42.

17. "Lamp of Memory," section 10, in *John Ruskin, Seven Lamps of Architecture* (New York: Noonday Press, 1961), p. 171.

18. Hollier, *Against Architecture*, p. 49.

19. Rossi, *A Scientific Autobiography*, p. 50.

20. Steven Groák, *The Idea of Building: Thought and Action in the Design and Production of Buildings* (London: E. & F. N. Spon, 1992), p. 6.

21. Hollier, *Against Architecture*, p. 46.

22. This then becomes the slogan for Heidegger's famous 1924 lecture which formed the basis for *Being and Time*. As Françoise Dastur notes, for Heidegger it is no longer a question of considering that "time finds its meaning in eternity but on the contrary of 'understanding time on the basis of time itself.'" Françoise Dastur, *Heidegger and the Question of Time*, trans. François Raffoul and David Pettigrew (Amherst, N.Y.: Humanity Books, 1990), p. 3.

23. Sigfried Giedion, *Space, Time and Architecture* (Cambridge, Mass.: Harvard University Press, 1946), p. 360.

24. Ibid., p. 392. My emphasis.

25. Henri Lefebvre, *The Production of Space,* trans. Donald Nicholson-Smith (Oxford: Blackwell, 1991), pp. 95–96.

26. Zygmunt Bauman, *Liquid Modernity* (Cambridge: Polity Press, 1997), p. 110.

27. Osborne, *The Politics of Time*, p. 9.

28. For the relationship of modernity to progress, see Zygmunt Bauman, *Modernity and Ambivalence* (Cambridge: Polity Press, 1991), pp. 10–11. Octavio Paz notes that the linear construction of modernity is a peculiarly Western phenomenon. See Heynen, *Architecture and Modernity*, p. 9.

29. Le Corbusier, *Precisions on the Present State of Architecture and City Planning,* trans. Edith Schreiber Aujame (Cambridge, Mass.: MIT Press, 1991), p. 72.

30. The terms, out of Pierre Bourdieu, are used by Garry Stevens, who argues that architects tend to satisfy either the demands of the external market or those of the internal market, but not both at the same time (in that satisfying economic demands is seen as a corruption of the symbolic demand). The internal market, driven as it is by an autonomous value system of aesthetic codes and intellectual ideologies, is defined through its symbolic capital. Garry Stevens, *The Favored Circle: The Social Foundations of Architectural Distinction* (Cambridge, Mass.: MIT Press, 1998), pp. 88–95. A similar argument is made by Dana Cuff in *Architecture: The Story of Practice* (Cambridge, Mass.: MIT Press, 1991). Recent trends are indicating that the barrier between symbolic and economic capital is less firm than Stevens and Cuff would have it, as architects such as Daniel Libeskind first establish their cultural capital in the internal marketplace before exploiting it in the external marketplace.

31. This is a hopelessly short summary of Marx's fundamental argument in *Das Capital*. See especially vol. 2, IV, 19.

32. Stewart Brand, *How Buildings Learn: What Happens after They're Built* (New York: Viking, 1994), p. 63.

33. Ignasi de Solà-Morales, *Differences: Topographies of Contemporary Architecture*, trans. Graham Thompson (Cambridge, Mass.: MIT Press, 1997), p. 68.

34. Kwinter, *Architectures of Time*, p. 6.

35. As quoted in Stan Allen, *Points + Lines* (New York: Princeton Architectural Press, 1999), p. 50.

36. Bruno Schulz, *Sanatorium under the Sign of the Hourglass* (London: Picador, 1987), p. 137.

37. For the various forms of critique, see Andrew Ross, *The Celebration Chronicles: Life, Liberty, and the Pursuit of Property Value in Disney's New Town* (London: Verso, 2000), p. 329.

38. See especially chapter 7, "The Siege of the School," in ibid.

39. For the trajectory of Le Corbusier's politics, see Robert Fishman, "From Radiant City to Vichy: Le Corbusier's Plans and Politics 1928–1942," in *The Open Hand: Essays on Corbusier*, ed. Russell Walden (Cambridge, Mass.: MIT Press, 1977). For an interpretation of the motives behind Le Corbusier's Vichy alliance, see Simon Richards, *Le Corbusier and the Concept of Self* (New Haven: Yale University Press, 2003), pp. 54–65.

40. Hans Jonas, *The Imperative of Responsibility: In Search of an Ethics for the Technological Age* (Chicago: University of Chicago Press, 1984), p. 125.

41. Ibid.

42. Bruno Latour, *We Have Never Been Modern*, trans. Catherine Porter (New York: Harvester Wheatsheaf, 1993), p. 78.

43. Ibid., p. 69.

44. Kenzo Tange, "Creation in Present-Day Architecture and the Japanese Tradition," in *Kenzo Tange,* ed. Robin Boyd (London: Prentice-Hall, 1962), p. 114.

6 In Time

1. Michel Serres and Bruno Latour, *Conversations on Science, Culture, and Time,* trans. Roxanne Lapidus (Ann Arbor: University of Michigan Press, 1995), p. 49.

2. Ibid., p. 58.

3. Alberto Melucci, *The Playing Self: Person and Meaning in the Planetary Society* (Cambridge: Cambridge University Press, 1996), p. 12.

4. The terms are from Johannes Fabian, *Time and the Other: How Anthropology Makes Its Subject* (New York: Columbia University Press, 1983), pp. 22–23.

5. Ibid., p. 26 and passim.

6. Fabian is particularly critical of Claude Lévi-Strauss, the French anthropologist who brought structuralist methods to anthropology, and in so doing "excludes" time. See ibid., pp. 54–56.

7. Karl Marx, "Critique of Hegel's Philosophy of Right," in Marx, *Early Writings* (London: Penguin, 1992), p. 247.

8. See Gary Shapiro, *Earthwards: Robert Smithson and Art after Babel* (Berkeley: University of California Press, 1995), p. 39.

9. Ignasi de Solà-Morales, *Differences: Topographies of Contemporary Architecture,* trans. Graham Thompson (Cambridge, Mass.: MIT Press, 1997), p. 68.

10. For issues arising from the assertion of time over space in modernity see, among many texts, Stephen Kern, *The Culture of Time and Space 1880–1918,* 2nd edn. (Cambridge, Mass.: Harvard University Press, 2003); and Zygmunt Bauman, *Liquid Modernity* (Cambridge: Polity Press, 1997), pp. 100–118. For the assertion of space over time, see Edward W. Soja, *Postmodern Geographies: The Reassertion of Space in Critical Social Theory* (London: Verso, 1989). It was Foucault who did more than anyone in his critique of time-based historicism and his analysis of space as the vector of power. It should be noted that neither Soja nor Foucault argues for an exclusive, atemporal sense of space.

11. Henri Lefebvre, *The Production of Space,* trans. Donald Nicholson-Smith (Oxford: Blackwell, 1991), p. 95.

12. Steven Groák, *The Idea of Building: Thought and Action in the Design and Production of Buildings* (London: E. & F. N. Spon, 1992), p. 11. He then goes on to describe the nature of "time in building affairs": 1. Fabric of buildings degrades through physical and chemical change over time; 2. Ordinary wear and tear; 3. Social

change; 4. Economic life of the building; 5. Everyday changes in level of internal comfort.

13. As Zygmunt Bauman notes: "I personally learned more about the society we live in from Balzac, Zola, Kafka, Musil, Frisch, Perec, Kundera, Beckett . . . than, say, from Parsons and quite a few other in and out footnote stalwarts." Tony Blackshaw, "An Interview with Professor Zygmunt Bauman," *Network: The Newsletter of the British Sociological Association,* no. 83 (2002).

14. James Joyce as quoted in Richard Ellmann, *James Joyce,* rev. edn. (Oxford: Oxford University Press, 1983), p. 83.

15. Henri Lefebvre, "The Everyday and Everydayness," *Yale French Studies* 73 (1987): 10.

16. For the relationship between Joyce, time, and the everyday, see in particular Henri Lefebvre, *Everyday Life in the Modern World,* trans. Sacha Rabinovitch (New Brunswick: Transaction Publishers, 1984), pp. 2–8.

17. Peter Osborne, *The Politics of Time: Modernity and the Avant-Garde* (London: Verso, 1995), p. 196.

18. Lefebvre, *Everyday Life in the Modern World,* p. 18.

19. Melucci, *The Playing Self,* p. 7.

20. See Zygmunt Bauman, *Globalization: The Human Consequences* (Cambridge: Polity Press, 1998), pp. 35–38.

21. Quoted in Bruno Latour, *We Have Never Been Modern,* trans. Catherine Porter (New York: Harvester Wheatsheaf, 1993), p. 75.

22. Stewart Brand, *How Buildings Learn: What Happens after They're Built* (New York: Viking, 1994), p. 2.

23. Brian Eno, *A Year with Swollen Appendices* (London: Faber and Faber, 1996), p. 133.

24. Brand, *How Buildings Learn,* p. 221.

25. As quoted in ibid., p. 77.

26. As quoted in Luigi Prestinenza Puglisi, *Hyper Architecture: Spaces in the Electronic Age* (Basel: Birkhäuser, 1999), p. 6.

27. As quoted in Colin Amery, "The Architecture of Renzo Piano," in *Pritzker Prize for Architecture: Renzo Piano* (Los Angeles: Jensen and Walker, 1999), p. 33. In an interview on BBC Radio, Piano is quoted as saying the Beaubourg is a "parody of hi-tech."

28. The story is from Carola Giedion-Welcker's memoir of the last days of Joyce, as repeated by Richard Ellmann in his authoritative biography of Joyce. I have only

added the surmise about Giedion's admonishment of Joyce's love of tradition. Ellmann, *James Joyce*, p. 740. *Space, Time and Architecture* was based on the Norton Lectures at Harvard 1938–1939, and first published in 1941.

29. Le Corbusier, *When the Cathedrals Were White: A Journey to the Country of Timid People*, trans. Francis Hyslop (London: Routledge, 1947). As we shall see in chapter 10, the call for whiteness is wrapped up with a call for morality.

30. Le Corbusier, *The Decorative Art of Today*, trans. James Dunnett (London: Architectural Press, 1987), pp. 188–189.

31. Le Corbusier, *When the Cathedrals Were White*, p. 4.

32. Mark Wigley, *White Walls, Designer Dresses: The Fashioning of Modern Architecture* (Cambridge, Mass.: MIT Press, 1995), p. 330.

33. Le Corbusier, *The Decorative Art of Today*, p. 188.

34. See Solà-Morales's careful unpicking of the rhetoric of the hi-tech movement in *Differences*, pp. 116–131.

35. The restoration was also needed to cope with the effects of the huge influx of visitors who exceeded by a factor of five the initial estimates for visitor numbers. In this sense, the building was a victim of its own extraordinary success.

36. Manfredo Tafuri, *The History of Italian Architecture 1944–1985* (Cambridge, Mass.: MIT Press, 1989), p. 51. There is an irony here that a main protagonist of BPR, Ernesto Rogers, was a cousin of Richard Rogers's father.

37. Mohsen Mostafavi and David Leatherbarrow, *On Weathering* (Cambridge, Mass.: MIT Press, 1993), p. 45. This book, with its exquisite duotone photographs of staining and weathering in architecture, does at times get close to promoting an aesthetics of dirt.

38. Nancy Holt, ed., *The Writings of Robert Smithson* (New York: New York University Press, 1979), p. 181.

39. Ibid., p. 10.

40. Ibid., pp. 9–11. Smithson does, however, enjoy the way that the architecture of entropy cocks a snook at all traditional artistic and architectural values.

41. Lars Lerup, *Building the Unfinished: Architecture and Human Action* (Beverly Hills: Sage, 1977).

42. Ibid., p. 166.

43. Ibid., p. 21.

44. These arguments are set out in Herman Hertzberger, *Lessons for Students in Architecture*, trans. Ina Rike, 4th rev. edn. (Rotterdam: 010 Publishers, 2001). For

example, he notes: "Our architecture must be capable of accommodating all those different situations which affect the way a building is understood and used. Not only must it be capable of adapting itself to changing weather conditions and different seasons as well as being suitable for use during both day and night, it must be deliberately designed to respond to all these phenomena" (pp. 229–230).

45. Ibid., p. 157.

46. Ibid., p. 146.

47. Winfried Nerdinger, *Dinner for Architects* (New York: Norton, 2005).

48. This is a quote from Ivan Harbour, a director at Richard Rogers's practice Rogers, Stirk, Harbour.

49. Lefebvre, *The Production of Space*.

50. A fixation explained by Bob Evans in his seminal essay: Robin Evans, "Translations from Drawing to Building," in Evans, *Translations from Drawing to Building and Other Essays* (London: Architectural Association, 1997).

51. Dalibor Vesely, *Architecture in the Age of Divided Representation: The Question of Creativity in the Shadow of Production* (Cambridge, Mass.: MIT Press, 2004), p. 6. The development of perspective is traced in chapter 3, "The Perspectival Transformation of the Medieval World." Vesely argues that the use of perspective in the late Renaissance heralds the age of divided representation in the Baroque period, which in turn sets the conditions for modernity. The division in the title of his book refers to the separation of the "symbolic-communicative and the instrumental-noncommunicative representations of reality" (pp. 177–178).

52. Ibid., p. 18.

53. Evans, "Translations from Drawing to Building," p. 181.

54. Ibid., p. 182.

55. Ibid., p. 181.

56. Ibid., p. 172.

57. Lefebvre, *The Production of Space*, p. 361.

58. The Dutch firm MVRDV have led the way in datascapes. At the end of a brilliant lecture by Winy Maas of MVRDV, I asked him if the datascapes might be better termed *dadascapes* (to reflect what I thought was the absurdity and arbitrariness in his method of data collection). I did not get an answer.

59. Vesely, *Architecture in the Age of Divided Representation*, pp. 348–352.

60. Roger Connah, *How Architecture Got Its Hump* (Cambridge, Mass.: MIT Press, 2001), pp. 43–44.

61. Ibid., p. 47.

62. As quoted in Mary Ann Doane, *The Emergence of Cinematic Time: Modernity, Contingency, the Archive* (Cambridge, Mass.: Harvard University Press, 2002), p. 142.

63. Kristin Ross, introduction to Jacques Rancière, *The Ignorant Schoolmaster* (Stanford: Stanford University Press, 1991).

64. Vesely, *Architecture in the Age of Divided Representation*, p. 4.

65. Including one author who apparently liked them so much that he claimed them as his own. Manuel Gausa, *The Metapolis Dictionary of Advanced Architecture* (Barcelona: Actar, 2003).

66. Most famously by Kant in the *Critique of Pure Reason*, but maybe more poignantly by Heidegger in his privileging of time over space—or, more specifically, temporality over spatiality—in *Being and Time*, a privileging which results in the suppression of space. He addresses this artificial separation in one of his last texts with the introduction of the term "time-space." Martin Heidegger, *On Time and Being*, trans. Joan Stambaugh (New York: Harper, 1972). See Edward Casey's brilliant unraveling of the complexities of treating space as atemporal. Edward S. Casey, *The Fate of Place: A Philosophical History* (Berkeley: University of California Press, 1997), p. 277.

7 Slack Space

1. Anthony Giddens, *The Consequences of Modernity* (Cambridge: Polity Press, 1990), pp. 16–20. In the same vein is David Harvey's famous identification of time-space compression with the condition of postmodernity. David Harvey, *The Condition of Postmodernity* (Oxford: Basil Blackwell, 1989).The issue is further complicated by the rise of virtual networks since Giddens and Harvey wrote, with the confusion of time and space now becoming a commonplace on the Internet.

2. Le Corbusier, *The Modulor*, trans. Peter De Francia and Anna Bostock (London: Faber and Faber, 1961), p. 32.

3. All these quotes are taken from Cornelis van de Ven, *Space in Architecture* (Amsterdam: Van Gorcum Assen, 1978).

4. As quoted in ibid., p. 90. The German term is *Raumgestalterin*, a more contemporary translation of which might be "shaper of space."

5. Adrian Forty, *Words and Buildings: A Vocabulary of Modern Architecture* (London: Thames and Hudson, 2000), p. 256.

6. Edward S. Casey, *The Fate of Place: A Philosophical History* (Berkeley: University of California Press, 1997), p. 2.

7. As quoted in Martin Heidegger, *Being and Time*, trans. John Macquarrie and Edward Robinson (New York: Harper, 1962), p. 123.

8. For the distinction between the geometrical and the physical conceptions of space, see Van de Ven, *Space in Architecture*, p. 30.

9. David Adler, ed., *Metric Handbook*, 2nd edn. (Oxford: Architectural Press, 1999); Ernst Neufert, *Architects' Data* (Oxford: Blackwell Science Publisher, 2000). Some version of Neufert has been in print since the first edition in 1936: Ernst Neufert, *Bau-Entwurfslehre . . . Handbuch für den Baufachmann, Bauherrn, Lehrenden und Lernenden* (Berlin: Bauwelt-Verlag, 1936).

10. Ministry for Housing and Local Government, *Space in the Home*, Design Bulletin 6 (London: HMSO, 1968).

11. See Richard Rorty, *Philosophy and the Mirror of Nature* (Princeton: Princeton University Press, 1979), for the mirroring nature of Enlightenment thought and other versions of philosophical thought. See chapter 2 of this book, especially the section "Bauman's Order," for the ordering tendencies of modernism.

12. William E. Connolly, *Politics and Ambiguity* (Madison: University of Wisconsin Press, 1987), p. 8.

13. Zygmunt Bauman, *Postmodern Ethics* (Oxford: Blackwell, 1993), p. 145.

14. Heidegger, *Being and Time*, §§19–21.

15. Henri Lefebvre, *The Production of Space*, trans. Donald Nicholson-Smith (Oxford: Blackwell, 1991).

16. Bauman, *Postmodern Ethics*, p. 145.

17. See Forty, *Words and Buildings*, p. 275.

18. Lefebvre, *The Production of Space*, p. 360. Adrian Forty has an excellent summary of the issues at stake in this Lefebvrian analysis of the relationship of architecture and space. Forty, *Words and Buildings*, pp. 271–275.

19. David Harvey, *Spaces of Hope* (Edinburgh: Edinburgh University Press, 2000), p. 182.

20. Zygmunt Bauman, *Modernity and Ambivalence* (Cambridge: Polity Press, 1991), p. 15.

21. Lefebvre, *The Production of Space*, p. 26.

22. Henri Lefebvre, *Writings on Cities*, trans. Eleonore Kofman and Elizabeth Lebas (Oxford: Blackwell, 1996), p. 23.

23. See Stuart Elden, *Mapping the Present* (London: Continuum, 2001), p. 151.

24. Heidegger, *Being and Time*, p. 146.

25. Immanuel Kant, *Critique of Pure Reason*, trans. Norman Kemp Smith (London: Macmillan, 1929), p. 71.

26. Heidegger, *Being and Time*, p. 146.

27. Kant, *Critique of Pure Reason*, p. 68.

28. Heidegger, *Being and Time*, p. 146.

29. Magda King, *Heidegger's Philosophy* (New York: Macmillan, 1964), p. 86.

30. In the original German *Ent-fernung*, translated by Macquarrie and Robinson as "deseverance." De-distancing, the translation of Joan Stambaugh, reintroduces Heidegger's active use of the hyphen.

31. Heidegger, *Being and Time*, p. 141.

32. Martin Heidegger, "Building, Dwelling, Thinking," in Heidegger, *Poetry, Language, Thought* (New York: Harper, 1971).

33. Casey, *The Fate of Place*, p. 254.

34. Hilde Heynen, *Architecture and Modernity: A Critique* (Cambridge, Mass.: MIT Press, 1999), p. 94.

35. "Hence Being-in is not to be explained ontologically by some ontical characterization, as if one were to say, for instance, that . . . man's 'spatiality' is a result of his bodily nature (which, at the same time, gets 'founded' upon corporeality)." Heidegger, *Being and Time*, p. 82. When reminded of Sartre's criticism that *Being and Time* contained only six lines on the body, Heidegger "replies that this for him had been the hardest thing to solve and he knew no way to say more about it at the time." As quoted in William Richardson, "Heidegger among the Doctors," in *Reading Heidegger*, ed. John Sallis (Bloomington: Indiana University Press, 1993), p. 52.

36. Maurice Merleau-Ponty, *Phenomenology of Perception*, trans. Colin Smith (London: Routledge, 1962), p. 102.

37. The reason for this is that it is the phenomenal body of early Merleau-Ponty (as set out in *Phenomenology of Perception*) that is the subject of most architectural attention, and not so much the fleshly body of later Merleau-Ponty (as set out in *The Visible and the Invisible*). This fleshly body becomes the site of social and political spatial control. Maurice Merleau-Ponty, *The Visible and the Invisible* (Evanston: Northwestern University Press, 1968).

38. In an interview he says: "If I read a crazy guy like Heidegger . . . he's too much for me, but sometimes I read something and do read what he's trying to say. I understand him as trying to look for the essential and not for fashion." Jeremy Melvin, "Zumthor Goes to the Essence of Things: An Interview with Peter Zumthor" (Royal Academy of Arts, 2006 [cited June 2007]); available from <http://www.royalacademy.org.uk/architecture/interviews/zumthor,267,AR.html>.

39. Heidegger, *Being and Time*, p. 165.

40. See "Situated Knowledge," chapter 3 above.

41. See Trent Schoyer's foreword to Theodor W. Adorno, *The Jargon of Authenticity* (Evanston: Northwestern University Press, 1973), p. xiv.

42. For the "idealist" tendencies of Frampton's reading of tectonics, see Andrew Benjamin, "Plans to Matter: Towards a History of Material Possibility," in *Material Matters,* ed. Katie Lloyd Thomas (Abingdon: Routledge, 2007), pp. 13–28.

43. Kenneth Frampton, "Towards a Critical Regionalism: Six Points for an Architecture of Resistance," in *The Anti-Aesthetic: Essays on Postmodern Culture,* ed. Hal Foster (Seattle: Bay Press, 1983), p. 27.

44. Michel Foucault, "The Masked Philosopher," in Foucault, *Politics, Philosophy, Culture: Interviews and Other Writings 1977–1984,* ed. Lawrence Kritzman (London: Routledge, 1988), p. 328.

45. *Bruno Latour, We Have Never Been Modern,* trans. Catherine Porter (New York: Harvester Wheatsheaf, 1993), p. 65.

46. As appears to happen, despite all the editors' good intentions, in *Softspace,* ed. Sean Lally and Jessica Young (Abingdon: Routledge, 2007).

47. Connolly, *Politics and Ambiguity,* pp. 114–115.

48. The term "slack space" is also used by the architect Peter Barber in relation to his housing design. He in turn credits Cedric Price for the general concept if not the actual term. See Tatjana Schneider and Jeremy Till, *Flexible Housing* (Oxford: Architectural Press, 2007), pp. 137–138. The principles of slack space are based on the work done in a MArch studio that I ran with Tatjana Schneider at the School of Architecture, University of Sheffield in 2005. Many examples of slack space can be found in our book on flexible housing.

49. Jonathan Hill, *Actions of Architecture: Architects and Creative Users* (London: Routledge, 2003). For further examples of slack space, see also Bernard Leupen's brilliant analysis of the frame in relation to generic space: Bernard Leupen, *Frame and Generic Space: A Study into the Changeable Dwelling Proceeding from the Permanent* (Rotterdam: 010 Publishers, 2006).

8 Lo-Fi Architecture

1. Graeme Thomson, *Complicated Shadows: The Life and Music of Elvis Costello* (Edinburgh: Canongate, 2005), p. 188.

2. "Is it worth it / A new winter coat and shoes for the wife / And a bicycle on the boy's birthday / It's just a rumour that was spread around town / By the women and children / Soon we'll be shipbuilding / Well I ask you / The boy said 'DAD THEY'RE

GOING TO TAKE ME TO TASK / BUT I'LL BE BACK BY CHRISTMAS' / It's just a rumour that was spread around town / Somebody said that someone got filled in / For saying that people get killed in / The result of this shipbuilding / With all the will in the world / Diving for dear life / When we could be diving for pearls / It's just a rumour that was spread around town / A telegram or a picture postcard / Within weeks they'll be re-opening the shipyards / And notifying the next of kin / Once again / It's all we're skilled in / We will be shipbuilding / WITH ALL THE WILL IN THE WORLD / DIVING FOR DEAR LIFE / WHEN WE COULD BE DIVING FOR PEARLS"

3. Or words to that effect.

4. Le Corbusier, *Towards a New Architecture* (London: Architectural Press, 1946), p. 115.

5. Michael Bérubé, "The Elvis Costello Problem," in Bérubé, *Rhetorical Occasions: Essays on Humans and the Humanities* (Chapel Hill: University of North Carolina Press, 2006), p. 226. The "problem" he refers to is the "difficulty of communicating to students by the touchstones of popular culture" when those touchstones are of a previous generation, even year, whose immanent relevance appears to have passed. He is with me in seeing Costello as someone whose relevance is more than transitory. Finding Bérubé was one of those happy accidents of the contingent researcher. I was drawn by the fact that the electronic catalogue listed two of his book chapters as "The Future of Contingency" and "The Elvis Costello Problem." Irresistible.

6. For example, in 11 years of the RIBA Stirling Prize, the pinnacle of probably the most exhaustive architectural awards system in the world, there have been 82 shortlisted entries. Of these just one has been a public housing scheme, versus 4 private houses. The most represented building type is the museum (15). Parliament or government buildings (6) come fourth. There has been just one hospital, and one doctor's surgery, and no retail at all. As a member and then chair of the Awards Group from 2000 to 2006, I have to take some responsibility.

7. Denise Scott Brown, quoted in Dell Upton, "Architecture in Everyday Life," *New Literary History* 33, no. 4 (2003): 710–711.

8. Mary McLeod's brilliant article on the way that the various forms of postmodernism and deconstruction are merely distractions from the underlying capitulation to the rise of neoconservatism is sobering. See Mary McLeod, "Architecture and Politics in the Reagan Era: From Postmodernism to Deconstructivism," *Assemblage* 8 (1989), pp. 13–58.

9. Henri Lefebvre, *Everyday Life in the Modern World*, trans. Sacha Rabinovitch (New Brunswick: Transaction Publishers, 1984), p. 37.

10. Henri Lefebvre, *Critique of Everyday Life*, trans. John Moore, vol. 1 (London: Verso, 1991), p. 86.

11. Ibid.

12. See Mary McLeod's excellent introduction to the relationship of Lefebvre's theories of the everyday to architecture. Mary McLeod, "Henri Lefebvre's Critique of Everyday Life: An Introduction," in *Architecture of the Everyday*, ed. Steven Harris and Deborah Berke (New York: Princeton Architectural Press, 1997), pp. 9–29.

13. We thought that we had invented this formulation in Sarah Wigglesworth and Jeremy Till, *The Everyday and Architecture* (London: Academy Editions, 1998), pp. 7–9, but subsequently found out that Mark Rakatansky had beaten us to it. "Thus architecture that ignores the everyday allows itself—sets itself up—to be ignored in the everyday, or you could say, to be ignored everyday." Mark Rakatansky, "Identity and the Discourse of Politics in Contemporary Architecture," *Assemblage* 27 (1995): 15.

14. Lefebvre, *Everyday Life in the Modern World*, p. 14.

15. Joan Ockman summarizes this dilemma very well. Joan Ockman, "Toward a Theory of Normative Architecture," in *Architecture of the Everyday*, ed. Harris and Berke, pp. 144–147.

16. Lefebvre, *Critique of Everyday Life*, vol. 1, p. 87.

17. Manfredo Tafuri, "L'Architecture dans le Boudoir," in *Oppositions Reader*, ed. K. Michael Hays (New York: Princeton Architectural Press, 1998), p. 310.

18. See Upton, "Architecture in Everyday Life," pp. 720–721. Upton is very good at identifying the false dichotomy that is set up between architecture and the everyday, and uses the agency of the body to overcome the problem. In this I agree with him—even his criticism of our own work on the everyday stings (a misreading of our intentions, I would say). Wigglesworth and Till, *The Everyday and Architecture*.

19. Peter Stallybrass and Allon White, *The Politics and Poetics of Transgression* (London: Methuen, 1986), p. 3.

20. The two articles were published in 1955 and 1956 in the *Architectural Review*. They were subsequently republished: James Stirling, "Garches to Jaoul: Le Corbusier as Domestic Architect in 1927 and 1953," and "Ronchamp: Le Corbusier's Chapel and the Crisis of Rationalism," both in *Le Corbusier in Perspective*, ed. Peter Serenyi (Englewood Cliffs, N.J.: Prentice-Hall, 1975). Of course Stirling's later career shows all the same hallmarks of moving away from the "rational" precepts of modernism. See also Tafuri for the "mindless prejudice" with which Le Corbusier's late work was met. Manfredo Tafuri, *The History of Italian Architecture 1944–1985* (Cambridge, Mass.: MIT Press, 1989), pp. 55–56.

21. Stirling, "Garches to Jaoul," p. 63.

22. "The forms which have developed from the rationale and the initial ideology of the modern movement are being mannerised and changed in a conscious imperfection." Stirling, "Ronchamp," p. 67.

23. Ibid., p. 66.

24. Stirling, "Garches to Jaoul," p. 63.

25. Zygmunt Bauman, *Modernity and Ambivalence* (Cambridge: Polity Press, 1991), p. 14.

26. Bruno Latour, *We Have Never Been Modern*, trans. Catherine Porter (New York: Harvester Wheatsheaf, 1993), p. 112.

27. Ibid., p. 50.

28. Ibid., p. 142.

29. Ibid., p. 141.

30. The term "monstrous hybrids" is used by Jane Jacobs, *Systems of Survival: A Dialogue on the Moral Foundations of Commerce and Politics* (New York: Random House, 1992), chapter 6.

31. Latour, *We Have Never Been Modern*, p. 121.

32. The term "local knowledge" comes from Clifford Geertz, who writes: "Like gardening, politics, and poetry, law and ethnography are crafts of place: they work by the light of local knowledge. Whatever else anthropology and jurisprudence may have in common, they are alike absorbed with the artisan task of seeing broad principles in parochial facts. 'Wisdom,' as an African proverb has it, 'comes out of an ant heap.'" There is no reason not to add architecture to his list of disciplines. Clifford Geertz, *Local Knowledge: Further Essays in Interpretive Anthropology* (London: Fontana, 1983), p. 169.

33. Duncan McCorquodale, Katerina Ruëdi, and Sarah Wigglesworth, eds., *Desiring Practices: Architecture, Gender and the Interdisciplinary* (London: Black Dog Publishing, 1996), p. 284.

34. An extended version of which was subsequently published as Jane Rendell, *The Pursuit of Pleasure: Gender, Space and Architecture in Regency London* (London: Athlone Press, 2002).

9 Architectural Agency

1. See Burton Bledstein, *The Culture of Professionalism: The Middle Class and the Development of Higher Education in America* (New York: Norton, 1976), pp. 88–97.

2. The two main exceptions among the affiliated bodies of the UIA (Union Internationale des Architectes) are the Royal Architectural Institute of Canada and the Architectural Society of China.

3. Royal British Institute of Architects, *Transactions of the RIBA*, vol. 1/1 (London: John Weale, 1836), p. vii.

4. It is only since 2003 that the RIBA has tried to clarify this mix by the establishment of a tripartite organization: the RIBA Trust, which deals with the knowledge;

Professional Services, which deals with the professional and practice aspects of the Institute; and Enterprises, which deals with the commercial aspects. Whether these distinctions are clear to the members, let alone the public, is less evident.

5. This is why the clichéd figure of the architect as an artist is such a double-edged sword. On the one hand the artist is seen as a paradigm of cultural redemption (good for architects to be linked with), but the cost of this is their very association with the things that they create; artists are seen not as professionals grounded in abstract knowledge but as muses impulsively producing objects. The architect-artist thus fails the test of professional credibility.

6. Garry Stevens, *The Favored Circle: The Social Foundations of Architectural Distinction* (Cambridge, Mass.: MIT Press, 1998), pp. 93–95. Some reviewers have criticized Stevens's overreliance on Bourdieu in his analysis. I like the book not for whether it gets Bourdieu right or wrong, but for the way that a cussedness breaks through the surface of academic propriety, and for the fact that it is prepared to issue challenges to a number of the holy cows of architecture.

7. Ibid., p. 82.

8. Zygmunt Bauman, *Modernity and Ambivalence* (Cambridge: Polity Press, 1991), p. 212.

9. Randall Collins, "Changing Conceptions in the Sociology of Professions," in *The Formation of Professions*, ed. Rolf Torstendahl and Michael Burrage (London: Sage, 1990). See also the essay by Larson in the same book, as well as the companion volume: Rolf Torstendahl and Michael Burrage, eds., *Professions in Theory and History* (London: Sage, 1990).

10. Bauman, *Modernity and Ambivalence*, p. 218.

11. Indra Kagis McEwen, *Vitruvius: Writing the Body of Architecture* (Cambridge, Mass.: MIT Press, 2003), p. 28. The Vitruvius quotes are from Book 1.1.2 of the *Ten Books of Architecture*. Theory and practice are the normal translations of the Vitruvian terms *ratiocinatio* and *fabrica*: McEwen interprets them more clearly as two forms of making—written and practical.

12. Anthony Giddens, *The Consequences of Modernity* (Cambridge: Polity Press, 1990), pp. 83–90.

13. Bauman, *Modernity and Ambivalence*, p. 224.

14. Giddens, *The Consequences of Modernity*, p. 89.

15. Ibid., p. 90.

16. Peter Eisenman, *Eisenman Inside Out: Selected Writings 1963–1988* (New Haven: Yale University Press, 2004), p. 38. My emphasis.

17. Bledstein, *The Culture of Professionalism*, p. 88.

18. Ivan Illich, *Limits to Medicine: Medical Nemesis, the Expropriation of Health* (London: Marion Boyars, 1976). Against medical advice, Illich self-medicated in his final illness.

19. Bryan Lawson, May Bassanino, et al., "Intentions, Practices and Aspirations: Understanding Learning in Design," *Design Studies* 24, no. 4 (2003).

20. One of the better analyses of the workings of elite practice in relation to the marketplace is Magali Sarfatti Larson, *Behind the Postmodern Façade: Architectural Change in Late Twentieth-Century America* (Berkeley: University of California Press, 1993), pp. 98–137.

21. Lucius Seneca, *Moral Epistles*, trans. Richard Gummere, vol. 2 (Cambridge, Mass.: Harvard University Press, 1917), p. 399.

22. Zygmunt Bauman, *Legislators and Interpreters: On Modernity, Post-modernity, and Intellectuals* (Ithaca: Cornell University Press, 1987), p. 3.

23. Zygmunt Bauman, *Intimations of Postmodernity* (London: Routledge, 1992), p. 204.

24. John D. Caputo, *Radical Hermeneutics: Repetition, Deconstruction, and the Hermeneutic Project* (Bloomington: Indiana University Press, 1987), p. 213.

25. Nicholas H. Smith, *Strong Hermeneutics: Contingency and Moral Identity* (London: Routledge, 1997), p. 35.

26. As John Caputo concludes his brilliant book: "If I have argued anything, it is that addressing our sociology is ultimately a matter of getting down to cases, of getting a lot of heads together—specialists and non-specialists, perpetrators and victims, dreamers and pragmatists, professionals and amateurs—and letting them hammer something out for the time being, which may even last quite a while—to their surprise." Caputo, *Radical Hermeneutics*, p. 264.

27. Roberto Mangabeira Unger, *Social Theory: Its Situation and Its Task* (Cambridge: Cambridge University Press, 1987), p. 30.

28. Gillian Rose, "Athens and Jerusalem: A Tale of Two Cities," *Social and Legal Studies* 3 (1994): 337. For a development of this argument, see Jeremy Till, "Architecture of the Impure Community," in *Occupying Architecture: Between the Architect and the User*, ed. Jonathan Hill (London: Routledge, 1998).

29. Henri Lefebvre, *Critique of Everyday Life*, trans. John Moore, vol. 1 (London: Verso, 1991), p. 86.

30. Bruno Latour speaks of the importance of recognizing such conjoined networks, but also of the way that they are dismissed under the separating habit of modernity. "Epistemology, the social sciences, the sciences of texts—all have their privileged vantage point, provided that they remain separate. . . . That a delicate shuttle should have woven together the heavens, industry, texts, souls and moral

law—this remains uncanny, unthinkable, unseemly." Bruno Latour, *We Have Never Been Modern,* trans. Catherine Porter (New York: Harvester Wheatsheaf, 1993), p. 5.

31. Roberto Mangabeira Unger, *False Necessity: Anti-Necessitarian Social Theory in the Service of Radical Democracy* (Cambridge: Cambridge University Press, 1987), p. 396.

32. John Shotter, *Cultural Politics of Everyday Life: Social Constructionism, Rhetoric and Knowing of the Third Kind* (Buckingham: Open University Press, 1993), p. xiii. The terms "knowing how" and "knowing what" are initially from Gilbert Ryle, *The Concept of Mind* (New York: Barnes and Noble, 1962).

33. Reyner Banham, "Opening Remarks," in *Design Participation,* ed. Nigel Cross (London: Academy Editions, 1972).

34. N. J. Habraken, *The Structure of the Ordinary* (Cambridge, Mass.: MIT Press, 1998), p. 2.

35. J. Christopher Jones, *Design Methods,* 2nd edn. (New York: Van Nostrand Reinhold, 1992), p. xxix.

36. This was an ongoing concern in Price's work. It is best summarized in the introduction to Cedric Price, *Cedric Price: Works II* (London: Architectural Association, 1984), p. 18.

37. Jonathan Hill, *Actions of Architecture: Architects and Creative Users* (London: Routledge, 2003), p. 135.

38. John Forester, "Designing: Making Sense Together in Practical Conversations," *Journal of Architectural Education* 38, no. 3 (1985). See also John Forester, *Planning in the Face of Power* (Berkeley: University of California Press, 1989), pp. 119–133.

39. Forester, "Designing," p. 14.

40. See Alistair Blyth and John Worthington, *Managing the Brief for Better Design* (London: Taylor and Francis, 2001), p. xii. The work of John Worthington and his colleagues at DEGW has been seminal in seeing the briefing process and the production of the brief as an essential and creative part of the architectural process. See also Francis Duffy, *Design for Change: The Architecture of DEGW* (Basel: Birkhäuser, 1998).

41. Harold Perkin, *The Third Revolution: Professional Elites in the Modern World* (London: Routledge, 1996), p. 1.

42. Caputo, *Radical Hermeneutics,* p. 258.

10   Imperfect Ethics

1. Greg Lynn, *Animate Form* (New York: Princeton Architectural Press, 1999).

2. Karsten Harries, *The Ethical Function of Architecture* (Cambridge, Mass.: MIT Press, 1997), p. 291.

3. This is Mark C. Taylor talking about the morphologically driven work of students of Greg Lynn and Hani Rashid. Mark C. Taylor, "Deregulation," in *Architectural Laboratories,* ed. Greg Lynn and Hani Rashid (Rotterdam: NAi Publishers, 2003), p. 169.

4. "Reconciling Poetics and Ethics in Architecture," McGill University, Montreal, September 2007.

5. Roger Scruton, *The Aesthetics of Architecture* (London: Methuen, 1979), p. 230. Scruton argues that "the sense of the appropriate exists as an embodiment of moral thought."

6. Le Corbusier, *The Decorative Art of Today,* trans. James Dunnett (London: Architectural Press, 1987), p. 192.

7. Manfredo Tafuri, *Architecture and Utopia: Design and Capitalist Development* (Cambridge, Mass.: MIT Press, 1975), p. 178.

8. Sometimes misquoted as "God is in the details," the attachment to Mies is given through the assurances of Philip Johnson; see Philip Johnson, "Architectural Details," *Architectural Record* (April 1964), pp. 137–147.

9. There is continuing discussion on Mies's exact relationship with the Nazis. The most damning evidence is in the designs themselves, particularly those for the Reichsbank and the German Pavilion for the 1935 Brussels World Fair (both unbuilt), the latter of which Mies explicitly linked to the representation of the Reich. See Franz Schulze, *Mies van de Rohe: A Critical Biography* (Chicago: University of Chicago Press, 1985), pp. 199–200.

10. Ibid., p. 201.

11. This is the way that Solà-Morales describes the autonomous project of Mies. Ignasi de Solà-Morales, *Differences: Topographies of Contemporary Architecture,* trans. Graham Thompson (Cambridge, Mass.: MIT Press, 1997), p. 36.

12. Harries, *The Ethical Function of Architecture,* p. 4.

13. Zygmunt Bauman, *Alone Again: Ethics after Certainty* (London: Demos, 2000), p. 15.

14. Geoffrey Scott, *Architecture of Humanism* (London: Methuen, 1961), pp. 161–162.

15. Bruno Taut, *Modern Architecture* (London: The Studio, 1929), p. 9.

16. Frank Lloyd Wright, *Autobiography* (London: Faber and Faber, 1945), p. 293.

17. Le Corbusier, *Precisions on the Present State of Architecture and City Planning,* trans. Edith Schreiber Aujame (Cambridge, Mass.: MIT Press, 1991), p. 31.

18. Walter Gropius, *Apollo in the Democracy: The Cultural Obligation of the Architect* (New York: McGraw-Hill, 1968), p. 36.

19. Le Corbusier, *Towards a New Architecture* (London: Architectural Press, 1946), p. 210.

20. As quoted in David Watkin, *Morality and Architecture Revisited* (London: John Murray, 2001), p. 18. Many of these quotes can also be found in Watkin's book. He uses them to great effect in demolishing the false moral pretensions of the modern-movement architects and their champions, though less edifying is the ideological basis of his critique, which implies the equation *modernism (as style) = false morals = socialism = bad.* His response just compounds the problem in suggesting that "morality in architecture" can be found only in the restitution of a classically based aesthetic. He thus dismisses one aesthetic = ethics formulation only to replace it with another.

21. James Stirling, *James Stirling: Buildings and Projects 1950–1974* (London: Thames and Hudson, 1975), p. 14.

22. Jonathan Keates, "David Chipperfield Architects," in *4 City Visionaries* (London: British Council, 2000), p. 29.

23. Quoted in Watkin, *Morality and Architecture Revisited*, p. 9.

24. Kenneth Frampton, "Rappel à l'ordre: The Case for the Tectonic," in *Theorizing a New Agenda for Architecture: An Anthology of Architectural Theory 1965–1995*, ed. Kate Nesbitt (New York: Princeton Architectural Press, 1996).

25. This is Frampton quoting Stanford Anderson: Kenneth Frampton, "Towards a Critical Regionalism: Six Points for an Architecture of Resistance," in *The Anti-Aesthetic: Essays on Postmodern Culture*, ed. Hal Foster (Seattle: Bay Press, 1983), p. 26.

26. Beatriz Colomina, "Mies Not," in *The Presence of Mies*, ed. Detlef Mertins (New York: Princeton Architectural Press, 1994), p. 201. Colomina doubts whether Mies actually ever said this.

27. Le Corbusier, *When the Cathedrals Were White: A Journey to the Country of Timid People*, trans. Francis Hyslop (London: Routledge, 1947), p. 46.

28. Alice Coleman, *Utopia on Trial* (London: Hilary Shipman, 1985). Although Coleman writes in the introduction that "this is not to be construed as a claim that design is the only fact in the prevention or promotion of social behaviour," the rest of the book is more or less spent attempting to substantiate that claim. The most damning critiques of Coleman's work came from sociologists who found systematic failings in her analytical methods, which revealed an underlying ideological bias. Paul Spicker, "Poverty and Depressed Estates: A Critique of Utopia on Trial," *Housing Studies* 2, no. 4 (1987): 283–292.

29. This was the tactic that we used in the British Pavilion at the 2006 Venice Architecture Biennale, in the show that I curated with a team from Sheffield. Our exhibition *Echo/City* presented Sheffield as an "urban register" at four different

scales: 1:1, 1:100, 1:10,000, and 1:10,000,000. Each scale was seen as both metric and social. For more on this, see Jeremy Till, *Echo/City: An Urban Register* (London: British Council, 2006). The team was Ian Anderson, Ruth Ben-Tovim, Tim Etchells, Hugo Glendinning, Jim Prevett, Trish O'Shea, Jeremy Till, Martyn Ware, and Sarah Wigglesworth, with Emily Campbell of the British Council as commissioner.

30. Michel de Certeau, *The Practice of Everyday Life* (Berkeley: University of California Press, 1984), p. 92.

31. Architects Registration Board, "Code of Conduct" (ARB, 2002), 3. My emphasis.

32. Tom Spector, "Codes of Ethics and Coercion," in *Architecture and Its Ethical Dilemmas*, ed. Nicholas Ray (London: Routledge, 2005), p. 102. Some of the argument in these paragraphs is taken from Spector's cogent essay. His book *The Ethical Architect*, while opening up the discussion way beyond professional codes, always remains within the terms and values of the Vitruvian triad around which it is constructed. Tom Spector, *The Ethical Architect: The Dilemma of Contemporary Practice* (New York: Princeton Architectural Press, 2001).

33. That they are indeed minimum is shown by the fact that only a handful of architects have been struck off the ARB register in the past few years, the majority for failing to maintain professional indemnity insurance.

34. See in particular Roberto Mangabeira Unger, *False Necessity: Anti-Necessitarian Social Theory in the Service of Radical Democracy* (Cambridge: Cambridge University Press, 1987), p. 331.

35. For example Žižek, who writes: "Every concrete ecological concern and project to change technology in order to improve the state of our natural surroundings is thus devalued as relying on the very source of the trouble." Slavoj Žižek, *The Ticklish Subject: The Absent Centre of Political Ontology* (London: Verso, 2000), p. 12. It is the neoliberal insistence that technology can "solve the problem" that is at the heart of the problem.

36. Alasdair Macintyre, *After Virtue* (London: Duckworth, 1981), p. 245.

37. See in particular John D. Caputo, *Radical Hermeneutics: Repetition, Deconstruction, and the Hermeneutic Project* (Bloomington: Indiana University Press, 1987), pp. 240–242; Barbara Herrnstein Smith, *Contingencies of Value: Alternative Perspectives for Critical Theory* (Cambridge, Mass.: Harvard University Press, 1988), pp. 92–94; and Jeffrey Stout, *Ethics after Babel: The Languages of Morals and Their Discontents* (Boston: Beacon Press, 1988), pp. 190–224. As Stout notes, Macintyre's argument depends on "greatly exaggerated descriptions of our predicament" (p. 216). Caputo's critique is particularly coruscating.

38. Smith, *Contingencies of Value*, p. 94.

39. The term "originary ethics" is taken from John Caputo: "Heidegger's more originary ethos is a higher version, an eschatological version, of metaphysics. For it tells

the story of the primordial ethos and the great beginning, prior to the subject-object split, and looks ahead to a new dawn." Caputo, *Radical Hermeneutics*, p. 237.

40. Ibid., p. 240. Caputo introduces his critique as being "flippant," but this should not detract from its poignancy.

41. Harries, *The Ethical Function of Architecture*, p. 291.

42. Ibid. Most telling is that this section is illustrated with a picture of the US Capitol in Washington: "What Heidegger says of the Greek temple, that it lets the god be present, has its analogue in . . . the presence of shared values in civic monuments—think of the Capitol, of the Washington, Jefferson and Lincoln memorials, or of Civil War monuments." The suggestion that ethics is eventually overseen by the "shared" values represented by the US Capitol would be intolerable to many.

43. Caputo, *Radical Hermeneutics*, p. 240.

44. Zygmunt Bauman, *Intimations of Postmodernity* (London: Routledge, 1992), p. xxii.

45. Ibid. It should be noted that Bauman identifies negative connotations in this paradox, insofar as in handing back ethical responsibility to the individual, "morality has been privatised." My more positive interpretation is taken from his slightly later book, *Postmodern Ethics*.

46. Zygmunt Bauman, *Postmodern Ethics* (Oxford: Blackwell, 1993), p. 3.

47. Ibid., p. 250.

48. Caputo, *Radical Hermeneutics*, p. 263. Caputo defines the ethics of dissemination as "an ethics bent on dispersing power clusters, constellations of power which grind us all under" (p. 259).

49. Hans Jonas, *The Imperative of Responsibility: In Search of an Ethics for the Technological Age* (Chicago: University of Chicago Press, 1984), p. 201.

50. As described in Stephen K. White, *Political Theory and Postmodernism* (Cambridge: Cambridge University Press, 1991), p. 96.

51. These ideas are developed in my essay on architecture and participation. Jeremy Till, "The Negotiation of Hope," in *Architecture and Participation*, ed. Peter Blundell Jones, Doina Petrescu, and Jeremy Till (London: Routledge, 2005), pp. 25–44.

52. Roberto Mangabeira Unger, "The Better Futures of Architecture," in *Anyone*, ed. Cynthia Davidson (New York: Rizzoli, 1991), p. 36.

11 Hope against Hope

1. Manfredo Tafuri, *Architecture and Utopia: Design and Capitalist Development* (Cambridge, Mass.: MIT Press, 1975), p. 182.

2. Ibid., p. 181.

3. Ibid., p. ix.

4. Manfredo Tafuri, *Theories and History of Architecture* (London: Granada, 1980), p. xxii.

5. Zygmunt Bauman, *Globalization: The Human Consequences* (Cambridge: Polity Press, 1998), p. 37.

6. Le Corbusier, *When the Cathedrals Were White: A Journey to the Country of Timid People,* trans. Francis Hyslop (London: Routledge, 1947), p. 217.

7. David Harvey, *Spaces of Hope* (Edinburgh: Edinburgh University Press, 2000), p. 174.

8. Ibid., p. 179.

9. Ibid., p. 182.

10. Ibid., p. 232.

11. Ibid., p. 200.

12. Roberto Mangabeira Unger, *False Necessity: Anti-Necessitarian Social Theory in the Service of Radical Democracy* (Cambridge: Cambridge University Press, 1987), p. 12.

13. Ibid., p. 330.

14. Ibid., pp. 6–7.

15. Roberto Mangabeira Unger, *Social Theory: Its Situation and Its Task* (Cambridge: Cambridge University Press, 1987), p. 6.

16. "Even the most entrenched formative context, productive of the most rigid, determining, and inclusive hierarchies, can be dissolved by escalating practical and imaginative conflict." Unger, *False Necessity,* p. 308.

17. Unger, *Social Theory,* p. 47.

18. For the idea of the transformative vocation, particularly in contrast to instrumental practice, see ibid., pp. 26–35. For its potential application to architecture, see Roberto Mangabeira Unger, "The Better Futures of Architecture," in *Anyone,* ed. Cynthia Davidson (New York: Rizzoli, 1991), pp. 28–36. The latter is also available online at <http://www.law.harvard.edu/faculty/unger/english/archi.php>.

19. Unger, *False Necessity,* p. 411.

20. Unger, *Social Theory,* p. 15.

21. G. W. F. Hegel, *Science of Logic,* trans. A. V. Miller (London: George Allen and Unwin, 1969), p. 545.

22. The phrase "ethical imagination" comes from Kearney. "An ethical imagination responsive to the demands of the other, refuses however to accept that the self is nothing but a heap of reified technique or commodified desire. The ethical imagination bids man to tell and retell the story of himself. . . . Ethics, in other words, presupposes the existence of a certain narrative identity: a self which remembers its commitments to the other and recalls that these commitments have not yet been met." Richard Kearney, *The Wake of Imagination* (London: Hutchinson, 1988), p. 395.

23. Maurice Merleau-Ponty, *In Praise of Philosophy* (Evanston: Northwestern University Press, 1963), p. 60. This comes from Merleau-Ponty's inaugural professorial address in which he outlines the tensions of the philosopher as someone moving between knowledge and ignorance, truth and ambiguity, philosopher and man, detached and engaged—tensions which are absolutely necessary for philosopher and architect alike.

24. Michel Serres, *Angels: A Modern Myth,* trans. Francis Cowper (Paris: Flammarion, 1995), p. 293.

Bibliography

Works cited are referenced in the notes. The following are sources that have been particularly useful in the construction of the argument for the book. If I was to name the five key texts they would be Bauman's *Modernity and Ambivalence,* Caputo's *Radical Hermeneutics,* Latour's *We Have Never Been Modern,* Lefebvre's *Production of Space,* and Mangabeira Unger's *Social Theory.*

Adorno, Theodor W. *The Jargon of Authenticity.* Evanston: Northwestern University Press, 1973.

Banham, Reyner. "A Black Box: The Secret Profession of Architecture." In Banham, *A Critic Writes,* ed. Mary Banham. Berkeley: University of California Press, 1996, 292–299.

Bauman, Zygmunt. *Alone Again: Ethics after Certainty.* London: Demos, 2000.

Bauman, Zygmunt. *Globalization: The Human Consequences.* Cambridge: Polity Press, 1998.

Bauman, Zygmunt. *Intimations of Postmodernity.* London: Routledge, 1992.

Bauman, Zygmunt. *Legislators and Interpreters: On Modernity, Post-modernity, and Intellectuals.* Ithaca: Cornell University Press, 1987.

Bauman, Zygmunt. *Liquid Modernity.* Cambridge: Polity Press, 1997.

Bauman, Zygmunt. *Modernity and Ambivalence.* Cambridge: Polity Press, 1991.

Bauman, Zygmunt. *Modernity and the Holocaust.* Cambridge: Polity Press, 1989.

Bauman, Zygmunt. *Postmodern Ethics.* Oxford: Blackwell, 1993.

Bauman, Zygmunt. *Wasted Lives: Modernity and Its Outcasts.* Cambridge: Polity Press, 2004.

Berman, Marshall. *All That Is Solid Melts into Air: The Experience of Modernity.* New York: Viking Penguin, 1988.

Bernstein, Richard J. *Beyond Objectivism and Relativism*. Oxford: Blackwell, 1983.

Bernstein, Richard J. *The New Constellation: The Ethical-Political Horizons of Modernity/Postmodernity*. Cambridge: Polity Press, 1991.

Billig, Michael. *Ideological Dilemmas: A Social Psychology of Everyday Thinking*. London: Sage, 1988.

Bledstein, Burton. *The Culture of Professionalism: The Middle Class and the Development of Higher Education in America*. New York: Norton, 1976.

Bloch, Ernst. *The Principle of Hope*. Trans. Neville Plaice, Stephen Plaice, and Paul Knight. 3 vols. Oxford: Blackwell, 1986.

Brand, Stewart. *How Buildings Learn: What Happens after They're Built*. New York: Viking, 1994.

Callinicos, Alex. *Making History: Agency, Structure, and Change in Social Theory*. Cambridge: Polity Press, 1987.

Caputo, John D. *Radical Hermeneutics: Repetition, Deconstruction, and the Hermeneutic Project*. Bloomington: Indiana University Press, 1987.

Casey, Edward S. *The Fate of Place: A Philosophical History*. Berkeley: University of California Press, 1997.

Connah, Roger. *How Architecture Got Its Hump*. Cambridge, Mass.: MIT Press, 2001.

Connolly, William E. *Politics and Ambiguity*. Madison: University of Wisconsin Press, 1987.

Cuff, Dana. *Architecture: The Story of Practice*. Cambridge, Mass.: MIT Press, 1991.

de Certeau, Michel. *The Practice of Everyday Life*. Berkeley: University of California Press, 1984.

Dewey, John. *The Quest for Certainty*. London: George Allen and Unwin, 1930.

Doane, Mary Ann. *The Emergence of Cinematic Time: Modernity, Contingency, the Archive*. Cambridge, Mass.: Harvard University Press, 2002.

Dutton, Thomas A., ed. *Voices in Architectural Education: Cultural Politics and Pedagogy*. New York: Bergin and Garvey, 1991.

Eno, Brian. *A Year with Swollen Appendices*. London: Faber and Faber, 1996.

Evans, Robin. *The Projective Cast: Architecture and Its Three Geometries*. Cambridge, Mass.: MIT Press, 1995.

Fabian, Johannes. *Time and the Other: How Anthropology Makes Its Object*. New York: Columbia University Press, 1983.

Forester, John. *The Deliberative Practitioner: Encouraging Participatory Planning Processes*. Cambridge: MIT Press, 1999.

Forty, Adrian. *Words and Buildings: A Vocabulary of Modern Architecture*. London: Thames and Hudson, 2000.

Freire, Paulo. *Pedagogy of the Oppressed*. Trans. Myra Ramos. London: Penguin, 1996.

Geertz, Clifford. *Local Knowledge: Further Essays in Interpretive Anthropology*. London: Fontana, 1983.

Ghirardo, Diane, ed. *Out of Site: A Social Criticism of Architecture*. Seattle: Bay Press, 1991.

Giddens, Anthony. *The Consequences of Modernity*. Cambridge: Polity Press, 1990.

Gramsci, Antonio. *Selections from the Prison Notebooks of Antonio Gramsci*. Trans. Quintin Hoare and Geoffrey Nowell-Smith. London: Lawrence and Wishart, 1971.

Groák, Steven. *The Idea of Building: Thought and Action in the Design and Production of Buildings*. London: E. & F. N. Spon, 1992.

Habraken, N. J. *The Structure of the Ordinary: Form and Control in the Built Environment*. Cambridge, Mass.: MIT Press, 1998.

Habraken, N. J. *Supports: An Alternative to Mass Housing*. London: Architectural Press, 1972.

Haraway, Donna. *Simians, Cyborgs and Women: The Reinvention of Nature*. London: Free Association Books, 1991.

Harries, Karsten. "Building and the Terror of Time." *Perspecta* 19 (1982): 52–69.

Harries, Karsten. *The Ethical Function of Architecture*. Cambridge, Mass.: MIT Press, 1997.

Harvey, David. *Spaces of Hope*. Edinburgh: Edinburgh University Press, 2000.

Heidegger, Martin. *Being and Time*. Trans. John Macquarrie and Edward Robinson. New York: Harper, 1962.

Heller, Agnes. "From Hermeneutics in Social Science toward a Hermeneutics of Social Science." *Theory and Society* 18 (1989): 291–322.

Hertzberger, Herman. *Lessons for Students in Architecture*. Trans. Ina Rike. 4th rev. edn. Rotterdam: 010 Publishers, 2001.

Heynen, Hilde. *Architecture and Modernity: A Critique*. Cambridge, Mass.: MIT Press, 1999.

Hill, Jonathan. *Actions of Architecture: Architects and Creative Users*. London: Routledge, 2003.

Hodges, Michael, and John Lachs. *Thinking in the Ruins: Wittgenstein and Santayana on Contingency*. Nashville: Vanderbilt University Press, 2000.

Hollier, Denis. *Against Architecture: The Writings of Georges Bataille*. Trans. Betsy Wing. Cambridge, Mass.: MIT Press, 1989.

Holt, Nancy, ed. *The Writings of Robert Smithson*. New York: New York University Press, 1979.

Illich, Ivan. "Disabling Professions." In Illich et al., *Disabling Professions*. London: Marion Boyars, 1977, 11–40.

Jonas, Hans. *The Imperative of Responsibility: In Search of an Ethics for the Technological Age*. Chicago: University of Chicago Press, 1984.

Karatani, Kojin. *Architecture as Metaphor: Language, Number, Money*. Trans. Sabu Kohso. Cambridge, Mass.: MIT Press, 1995.

Kern, Stephen. *The Culture of Time and Space 1880–1918*. 2nd edn. Cambridge, Mass.: Harvard University Press, 2003.

Koolhaas, Rem, and Bruce Mau. *S, M, L, XL*. Rotterdam: 010 Publishers, 1995.

Kubler, George. *The Shape of Time: Remarks on the History of Things*. New Haven: Yale University Press, 1962.

Kwinter, Sanford. *Architectures of Time: Toward a Theory of the Event in Modernist Culture*. Cambridge, Mass.: MIT Press, 2001.

Larson, Magali Sarfatti. *Behind the Postmodern Façade: Architectural Change in Late Twentieth-Century America*. Berkeley: University of California Press, 1993.

Latour, Bruno. *We Have Never Been Modern*. Trans. Catherine Porter. New York: Harvester Wheatsheaf, 1993.

Lefebvre, Henri. *Critique of Everyday Life*. Trans. John Moore. Vol. 1. London: Verso, 1991.

Lefebvre, Henri. "The Everyday and Everydayness." *Yale French Studies* 73 (1987): 2–20.

Lefebvre, Henri. *Everyday Life in the Modern World*. Trans. Sacha Rabinovitch. New Brunswick: Transaction Publishers, 1984.

Lefebvre, Henri. *The Production of Space*. Trans. Donald Nicholson-Smith. Oxford: Blackwell, 1991.

Lefebvre, Henri. *Writings on Cities*. Trans. Eleonore Kofman and Elizabeth Lebas. Oxford: Blackwell, 1996.

Lerup, Lars. *Building the Unfinished: Architecture and Human Action*. Beverly Hills: Sage, 1977.

Leupen, Bernard. *Frame and Generic Space: A Study into the Changeable Dwelling Proceeding from the Permanent.* Rotterdam: 010 Publishers, 2006.

Luhmann, Niklas. *Observations on Modernity.* Trans. William Whobrey. Stanford: Stanford University Press, 1998.

McCorquodale, Duncan, Katerina Ruëdi, and Sarah Wigglesworth, eds. *Desiring Practices: Architecture, Gender and the Interdisciplinary.* London: Black Dog Publishing, 1996.

McEwen, Indra Kagis. *Vitruvius: Writing the Body of Architecture.* Cambridge, Mass.: MIT Press, 2003.

Melucci, Alberto. *The Playing Self: Person and Meaning in the Planetary Society.* Cambridge: Cambridge University Press, 1996.

Merleau-Ponty, Maurice. *In Praise of Philosophy.* Evanston: Northwestern University Press, 1963.

Misak, C. J. *Truth, Politics, Morality: Pragmatism and Deliberation.* London: Routledge, 1999.

Osborne, Peter. *The Politics of Time: Modernity and the Avant-Garde.* London: Verso, 1995.

Paz, Octavio. *Convergences: Essays on Art and Literature.* Trans. Helen Lane. London: Bloomsbury, 1987.

Perkin, Harold. *The Third Revolution: Professional Elites in the Modern World.* London: Routledge, 1996.

Rasch, William. *Niklas Luhmann's Modernity: The Paradoxes of Differentiation.* Stanford: Stanford University Press, 2000.

Rorty, Richard. *Contingency, Irony, and Solidarity.* Cambridge: Cambridge University Press, 1989.

Rorty, Richard. *Philosophy and the Mirror of Nature.* Princeton: Princeton University Press, 1979.

Rose, Gillian. "Athens and Jerusalem: A Tale of Two Cities." *Social and Legal Studies* 3 (1994): 337.

Scanlan, John. *On Garbage.* London: Reaktion Books, 2005.

Serres, Michel, and Bruno Latour. *Conversations on Science, Culture, and Time.* Trans. Roxanne Lapidus. Ann Arbor: University of Michigan Press, 1995.

Shapiro, Gary. *Earthwards: Robert Smithson and Art after Babel.* Berkeley: University of California Press, 1995.

Shields, Rob. *Lefebvre, Love and Struggle: Spatial Dialectics.* London: Routledge, 1999.

Shotter, John. *Cultural Politics of Everyday Life: Social Constructionism, Rhetoric and Knowing of the Third Kind.* Buckingham: Open University Press, 1993.

Smith, Barbara Herrnstein. *Contingencies of Value: Alternative Perspectives for Critical Theory.* Cambridge, Mass.: Harvard University Press, 1988.

Smith, Nicholas H. *Strong Hermeneutics: Contingency and Moral Identity.* London: Routledge, 1997.

Soja, Edward W. *Thirdspace: Journeys to Los Angeles and Other Real-and-Imagined Places.* Oxford: Blackwell, 1996.

Solà-Morales, Ignasi de. *Differences: Topographies of Contemporary Architecture.* Trans. Graham Thompson. Cambridge, Mass.: MIT Press, 1997.

Sontag, Susan. *Illness as Metaphor.* London: Penguin, 1979.

Spector, Tom. *The Ethical Architect: The Dilemma of Contemporary Practice.* New York: Princeton Architectural Press, 2001.

Stallybrass, Peter, and Allon White. *The Politics and Poetics of Transgression.* London: Methuen, 1986.

Stevens, Garry. *The Favored Circle: The Social Foundations of Architectural Distinction.* Cambridge, Mass.: MIT Press, 1998.

Stout, Jeffrey. *Ethics after Babel: The Languages of Morals and Their Discontents.* Boston: Beacon Press, 1988.

Tafuri, Manfredo. *Architecture and Utopia: Design and Capitalist Development.* Cambridge, Mass.: MIT Press, 1975.

Tafuri, Manfredo. "L'Architecture dans le Boudoir." In *Oppositions Reader,* ed. K. Michael Hays. New York: Princeton Architectural Press, 1998, 291–316.

Tafuri, Manfredo. *The Sphere and the Labyrinth: Avant-Gardes and Architecture from Piranesi to the 1970s.* Cambridge, Mass.: MIT Press, 1987.

Taylor, Charles. *Human Agency and Language.* Cambridge: Cambridge University Press, 1985.

Thompson, Michael. *Rubbish Theory: The Creation and Destruction of Value.* Oxford: Oxford University Press, 1979.

Turner, John F. C., and Robert Fichter. *Freedom to Build: Dweller Control of the Housing Process.* New York: Macmillan, 1972.

Unger, Roberto Mangabeira. "The Better Futures of Architecture." In *Anyone,* ed. Cynthia Davidson. New York: Rizzoli, 1991, 28–36.

Unger, Roberto Mangabeira. *False Necessity: Anti-Necessitarian Social Theory in the Service of Radical Democracy.* Cambridge: Cambridge University Press, 1987.

Unger, Roberto Mangabeira. *Social Theory: Its Situation and Its Task*. Cambridge: Cambridge University Press, 1987.

Vesely, Dalibor. *Architecture in the Age of Divided Representation: The Question of Creativity in the Shadow of Production*. Cambridge, Mass.: MIT Press, 2004.

Wellmer, Albrecht. "Truth, Contingency, and Modernity." In Wellmer, *Endgames: The Irreconcilable Nature of Modernity*. Cambridge, Mass.: MIT Press, 1998, 137–154.

White, Stephen K. *Political Theory and Postmodernism*. Cambridge: Cambridge University Press, 1991.

Wihl, Gary. *The Contingency of Theory: Pragmatism, Expressivism, and Deconstruction*. New Haven: Yale University Press, 1994.

Winner, Langdon. *Autonomous Technology: Technics-Out-of-Control as a Theme in Political Thought*. Cambridge, Mass.: MIT Press, 1977.

Figure Credits

Page 11   Paternoster, University of Sheffield: © Peter Lathey.

Page 16   Beaux-Arts Mao, Tsinghua University School of Architecture, 2003: © Jeremy Till and Sarah Wigglesworth.

Page 24   Civic Center, Perugia, 1988, Aldo Rossi: © Jeremy Till and Sarah Wigglesworth.

Page 25   Fountain with graffiti, Civic Center, Perugia, 1988, Aldo Rossi: © Jeremy Till and Sarah Wigglesworth.

Page 29   New Blahblah: © Jeremy Till.

Page 36   Two views of Rome: from Edmund Bacon, *Design of Cities* (London: Thames and Hudson, 1967).

Page 40   McLaren Headquarters, 2005, Foster Associates: © Jeremy Till.

Page 41   Pessac, Le Corbusier, picture taken in 1980s: © Peter Blundell Jones.

Page 75   Great Salt Lake, Utah: *Spiral Jetty*, Robert Smithson, photographed in August 2007: © Shelley Bernstein.

Page 78   Interior with fish on table, Villa Savoye, Poissy, 1928, Le Corbusier: © FLC/ADAGP, Paris and DACS, London 2007.

Page 78   Interior with bread on table, Villa Stein De Monzie, Garches, 1926, Le Corbusier: © FLC/ADAGP, Paris and DACS, London 2007.

Page 81   Stone garden, Ryoanji Temple, Kyoto: © Florian Kossak and Tatjana Schneider.

Page 87   Les K Architectures: © Les K Architectures.

Page 90   Poundbury, Dorset: © Malcolm Miles.

Page 102   Cleaning cradle, Lloyds Building, London, Richard Rogers Partnership: © Don Brubacher.

Page 103   Glass cleaners, Louvre Pyramid, Paris: © 1989 Musée du Louvre/Michel Chassat.

Page 105   Torre Velasca, Milan, 1957, BBPR: © Peter Blundell Jones.

Page 107   Great Salt Lake, Utah: *Spiral Jetty*, Robert Smithson, photographed in August 2007: © Shelley Bernstein.

Page 121   Space in the home: Ministry for Housing and Local Government, *Space in the Home*, Design Bulletin 6 (London: HMSO, 1968).

Page 130   Thermal baths, Vals, 1996, Peter Zumthor: © Lukas Barry.

Page 139   Housing estate in Dubai: © Jeremy Till and Sarah Wigglesworth.

Page 142   9 Stock Orchard Street, 2001, Sarah Wigglesworth Architects and Jeremy Till: © Paul Smoothy.

Index

Adorno, Theodor W., 131
Aesthetics, 65, 84, 88, 89, 104, 138, 144, 174–175. *See also* Ethics: and aesthetics
Agency, architectural, 151, 164–165, 167, 168
Alberti, Leon Battista, 44, 110
Ambiguity, 39, 122, 131, 132
Anderson, Laurie, 87
Angels with Dirty Faces, 194–195
Architects
  as gymnasts, 11, 189–190
  as tribe, 9, 10, 17–18
Architects Registration Board (ARB), 179–180
Architectural education, 8, 11, 13, 111–112, 135, 168
  detachment of, 9, 14, 15
  power structures, 14
  in relation to profession, 17
  stasis of, 15
Architectural profession, 16–18, 28, 153–156, 161–162
  difference from architectural practice, 18, 154–155, 161, 164
Architecture
  as art, 109, 137, 230 (n.5)
  with capital A, 19, 20, 41
  as commodity, 85, 92, 123, 138
  and control, 18, 40
  gap between ideals and reality, 2, 19, 32, 42, 46, 48, 138

as metaphor, 43–44
as waste, 67–69, 72
Aristotle, 38, 42, 173, 184
Aulenti, Gae, 99
Authenticity, 129, 131, 132, 185. *See also* Inauthenticity
Autonomy, architectural, 10, 17–21, 25, 61, 87, 155
Avant-garde, failure of, 15, 140, 203 (n.26)

Bacon, Edmund, 35
Banham, Reyner, 7, 8, 18, 166
Barthes, Roland, 113
Bataille, Georges, 19, 79, 82
Bauman, Irena, 206 (n.25)
Bauman, Zygmunt, 31–32, 48, 85, 122, 163, 220 (n.13)
  on contingency, 38, 54–55
  on ethics, 173, 185–186
  on expertise, 156–157, 159
  Modernity and Ambivalence, 47, 124, 159
  on order and disorder, 33, 34, 37, 74, 190
  on postmodernity, 51, 185
Beauty, 29, 30, 53, 175
Beaux-Arts, École des, 11
  founding, 12
  rituals, 12–13, 16–17, 202 (n.22)
Behrens, Peter, 53
Benjamin, Walter, 74, 114

Berger, John, 113
Berlage, Hendrik Petrus, 118
Bernstein, Richard, 53, 210 (n.18)
Bérubé, Michael, 137, 227 (n.5)
Bilbao, Guggenheim Museum, 119, 141
Bledstein, Burton, 161
Blobs, 13, 88, 171, 177
Body, 28, 30, 129–130, 132, 225 (n.37)
  and illness, 30
Boudon, Philippe, 41
BPR (Belgiojoso, Peressutti, Rogers),
  104, 221 (n.36)
Brand, Stewart, 86, 98–99
Breuer, Marcel, 100, 175
Briefing, 169, 183
British Library, 47, 156
Brown, Lancelot ("Capability"), 60
Burgin, Victor, 204 (n.42)

Calvino, Italo, 73–74
Cancer, 30–31
Capitalism, 49, 85, 90, 123, 138, 189
Caputo, John, 170, 184, 186, 231 (n.26),
  235 (n.39)
Casey, Edward, 129
Chipperfield, David, 175
Classification, 69, 71–72, 75, 140, 142–
  143
Cleanliness, 29–30, 69, 101, 177
Clients, 86, 123, 173–174, 180, 181–182
Coleman, Alice, 177–178, 234 (n.28)
Collins, Randall, 157
Colomina, Beatriz, 177, 216 (n.3)
Community Architecture, 165
Computers, 15, 86–87, 88, 110
Connah, Roger, 113, 114
Connolly, William, 39, 53, 121–122, 133
Connor, Steven, 213 (n.51)
Conover, Roger, 195
Conrad, Joseph, 46
Conservatism, 15
Context, for architecture, 96, 145, 165–
  166, 185–186. See also Formative
  contexts
Contingency, 38, 45. See also Dependency
  of architecture, 20, 45–46, 50, 53

coping with, 54–55
false, 15
and modernity, 32, 51
as opportunity, 47, 48, 52, 54, 55, 59,
  61, 191, 193
philosophy of, 38, 51–53, 54, 61
ridding of, 20, 36, 38, 56, 59, 111
summary of argument, 5
Costello, Elvis, 135–137, 139, 146
Crit. See Design jury
Curiosity, 47, 131, 132, 194

David, Jacques-Louis, 11
De Certeau, Michel, 7, 179
Deconstruction, 21
DeLillo, Don, 69, 74
Demolition, 68, 69, 72
Dependency, 1–2
  of architecture, 45–46, 161, 178
  denial of, 73, 79, 122
  as opportunity, 2, 151, 164, 183, 193
  as threat to profession, 155
Descartes, René, 42–43, 48, 120, 127
Design jury, 8, 14, 118
Design studio, 8–9, 12, 17, 136, 146,
  169
Detachment, architectural, 7, 161, 162,
  169, 176
Detailing, 176, 178
Dewey, John, 32, 61
Dirt, 65, 69, 87, 101, 104
Dirty realism, 44, 163, 182
Doesburg, Theo van, 118, 127
Douglas, Mary, 69, 71, 215 (n.10)
Dovey, Kim, 206 (n.23)
Drawing, architectural, 23, 110–112,
  118–119
  and time, 113–114
Drexler, Arthur, 20
Duany, Andrés, 12, 91

Eisenman, Peter, 21–22, 23, 160
Engagement, 2, 18, 128, 138, 164–165,
  176, 182
Enlightenment fundamentalism, 48,
  49, 51, 55, 185

Eno, Brian, 99
Entropy, 75, 104–106
Environmental crisis, 88, 182
Environmental responsibility, 180, 183, 195
Eternity, 82–83, 91, 92, 94
Ethics, 170, 171, 173
  and aesthetics, 174–175, 177–178
  and architecture, 171–172, 176, 182, 185
  false, 177, 180, 181
  originary, 173, 174, 184–185, 235 (n.39)
Evans, Robin, 88, 111
Everyday, the, 97–98, 114, 129, 137–140, 165, 185
Expertise, 134, 154–157, 159–160

Fabian, Johannes, 94
Fascism, 10, 25, 91, 172, 173, 233 (n.9)
Feminism, 60, 146, 147, 186
Forester, John, 168
Form, 30, 144, 190, 193
  fresh, 85, 88, 138
  making of, 15, 87, 113, 119
  purity of, 21, 189
Formative contexts, 191–193
Forty, Adrian, 118, 224 (n.18)
Foster, Norman, 39, 48, 85, 140
Foucault, Michel, 132, 165, 211 (n.22), 219 (n.10)
Frampton, Kenneth, 131, 176, 203 (n.35)
Freire, Paolo, 14
Fresh Conservatism, 15
Freud, Sigmund, 29, 52
Friedman, Thomas L., 49
Fuksas, Massimiliano, 174
Future Systems, 141

Geertz, Clifford, 229 (n.32)
Gehry, Frank O., 119, 141
Giddens, Anthony, 50, 51, 117, 159
Giedion, Sigfried, 82, 88, 96, 100–101, 151
  Space, Time and Architecture, 65, 84, 100
Giedion-Welcker, Carola, 100
Gilligan, Carol, 186

Graves, Michael, 140
Groák, Steven, 83, 96, 209 (n.5)
Gropius, Walter, 53, 80, 82, 84, 175
Guthrie, Peter, 67, 69

Habermas, Jürgen, 38, 48, 50, 211 (n.22), 212 (n.46)
Habraken, John, 167
Haraway, Donna, 60
Harries, Karsten, 79, 173, 184–185
Harvey, David, 46, 123, 190–191, 223 (n.1)
Hays, K. Michael, 20, 204 (n.36)
Hegel, Georg Wilhelm Friedrich, 38, 44, 193, 208 (n.53)
Heidegger, Martin, 43, 122, 129, 184, 217 (n.22)
  Being and Time, 131
  "Building, Dwelling, Thinking," 130, 132
  and space, 127–128, 129
Heller, Agnes, 35, 54, 55
Hermeneutics, 164, 170
Hertzberger, Herman, 107–108, 134, 146
Herzog and de Meuron, 104
Heynen, Hilde, 129, 206 (n.27), 216 (n.11)
Hill, Jonathan, 134, 168
Hope, 59, 98, 190, 191–193
  false, 111, 132, 144, 145, 185
Hybrid, 56, 140, 144–145, 165

Illich, Ivan, 162, 231 (n.18)
Imagination, 151, 192, 193
  ethical, 193, 195, 238 (n.22)
Inauthenticity, 131, 132
Intent, acting with, 48, 53, 58, 59, 69, 145, 194
Interpreters, versus legislators, 163–164, 169, 187
Isozaki, Arata, 27

Jacobs, Jane, 19
Johnson, Philip, 22
Jonas, Hans, 91, 186

Jones, John Chris, 167
Joyce, James, 90, 96–97, 100–101, 116

Kahn, Louis, 81, 118
Kant, Immanuel, 43, 44, 48, 127, 173, 212 (n.46)
Karatani, Kojin, 44, 45, 46
K Architectures, Les, 87
Kearney, Richard, 238 (n.22)
King, Magda, 127
Klima, Ivan, 70
Knowledge, professional, 110, 153–155, 161–162, 163, 165, 167
Knowledge, types of, 34–35, 43, 166. See also Situated knowledge
Koolhaas, Rem, 109, 126, 202 (n. 25), 215 (n.23)
Kwinter, Sanford, 88

Larson, Magali Sarfatti, 17
Las Vegas, 138
Latour, Bruno, 81, 91, 93, 132, 144, 145–146, 231 (n.30)
  We Have Never Been Modern, 47, 55–58
Lawson, Brian, 162, 209 (n.4)
Leatherbarrow, David, 104
Le Corbusier, 11, 25, 31, 53, 68, 77, 81, 136
  and Beaux-Arts, 13, 14
  housing at Pessac, 37, 41, 208 (n.59)
  and morals, 30, 101, 172, 175
  and order, 33, 37, 39, 117, 190
  and politics, 91, 218 (n.39)
  and transgression, 144–145
  When the Cathedrals Were White 13, 101
Lefebvre, Henri, 41, 84–85, 88, 96, 110, 112
  and the everyday, 97–98, 138–139, 165
  and space, 47, 122, 123, 125–126
Lerup, Lars, 107
Levinas, Emmanuel, 173
Lévi-Strauss, Claude, 219 (n.6)
Libeskind, Daniel, 218 (n.30)
Lo-fi architecture, 136–137, 139–140, 145, 146
Loos, Adolf, 97

Luhmann, Niklas, 49
Lyotard, Jean-François, 50

Macintyre, Alasdair, 184, 185
Marx, Karl, 33, 48, 95
Matta-Clark, Gordon, 87
McEwen, Indra Kagis, 28, 159
McLeod, Mary, 227 (n.8), 228 (n.12)
Melucci, Alberto, 59, 94, 98
Merleau-Ponty, Maurice, 129–130, 194
Mess, social, xi, xii, 35, 61, 190
Mies van der Rohe, Ludwig, xi, xii, 53, 81, 82, 172, 177
  and politics, 91, 172–173, 233 (n.9)
Modernism, as architectural movement, 19, 33, 65, 84, 101, 144, 206 (n.27)
Modernity, 49–51, 54, 65, 117
  in Latour, 56–57, 144
Moholy-Nagy, László, 118
Mostafavi, Mohsen, 104
Mulvey, Laura, 204 (n.42)
Musil, Robert, 54
MVRDV, 222 (n.58)

Neoliberalism, 15, 49
Neufert, Ernst, 120
New Urbanism, 90–91, 92
New York Five, 20
Nietzsche, Friedrich, 34, 52, 169

Ockman, Joan, 228 (n.15)
Oiticica, Hélio, 25
Oppositions (journal), 20, 23
Order, 30, 35–36
  conflation of visual and social, 28, 190
  and disorder, 34
  and modernity, 33–34, 37, 80
  in Vitruvius, 27–28, 29
Osborne, Peter, 82

Paris, Centre Pompidou, 99, 103
Parody, 42, 208 (n.61)
Participation, 115, 145
Pedagogy, critical, 14
Perfection, 30, 31, 57, 190

Perspective, 110
Pevsner, Nikolaus, 33, 176
Phenomenology, 128–129, 132, 133, 212
  (n.46)
Philosophy, 32, 42–43
Photography, 77, 85–86, 113–114
Piano, Renzo, 99, 100
Plans, 112, 116, 178
Plato, 30, 42, 44, 45, 51
Politics, of architecture, 122, 126, 162–
  163, 191
Postmodernism, architectural, 50, 58,
  92, 138, 144
Postmodernity, 50–51, 57, 163, 185, 209
  (n.61)
Poundbury, 89
Price, Cedric, 68, 146, 167
Problem, of the problem, 166–168
Professional codes, 179–181
  limits of, 180, 183
Professions, 50, 153–157, 161, 165–167,
  181
Progress, 57, 74, 75, 85, 217 (n.28)
  and architecture, 21, 33, 79, 85, 97
Purity, 30, 74
  as myth, 25, 35
Putnam, Hilary, 54

Quantity surveying, 157–158
Quasi-objects, 56

Rasch, William, 213 (n.54)
Reason, 43, 48–49, 121, 160
  as symptom of modernity, 33, 34, 58, 59
Relativism, 48, 58–59, 185
Rendell, Jane, 147
Responsibility
  abrogation of, 53, 92, 133
  taking, 60, 91, 124, 173, 179–180, 185–
  187
RIBA (Royal Institute of British Archi-
  tects), 153–155, 161, 181
  "Plan of Work," 157, 161
  Stirling Prize, 227 (n.6)
Rietveld, Gerrit, 118
Rinpoche, Sogyal, 54

Rogers, Richard, 99
Rorty, Richard, 47, 51–53, 211 (n.25,
  n.27)
Rose, Gillian, 165
Ross, Andrew, 90, 91
Ross, Kristin, 114
Rossi, Aldo, 22–24, 79, 82, 205 (n.50)
  Perugia, Civic Center, 23–25
Rubbish theory, 70–72
Ruskin, John, 82, 176

Scales, architectural, 178–179
Scanlan, John, 74, 75
Schmarsow, August, 118
Schneider, Tatjana, 226 (n.48)
Schulz, Bruno, 89, 91
Schulze, Franz, 172
Scott, Geoffrey, 174
Scott Brown, Denise, 138
Scully, Vincent, 23–25
Seneca, Lucius Annaeus, 163
Sense-making, 168
Serres, Michel, 81, 93, 98
Shapiro, Gary, 203 (n.26), 215 (n.20)
Sheffield, School of Architecture, 7, 8
Sherer, Daniel, 46
Shevtsov, Lev, 19, 35
Shotter, John, 166
Šik, Miroslav, 10
Situated knowledge, 60–61, 145, 165
Sketch, 109, 111, 119, 160–161
Smith, Barbara Herrnstein, 58, 184, 213
  (n.51)
Smith, Nicholas, 49, 164
Smithson, Robert, 68, 74–75, 95, 203
  (n.26)
Soja, Edward, 126
Solà-Morales, Ignasi de, 20, 23, 86, 95
Sontag, Susan, 30
Space
  abstract, 112, 123–124
  as measured, 120, 122
  as product, 118, 119–120, 122
  slack, 108, 133–134, 226 (n.48)
  social, 88, 96, 122, 125–127, 132, 190,
  195

Space in the Home, 120–121
Spatiality, 128–129
Spector, Tom, 42, 180, 235 (n.32)
Stability, 43, 72, 82–83, 95
Stallybrass, Peter, 30, 140
Stevens, Garry, 9, 12, 155, 218 (n.30), 230 (n.6)
Stirling, James, 143–144, 175, 228 (n.20)
Storytelling, 114–115
Structuralism, 20, 21, 95
Sustainability, 67, 69, 141, 182

Tafuri, Manfredo, 46, 140, 172, 189–190, 193
Tange, Kenzo, 92, 146
Taste, 12, 154, 155
Taut, Bruno, 174
Technological determinism, 15, 103
Technology, 57, 84, 85, 102
Tectonics, 131–132, 155, 176, 177, 183, 226 (n.42)
Thatcher, Margaret, 135, 177
Thompson, Michael, 70–71
Time, 75, 116
  dynamics of, 93–95, 117
  freezing of, 78, 82, 84, 85–86, 88, 89, 94
  lived, 96–97
  and modernity, 81, 85, 96, 216 (n.10)
  terror of, 79, 94, 99, 117
  thick, 95, 98
Toorn, Roemer van, 15
Transgression, 140–143

Unfinished, the, 107–108
Unger, Roberto Mangabeira, 165, 182, 187, 191–193
Utopia, 178, 189–191

Vals, Thermal Baths, 130–131
Venice, Biennale, 174, 234 (n.29)
Venturi, Robert, xi, 138
Vesely, Dalibor, 110, 113, 115, 222 (n.51)
Vitruvius Pollio, Marcus, 27–28, 30, 159

commodity, firmness, delight, 29, 50, 79, 90, 155
Vocation, transformative, 165, 192, 193, 237 (n.18)

Wallinger, Mark, xii
Waste, 67–68, 74–75
Watkin, David, 234 (n.20)
Wenders, Wim, 194
White, Allon, 30, 140
Whiteness, 30, 101
Wigglesworth, Gordon, 72
Wigglesworth, Sarah, 28, 80, 115, 146, 147
Wigley, Mark, 21, 43, 101, 205 (n.10)
Wollin, Peter, 204 (n.42)
Worthington, John, 232 (n.40)
Wright, Frank Lloyd, 53, 65, 174

Žižek, Slavoj, 235 (n.35)
Zumthor, Peter, 130–131